DREAM W[...]

Liz Bestic was born in Wuppertal, Germany, in 1953. She worked at the *Sunday Times* for seven years before becoming a freelance journalist. She researched the *Sunday Times* Good University Guide and writes for the national press and women's magazines. She is currently a member of the Guild of Health Writers and is deputy editor of *Parents* magazine.

Liz has two children and lives with her partner in north London, where she enjoys painting and printmaking, when she gets the time.

Jim Bewsher was born in Hammersmith, west London, in 1952. The son of a vicar, he was a trade union official for ten years before becoming deputy director of the Local Government Information Unit. He now runs a marketing and communications consultancy. He has written articles for the *Sunday Times* and various local government publications.

Jim lives with his partner and daughter in north London. He likes jazz, and is currently learning to play the piano.

DREAM WEDDINGS

The Hundred Best Places to Get Married in England and Wales

Liz Bestic and Jim Bewsher

A SIGNET BOOK

SIGNET

Published by the Penguin Group
Penguin Books Ltd, 27 Wrights Lane, London W8 5TZ, England
Penguin Books USA Inc., 375 Hudson Street, New York, New York 10014, USA
Penguin Books Australia Ltd, Ringwood, Victoria, Australia
Penguin Books Canada Ltd, 10 Alcorn Avenue, Toronto, Ontario, Canada M4V 3B2
Penguin Books (NZ) Ltd, 182–190 Wairau Road, Auckland 10, New Zealand

Penguin Books Ltd, Registered Offices: Harmondsworth, Middlesex, England

First published 1996
1 3 5 7 9 10 8 6 4 2

Copyright © Liz Bestic and Jim Bewsher, 1996
All rights reserved

The moral right of the authors has been asserted

Set in 10/12.5pt Monophoto Sabon
Typeset by Datix International Limited, Bungay, Suffolk
Printed in England by Clays Ltd, St Ives plc

Except in the United States of America, this book is sold subject
to the condition that it shall not, by way of trade or otherwise, be lent,
re-sold, hired out, or otherwise circulated without the publisher's
prior consent in any form of binding or cover other than that in
which it is published and without a similar condition including this
condition being imposed on the subsequent purchaser

Contents

Acknowledgements

There are a number of people without whose help this book would never have seen the light of day. Firstly, Patrick Watson at Wandsworth Council for his advice on the technicalities of the law and his humorous anecdotes of the weddings from hell! Martin Smith from Cheshire County Council who was instrumental in the drafting of Gyles Brandreth's Bill and gave us much needed help. Stan Abbott and Sue Crawford who kindly researched a number of the northern venues. Harriet Crowley who helped research London venues when we were tearing our hair out and Christian Timms who did the same as well as devising the database.

Additional thanks to Steve Bassam at the Association of Metropolitan Authorities, staff at the OPCS press office, Pat Newman at Cornwall County Council, the offices of MPs Harry Cohen and Gyles Brandreth and the staff of Coventry Tourist Information.

Finally, thanks to Alex Garland who happily stuffed envelopes and licked hundreds of stamps, Lesley and Tom Davey for unswerving support and encouragement and Mandy Bestic for putting up with it all while her home became a madhouse.

LIZ BESTIC and JIM BEWSHER

PICTURE ACKNOWLEDGEMENTS

The authors and publishers would like to thank the following for permission to reproduce photographs. They would be grateful to be informed of any omissions.

front cover
Herstmonceux Castle: Jo Brown. HMS *Warrior*: Warrior Preservation Trust, Portsmouth. Coventry City Football Club: Age Communications, London. Mr A. Thorpe, Priory Farm, Lavenham. Brighton Pavilion: Royal Pavilion, Art Gallery and Museums, Brighton. Christine Scott. Horse Racing: Copyright © Telegraph Colour Library.

back cover
Freeman's Press Agency

inset
4. City of Coventry, Chief Executive and Town Clerk's Department, Public Relations Unit. 11. Essex County Council, County Personnel Department. 12. Phyllis Court Club. 17. Letheby & Christopher Ltd, Zoo Hospitality, Zoological Gardens, London. 18. Chelsea Football Club.

The line drawing on p. 121 is reproduced by courtesy of Liverpool City Council.

PART ONE

The New Wedding Laws – Everything You Need to Know to Organize Your Dream Wedding

CHAPTER 1

An Introduction

If marriage is to achieve its possibilities, husbands and wives must learn to understand that whatever the law may say, in their private lives, they must be free.

BERTRAND RUSSELL

Fancy a dream wedding? Since the law changed in 1995 you can get married at any register office in the country and at hundreds of new wedding venues that have been licensed by their local authority.

So if you dream of getting hitched in a cottage or a castle, tying the knot on a boat or in a baronial hall or even kicking off your life together at a football club, it is now possible. *Dream Weddings* will show you not only the best places to marry but how to get the most out of your special day.

The success of the film *Four Weddings and a Funeral* has shown just how much the whole world loves an English wedding. And 1995 will surely go down in history as the year that changed the entire face of marriage.

Getting married is one of the most important decisions you ever make in your life and every year more than 350,000 prove it by tying the knot and saying 'I do'. Over half of these choose a civil wedding ceremony – that is around 175,000 people who, for whatever reason, have chosen not to marry in a church. And yet for more than a hundred years their only choice was to get married in a register office.

The British still have a rather peculiar attitude to marriage in general and civil marriage in particular. Civil weddings have always been viewed as the 'poor relation' to the more formal church wedding service. This view has endured not least because of a formidable church lobby which is happy to keep things just as they are. This attitude probably dates back as far as 1837 which was in fact the last time the laws on marriage substantially changed.

The word 'wedding' derives from the Anglo-Saxon word 'wed' which means 'a pledge' and it is this pledge in its modern form which constitutes a marriage. For a marriage to be legal in this country it has to take the form of a public declaration that the couple intend to live together as husband and wife. It has to be stated in front of two adult witnesses who then may say whether there is any reason legally why the couple are not free to marry.

During the 16th century people took a fairly laissez-faire attitude to marriage and couples were allowed to marry within their own community without much objection. But the government soon began to worry about the proliferation of clandestine marriages and, like the good bureaucrats that they were, they started to restrict people's freedoms.

They were also concerned about the rising number of so-called Fleet weddings. The Fleet was a notorious debtors' prison where because of a loophole in the law you could discharge your debts for a penny by getting married. You can imagine the scenes of degradation in the Fleet area – young girls were regularly abducted and prostitutes were paid a handsome sum to marry the hapless debtors and get them out of prison.

These marriages were all perfectly legal and often took place at dead of night. The law soon stepped in and in 1754 the rules were tightened up so that all weddings had to take place in daylight hours, in front of two witnesses and in a parish church. The new legislation also disenfranchised all the other religions. Jews and Quakers were both exempt and remain so today.

Then in 1837 it dawned on the government that there were hundreds of people who did not go to church but still wanted to marry. That was when civil marriages were formally legalized and had to be held in a place which was specially registered for the occasion. Sounds familiar? It was the beginning of the register office as we have known it ever since.

This liberalization of the law was bought at a price – the church insisted on strict demarkation so that civil marriages had to be secular and were prohibited by law from having any religious content whatsoever. Even today civil marriages must be entirely secular and have no religious content or connotations.

CHANGING THE MARRIAGE LAWS

When in 1994 Gyles Brandreth, Conservative MP for Chester, put forward his private member's Bill to up-date the Marriage Act it was the first real change affecting civil weddings since 1837. But although it was heralded as a triumph it was not such a big deal.

The two real changes which affect civil weddings in England are firstly that couples can now choose to marry in any register office in the country – they no longer have to marry in a register office in their place of residence.

Secondly, local authorities are now empowered to license suitable buildings, in addition to register offices, as venues for marriages. This will allow couples to marry by civil ceremony in any register office or approved building in England and Wales. What has not changed is the fact that weddings still have to take place indoors, in daylight hours, in front of two adult witnesses in keeping with that ancient law of 240 years ago!

This is not the first time there has been an attempt to change the wedding laws to bring them into line with other countries. In 1987 the government announced that new legislation should be introduced. A working group was set up and was asked to consider almost fifty recommendations for change to the present legislation. A Green Paper was then published called 'Registration: a modern service'. That Green Paper received more than 600 responses nationwide from individuals as well as public bodies. It was becoming more and more clear that couples wanted much more freedom to choose where they got married.

In 1990 the government's White Paper, 'Registration: proposals for change', aimed to introduce greater choice and flexibility for couples into where marriages could take place. This was a step in the right direction. The idea was to empower local authorities to license suitable buildings such as stately homes and hotels as venues for marriage and by freeing up couples to marry in any register office in the country.

HARRY COHEN'S BILL

In 1992 Harry Cohen, Labour MP for Leyton, introduced a Bill which aimed to give choices to couples about where and how their marriage vows were to be exchanged. He suggested that couples should be allowed to marry anywhere they liked, at any time of the day or night and in any language.

Cohen's Bill went much further than Gyles Brandreth's which followed. He wanted couples to have the choice of getting married in the Tower of London or even in their own home 'where they are going to live out their vows to each other'. He could not see why couples could not choose parks, gardens or other places of particular significance to them. In fact he wanted to liberate weddings totally from unnecessary restrictions so that lovers could have a proper choice for their own special day.

Although Harry privately thought his Bill was much better, this was politics and publicly he welcomed Gyles Brandreth's Bill which finally went through Parliament in 1994 before coming into effect in 1995. But some MPs were still keen to maintain the status quo; there was an outcry from others who were terrified the new Bill would mean the advent of 'Las Vegas-style' wedding parlours. Luckily most MPs kept their own counsel – realizing pretty rapidly the commercial potential of licensing some of the magnificent hotels and historic settings which existed in their very own constituencies.

Needless to say when the law changed the public was confused about what was going on. People had been crying out for this change for many years and were unsure why the British Government was unwilling to change a law which had clearly become outdated. What was so wrong with holding a civil wedding in a beautiful garden for example or even in your own home?

Many couples felt that the local register office was simply not an ideal place to get married. Some wanted more guests than the register office could accommodate. Others had moved away from their home but still wanted the option to go back there to get married. But the real truth was, more often than not, couples wanted a more stylish and memorable setting to make what is after all supposed to be a lifetime commitment.

GOING ABROAD

Many had already voted with their feet. Each year around 12,000 people go abroad to get married in ceremonies which are fully recognized under British law. In fact the sight of brides-to-be clutching their wedding frocks at Heathrow Airport has become as familiar as the sight of golfers with their clubs or surfers with their boards. At some resorts, marriages are so popular that you may see two or three couples hovering around the bar, in a holding pattern, while waiting for a wedding in the gazebo!

But the problem with these types of wedding is that although they may sound romantic in the travel brochures the reality is often very different. For one thing relatives miss out and for another, many couples long to take their vows somewhere that means something to them – perhaps where they went to college or first met – or where their families still live. These are the people for whom the new law will make a real difference.

A note of caution. If you do go abroad to get married do check that the ceremony will be recognized back in Britain and find out how easy it is to get a replacement marriage certificate when yours gets lost.

SCOTLAND

Couples have always been able to get married anywhere they like in Scotland. You can even ask a celebrant to marry you on the banks of Loch Ness if you want. Scotland's regulations on marriage are much less restrictive than those in England. Gretna Green has long been lodged in the public's imagination as the place for runaway couples and indeed young people do still elope to Gretna Green because it is the first place over the Scottish border. That may change now that couples are less restricted about where they marry. And, contrary to popular belief, couples getting married at Gretna Green always had to give notice of their intended marriage even if they did not actually have to be resident in Scotland at the time.

Scotland was outside the scope of the 1754 Marriage Act which governed England and Wales – in fact at one time it was possible to marry in Scotland simply by a declaration before two witnesses, but their own laws have been tightened up and are now bound by the Marriage (Scotland) Act of 1977.

That is why Scotland was at the forefront of everyone's minds when the law was about to change. Many people thought England would follow in Scotland's footsteps and allow couples to marry provided they were sixteen or over. In Scotland if you are under eighteen you do not even need the permission of your parents or guardian.

But come on – we are British after all – and the powers that be had their own ideas about just what the public should be allowed to do. The bureaucrats insisted that the new law would have some pretty strict guidelines. After all we need to be protected from the sort of charlatans who are hellbent on bringing the institution of marriage into disrepute!

So no open-air weddings or mid-air marriages. Definitely no weddings on Concorde – weddings can only take place in buildings which are 'readily identifiable'. They cannot take place in a temporary structure such as a marquee or folly in a garden. Some crafty places like Le Gothique Restaurant in London have tried (successfully) to get round the regulations by saying the cloisters constitute a fixed building and so ostensibly you can marry outdoors.

There must be access to the building so that the bride's spurned lover can sprint in the door and object to the wedding. No weddings in your own home or in a private house – it is not available to the public and may not comply with fire, health and safety requirements. Apparently the National Trust has had problems with this rule because some of their buildings are only open on certain days of the week.

No religious connotations or connections are allowed in the licensed room. Tullie House Museum in Carlisle fell foul of this one because they wanted to hold civil marriages at the Roman Altar. They had to abandon the plan because of their registrar's interpretation of religious images. Castell Coch in Wales had the same problem. The room they wanted to license had images of saints depicted on the walls — such a shame because a more fairytale setting for a wedding is hard to imagine. However, as we all know, rules are made to be broken and it cannot be long before shrewd hoteliers spy a loophole in the new law. Watch this space because we think things will evolve pretty quickly.

The general public were not the only ones who were confused about the new regulations either. Hoteliers in the Scilly Isles were left hopping mad after being accidentally omitted from the new regulations. The wording was such that it excluded both the Scilly Isles and the City of London as they did not come under the categories of 'county, metropolitan and London borough councils'.

One hotelier in particular had spent £10,000 transforming a bridal suite in Tresco ready for the new law. Gyles Brandreth had to rush back from holiday to table an amendment to put the anomaly right!

CHAPTER 2

Something for Everyone?

The new law may be a small step for the registration service but it's a giant leap for the marrying kind! Whatever your view on the change, it opens up all sorts of horizons to couples. It also means a whole new opportunity for hoteliers and people who run weddings up and down the country. Weddings are a multi-billion-pound industry. According to the latest surveys the average wedding costs more than £8,500 and for businesses like country house hotels, who traditionally held wedding receptions as a matter of course, the commercial potential is enormous. They now have the opportunity to offer a comprehensive service where everything is done in one place.

Naturally enough some local authorities are very worried about the new law. Not only because it means extra work for registrars but some see it as a bit of a threat – particularly where the register office is less than beautiful. But most registrars are welcoming the new law with open arms and a good deal of enthusiasm. From what we saw on our visits, they all seemed to be busy buying new outfits for their trips out to the local hotels and stately homes, and up-dating their register offices.

WANDSWORTH

Take Wandsworth in London, for example. Their register office is an attractive thirties building but it is smack in the middle of the Wandsworth one-way system. Are they worried? Not in the least. Even though there will probably be plenty of couples who will choose to wed either in a neighbouring borough or one of Wandsworth's many other licensed premises, Wandsworth simply want to see the greatest possible choice for couples looking to get married.

'We know our market and couples like getting married here because they know we go out of our way to make their day special.

As for the licensed premises we want to maximize the wedding business in Wandsworth and to make sure we maintain our market share. We can offer them a lovely register office or the chance to marry in an approved building. Whatever they choose we will help them plan their wedding ceremony so that they get a good service wherever. It is simply not in our interests to have people going around saying I got married in Wandsworth and it was a shambles – after all a good service from us reflects well on the council,' says Patrick Watson at Wandsworth.

LOCAL AUTHORITIES

Most local authorities are busy redecorating their marriage rooms, replanting their gardens and learning their scripts for their promotional videos which prospective couples will be getting, as part of their new found commercialism. Chester Register Office, for example, has already compiled a CD entitled 'Your Wedding' with suggested readings and music to accompany your special day. Brent has produced a video declaring itself a 'customer driven independent business' and is tempting new couples with promises of personalized wedding ceremonies.

The attitude of the registrar is a very important point to bear in mind when you are deciding where to marry. For example if you lived in Gloucester but have family in Wandsworth and want to marry at either Wandsworth Register Office or an approved building in the borough – no problem. Patrick Watson and his colleagues will bend over backwards to help you. But if you want to marry in some parts of the country like Devon for example – be warned. When we contacted them for their list of approved premises they wanted to charge us £5 for the privilege – something most authorities consider they should supply free of charge.

It is also true to say that it is very early days and a lot of places are flying by the seat of their pants in terms of the new law and how to interpret it. We found all sorts of discrepancies in the way local authorities were handling weddings. For example in some counties it was perfectly OK for the couples to choose any kind of music so long as it had no religious connotations. In others the registrar was determined to stay in control of the situation and was insistent he would choose the music or give them a list of recommended music. Although many local authorities are interpreting the rules differently it may well be up to you to make a stand and press for what you want. After all it is your day.

CHAPTER 3

So Why the Book?

Just as you may be, we were looking for somewhere attractive and memorable to tie the knot. We felt it was really important that we chose a setting which would form a very special backdrop to one of the most important days in our lives. Because neither of us are religious we had discounted the idea of marrying in church. Besides, one of us had been married before and the church in their wisdom will not countenance marrying second-time-arounders! Finally on discovering the law might change we decided to wait. And we are glad we did. Because now as you already know there is a huge selection of the most beautiful and interesting places in England and Wales to get married. From castles and towers to boats and a whole range of country house hotels.

We thought it would be useful for couples to have a list of the very best venues now offering a wedding service. We have included register offices as well because there are some very lovely ones dotted around the country and we are well aware that not everyone has a huge wedding budget. Besides, there will always be couples who want a low-key wedding and would rather opt for a beautiful register office ceremony followed by a modest 'do' in a local restaurant or pub.

IT'S YOUR CHOICE

While we are on the subject of the sort of wedding you want – we hope this book will help you make a good choice. After all it is your day but quite often family and friends forget and think it is theirs! Future parents-in-law are often guilty of taking over the organization of everything from the guest list to the readings at the ceremony. But it is important to think about what sort of day you want. For example a wild and wacky wedding may seem a really good idea over a bottle of wine with some friends but in the cold light of day it may seem ludicrous. And even though getting married in a castle may be your idea of a romantic wedding – think about it – do you really want to rattle around like peas in a pod after the ceremony? If you are determined to have a huge bash with loads of loud music and drunken friends you do not want to choose an élite little country house where they insist on a jacket and tie at dinner.

A country house hotel is a good choice for almost any kind of wedding because they are completely geared up for them. We had literally hundreds of replies from hotels to our questionnaire. For many, because they have already been organizing wedding receptions for donkey's years, the marriage ceremony is simply an add-on bonus for them. Many of them are extremely switched on and keen to attract the extra business. But with some we got the distinct impression that wedding ceremonies rather than being the icing on the cake were just one more hassle. So you pays your money and takes your choice.

Because of their size you may find hotels do not give you the same sort of personal attention you get in some of the smaller places who are keen to make a real go of weddings. We found the entrepreneurial spirit alive and kicking in many of the smaller venues. Most of them were willing to bend over backwards to be helpful and flexible and make sure you get the day of your dreams. However some do have to charge extra for the hire of the wedding room to cover their costs – whereas the larger hotels can absorb these costs into the reception. Very often when you book your wedding and reception at a hotel there is no charge at all for the wedding room.

ONLY THE BEST?

We arrived at the criteria for the 'hundred best' quite early on in our country-wide trawl. We realize the word 'best' means very different things to different people. Something which really appealed to us may not be another's cup of tea. So we decided 'best' does not necessarily mean 'grandest' or even 'most beautiful'; it means of a certain all-round standard. That was why we also knew we would have to visit every place in order to make that sort of judgement. We needed to see the wedding room and get a 'feel' for the atmosphere of the place. We certainly did not want to recommend somewhere which looked lovely in the brochure but actually had a gasworks partly obscured by the Cedar of Lebanon on the front lawn!

We also thought it was important you got some sense of what the owner was like. The named person is an important cog in the machinery of the new weddings as he or she deals with the registrar and should know the ins and outs of all the arrangements needed to make the day run smoothly. There seemed little point in recommending a fabulous castle, for example, where the owner had no idea of how to organize a good party.

The character who runs the place can make or break your big day – even in some of the best run hotels a Basil Fawlty character in charge of weddings can spell potential disaster. Although we found most to be totally sure they could handle anything there were one or two places where the venue was lovely but the owner was rude. We did not include these as we felt someone who could treat us with contempt would more than likely ruin your day. To be honest, though, the overall quality of the places we visited was extremely high; it was a real struggle to agree a short-list.

AN UNBIASED VIEW

Unlike other wedding guides which have come on the market we were not paid by any of the places for writing their entry and so they are recommended with absolutely no bias whatsoever. Indeed in many places we were lucky to get a free cup of coffee while we discussed the details of the wedding room and service!

We must stress that we have not sampled the food in most of the places and certainly have not tried out the honeymoon suite – apart from the Lygon Arms who very kindly put us up – so all the recommendations are purely on what we have seen or what we were told. Prices too are only a rough guide as many of the new venues had not yet drawn up a proper wedding package.

CHAPTER 4

Sorting Out the Practicalities

Getting married away from where you live means that two different register offices need to know about the arrangements. And if you are using an 'approved premises', also known as licensed premises, such as a hotel they also have to be involved. So the bureaucratic side of things is bound to be a little bit complicated. This chapter takes you through all the necessary procedures in the simplest possible way. As a general guide your day is likely to go more smoothly the earlier you start sorting out the red tape. And remember, the local registrar is always on hand to give advice.

If you have chosen a civil ceremony you need to contact the superintendent registrar of the district in which you want to marry. If you want to marry in an approved premises you also need to make arrangements with them. Each register office holds a list of buildings in its district which have been approved by the local council as venues for civil marriage. If you do not live in the district where the marriage is to take place you must give notice in your local register office as well.

For all civil marriages whether in a register office or approved building you must check in advance with the superintendent registrar about the formalities and agree a time and date before committing yourself to all the marriage plans and arrangements. When you go to your local register office to give notice of the wedding it will help if you can show your registrar that the appropriate arrangements have been made with the licensed premises and registrar in the other part of the country.

A legal notice of marriage must be completed at your local register office within a set number of days before the day of the wedding. There are two different types of notice and both are valid for three months.

MARRIAGE BY CERTIFICATE

The first, marriage by certificate, involves notifying the superintendent registrar of the district in which you have lived for the previous seven days. A minimum of twenty-one days must then elapse between giving the notice and the day of the marriage. If you live in different districts a notice must be given to the superintendent registrar of each district.

MARRIAGE BY LICENCE

Secondly you can get married by licence, commonly known as a special licence. It is more expensive but speeds up the whole process. Only one notice is then required even if you live in different districts. The notice should be given to the superintendent registrar of the district in which either of you has lived for at least the previous fifteen days.

You must allow a minimum of one clear working day to elapse between completing the notice and the day you intend to marry. For example if notice is given on Monday, the marriage may take place on Wednesday. This type of marriage is becoming more and more popular.

You must note that a notice by licence can only be given if either the bride or groom usually resides in England or Wales. If the other party is not usually resident he or she must be present in England or Wales on the day the notice is given.

The notice is only valid for three months which can create problems if you plan to book a popular venue. To get round these difficulties some register offices will give you a provisional booking up to a year in advance.

THE NECESSARY DOCUMENTS

When you go to the register office to complete the legal notice of marriage you may be asked to produce certain documents depending on your personal circumstances. You will need a birth certificate if you are under 23. Stories of faked birth certificates are legion amongst registrars. One sharp-eyed registrar at Wandsworth discovered a woman who had lied about her age. She was actually ten years older but had a dodgy birth certificate. They had to stop the marriage and challenge her. She broke down and admitted it while her hapless bridegroom's eyes grew larger and larger as her deceit was unravelled.

If you have been married before you will need to produce evidence of how your most recent marriage ended. For example, in the case of divorce you should take your Decree Absolute which must have on it an original stamp from the issuing court. If you have been widowed, the Death Certificate of your former spouse is normally required.

Anyone born outside the UK will need a passport or some other official identity document and deed poll documents will be needed if you have formally changed your name.

FEES

Fees for register office ceremonies are set nationally so you will pay the same whether you get married in Cornwall or Cumbria. In 1995 there was a fee of £19 for giving the notice of a wedding. If in a hurry you could pay £45 for the special licence, but either way you would then pay another £25.50 for the wedding ceremony and one copy of the marriage certificate. This fee has to be paid on the wedding day, so make sure that the bride, the groom or the best man has got the cash before setting off.

Where the ceremony is conducted outside the register office at an approved premises the registrar will charge a higher fee to reflect the additional administration, time and costs involved in travelling to the venue. These charges are set locally but are remarkably similar across the country. In 1995 you could probably expect to pay somewhere between £150 and £250 depending on whether the ceremony was held on a weekday, Saturday or Sunday. But if you are lucky enough to get married in Wandsworth you would only have to pay £120, the lowest fee in the country.

CHAPTER 5

The Wedding Ceremony

So much for the formalities but what about the ceremony itself? Wherever you choose to have a civil wedding most registrars offer a choice of wedding ceremonies. There is a standard ceremony in which you simply make the legal declarations to one another in the presence of your witnesses and invited guests. But some people prefer an 'enhanced' ceremony which includes a choice of additional words and readings. You should discuss this beforehand with your superintendent registrar.

Most register offices offer a choice of music to be played at your wedding. Many hold a selection of titles to choose from but some couples prefer to provide their own music. Bear in mind that it must not have any religious connections. Most registrars are happy to go along with anything from Meatloaf to Cliff Richard if they think it will make your day special.

Some couples prefer to have live music at the ceremony especially if it is being held in approved premises. Flutes, harps and even saxophones are now a regular part of the wedding scene. But, as always, do be sure to consult the registrar first. If your wedding is being held in a register office remember that they can run to a tight timetable, particularly on Saturdays. So if you want some special music or readings you may find it a lot easier if you have the wedding on a weekday when the register office will not be so busy.

Two witnesses are required to attend your wedding. They can be friends or relatives of either sex, normally over the age of sixteen, who will be able to understand the ceremony. Guests are usually very welcome to bring cameras or videos to record the occasion but they should consult with the registrar before taking pictures during the actual ceremony as it can be very distracting.

Indeed at Wakefield's Under the Clock Tower complex they have already captured on film for posterity the very first wedding ceremony in the country which was held not in a church or register office, but in the Old Court Room. The video shows very clearly how keen couples are to combine the solemnity of the occasion with a touch of fairytale fantasy. It was very much civil ceremony meets grand white wedding. Sharon wore a beautiful white satin gown while Robert wore the full morning suit and yet guests looked relaxed and informal in assorted wedding outfits. Babies were sitting in the 'aisle' in Moses baskets and once or twice someone wandered in as if they had stumbled in by mistake while looking for the council chamber.

The bride and groom looked very nervous and although they were in their full regalia, sat down throughout the ceremony. They had asked Sharon's brother to play a short recital on the piano and then her best friend read a short poem about love by W. H. Auden. The whole thing was over in about twenty minutes but it was still a moving and memorable occasion.

Finally, if a couple have very little English it is important to have an interpreter present when the legal notice of marriage is given and also during the ceremony. Likewise if one partner is hearing impaired it is usually possible to get a signer to be present for the wedding.

THE ORDER OF THE CEREMONY

Across the country registrars use a standard form of wedding ceremony. The basic words are the same although there may be some local variations in the detail. Many register offices publish useful leaflets explaining the procedure so you know what to expect when you get into the room. In addition register offices have suggested alternative forms of words that can be used in the ceremony. It is very important for all couples to spend a short time with the registrar before the ceremony sorting out the detail of what will happen on the day.

Below is an explanation of the standard ceremony taken from Cheshire's excellent guide 'Your Wedding'.

The superintendent registrar welcomes everyone and gives a little introduction. He addresses everyone present saying: 'This place in which we are now met has been duly sanctioned according to law for the celebration of marriage.'

Turning to the bride and groom he will then say: 'Before you are joined in matrimony, I have to remind you of the solemn and binding character of the vows you are about to make. Marriage, according to the law of this country, is the union of one man and one woman voluntarily entered into for life to the exclusion of all others.'

Then he turns to the assembled guests and says: 'If there is any person here who knows of any lawful impediment why these two people should not be married, they should declare it now.'

He then asks the bride and groom to state their full names and to make the first of the two legal declarations. No changes can be made to either declaration and the bride and groom have to repeat the words exactly.

'I do solemnly declare that I know not of any lawful impediment why I (full name) may not be joined in matrimony to (full name).' The registrar then says: 'Any union you enter into has to be done voluntarily and I ask each of you, therefore, this question. Do you (first name) by your own choice, freely enter into the union of marriage with (first name)?'

The bride and groom then respond by saying either 'yes' or 'I do'. They then make the second legal declaration to one another by repeating these words after the superintendent: 'I call upon these persons here present to witness that I (full name) do take thee (full name) to be my lawful wedded wife/husband.'

Although the exchange of one or two rings is a traditional part of the marriage ceremony, it is not a legal requirement. Couples who wish to include such an exchange in their ceremony may do so at this point.

In Cheshire the superintendent registrar will then ask the couple to turn and face one another and, where appropriate, say: 'We now come to the exchange of the wedding rings which is the outward sign of the lifelong promises you have made to each other. This is the traditional and ancient way of sealing the contract which you have just made.'

The bride and groom then repeat the words 'I give you this ring as a token of our marriage and as a symbol of all that we share'. If only one ring is given one person will say, 'I accept this ring as a token of our marriage and as a symbol of all that we share.'

The superintendent then concludes the ceremony by declaring that the bride and groom are now man and wife. At this point the couple, together with their witnesses, will be invited to sign the marriage register. The registrar will then issue the couple with the marriage certificate.

ADDITIONS TO THE CEREMONY

Some registrars have a list of optional enhancements to the marriage ceremony so that for example in his opening address to the couple he may say, 'the purpose of marriage is that you may always love, care for and support each other through all the joys and sorrows of life, and that love may be fulfilled in a relationship of permanent and continuing commitment. We trust that these things may come true for you both.'

Others are more flowery and include quotations from Mark Twain or John Donne. When it comes to the couple's vows to each other they may wish to say, 'I promise that I will always try to make our love and friendship last. I trust that our marriage will remain strong and look to our future together with hope, happiness and joy. May we treasure this day and never allow anything to destroy the feelings we share for each other.'

After the second legal declaration the couple may wish to say, 'I promise to care for you always and to keep our love and friendship as it is today. Please share my hopes and dreams and never allow anything to destroy the feelings we have for each other.'

During the exchange of rings they may say, 'I give you this ring as a token of my love and affection and in recognition of our shared life together. Wear it with a feeling of love and joy. I choose you to be my wife/husband this day and every day.'

Or perhaps: 'I give you this ring as a symbol of my love and affection, please wear it with a feeling of warmth and pride, now and always.'

Most registrars will agree to a short reading of a poem or a romantic quote being included at an appropriate part of the ceremony or at the end when the register is being signed. However you will need to discuss the details with the registrar beforehand.

PART TWO

The Hundred Best Places to Get Married

CHAPTER 6

The Entries Explained

Dream Weddings contains details of the 100 best places to get married in England and Wales. Each entry also includes all the basic information you need to organize your wedding, and is set out as follows:

Name: **The name of the venue**
Address: **The full postal address**
Tel: **The main telephone number**

DESCRIPTIVE TEXT

This includes a description of the venue and the wedding room together with some sense of the atmosphere of the place and the style of the owners.

All prices for hire of rooms and catering are those that applied in the summer of 1995 when the research for the book was carried out. When you find out today's prices remember to check whether VAT is included. Do not forget to add the registrar's fee.

The prices for catering are intended to give you a very rough indication of what you might actually pay and to allow some broad comparisons between venues. Nearly every venue in the book will tailor their catering to your individual needs. We have not commented on the quality of the food as we have not had the opportunity to taste it.

The text also includes information about the number of rooms or where to stay locally. As it is not a hotel guide we have not given a description of the rooms unless there is a special honeymoon suite.

Finally, we say what we think would be the best type of wedding to have at the venue. We do stress that it is our opinion and not necessarily the view of the proprietors.

Contact: The person responsible for weddings.

Main road: The nearest motorway or A road with distances if appropriate.

Station: The nearest main British Rail or Underground station.

Disabled access: Details of the type of disabled access. We are conscious that most weddings are likely to have an elderly or infirm relative present. Our comments are geared as much for them as they are for guests in wheelchairs.

Parking: Details of on-site or local parking.

Registrar tel no: The number of the relevant local registrar.

Bedrooms: The number of rooms if the venue has its own accommodation.

Wedding only: Some venues will only do a wedding if you have a reception as well. This section tells you if you can have a wedding only and go somewhere else for the reception.

. . . .

All the factual information in *Dream Weddings* is believed to be accurate at the time of writing. To the best of our abilities, it has been checked with the relevant establishment. Any comments on the establishments are our own.

However, because of the new law, the book was written to a very tight deadline and it is possible that some errors have crept into the copy. If so we apologize to our readers and the venues concerned.

Please contact us using the box number at the end of the book and we will be happy to make any necessary corrections to future editions of the book.

. . . .

Two different lists follow, one done by county or city, the second by theme. Chapter 2 gives the details.

LIST OF VENUES ARRANGED BY COUNTY OR CITY

County/City	Name	Page
Avon	Pump Room and Roman Baths	122
Avon	SS *Great Britain*	42
Avon	Thornbury Castle	75
Berkshire	Monkey Island Hotel	157
Berkshire	Oakley Court Hotel	151
Buckinghamshire	Pinewood Film Studios	51
Cheshire	Chester Register Office	146
Cheshire	Chester Town Hall	127
Cheshire	Finney Green Cottage	82
Cheshire	Peckforton Castle	71
Cheshire	Sandhole Farm	84
Cheshire	Tatton Park	99
Cornwall	Carlyon Bay Hotel	39
Cornwall	Polhawn Fort	45
Cornwall	St Austell Register Office	144
Cornwall	Trevigue Farm	47
County Durham	Lord Crewe Arms Hotel	117
Coventry	Coombe Abbey	59
Coventry	Coventry City Football Club	61
Coventry	Coventry Register Office	143
Coventry	Guildhall of St Mary	131
Cumbria	Armathwaite Hall	160
Cumbria	Naworth Castle	79
Cumbria	Tullie House Museum	115
Devon	Burgh Island	38
Dorset	Langtry Manor Hotel	92
Dyfed	Ty Penlan, the Old School	109
Essex	Braintree Register Office	141
Essex	The Fennes Estate	64
Essex	The Lawn	90

LIST OF VENUES ARRANGED BY THEME

SHIPS AND THE SEA

1 Burgh Island, Devon. Famous art deco hotel on an island
2 Carlyon Bay Hotel, Cornwall. Thirties seaside hotel
3 *Tuxedo Royale*, Gateshead. Nightclub on former cruise ship
4 SS *Great Britain*, Bristol. 1843 transatlantic passenger ship
5 HMS *Warrior*, Portsmouth. World's first iron battleship
6 Polhawn Fort, Cornwall. Napoleonic fort on the coast
7 Trevigue Farm, Crackington Haven, Cornwall. On the cliffs

SOMEWHERE SPECIAL – SOMEWHERE SPORTY

8 Pinewood Film Studios, Buckinghamshire
9 007 Bond Street, Warwickshire. James Bond theme nightclub
10 Heritage Park Hotel, mid-Glamorgan. Mining theme park
11 Finchcocks Musical Museum, Kent
12 Bentley Wildfowl Park and Motor Museum, East Sussex
13 Rivers Nightclub and Boaters Restaurant, Oxfordshire
14 Coombe Abbey, Coventry. Eccentric medieval themed hotel
15 Coventry City Football Club
16 Wentworth Club, Surrey. World famous golf club
17 The Fennes Estate, Essex
18 Sandown Park Racecourse, Esher, Surrey
19 London Zoo

FAIRYTALES CASTLES

20 Herstmonceux Castle, Hailsham, East Sussex
21 Peckforton Castle, Cheshire
22 Ripley Castle, Harrogate, North Yorkshire
23 Caerphilly Castle, South Wales
24 Thornbury Castle, Bristol, Avon
25 Amberley Castle, Arundel, West Sussex
26 Naworth Castle, Cumbria

HOME FROM HOME

27 Finney Green Cottage, Cheshire. Half-timbered guest house
28 Olde Stocks Restaurant, Leicestershire. On village green
29 Sandhole Farm, Congleton, Cheshire. Working farm
30 Tan Hill Inn, North Yorkshire. The highest pub in England
31 Boughton Monchelsea Place, Kent. Small Elizabethan manor
32 Ramblers Restaurant, Northumberland. Family-run restaurant
33 The Lawn, Rochford. Georgian house in Essex
34 Langtry Manor Hotel, Bournemouth. Former home of Lillie Langtry

FIT FOR A KING

35 Brighton Pavilion. Regency splendour by the sea
36 Alexandra Palace, Haringey, London. Italianate folly
37 Clandon Park, Surrey. Stately home with marble wedding room
38 Tatton Park, Cheshire. Stately home in its own deer park
39 Rhinefield House Hotel, New Forest, Hampshire. Exotic rooms
40 Lucknam Park, Wiltshire. Mix with the rich and famous
41 Lygon Arms, Worcestershire. Where Cromwell stayed

ARCHITECTURAL DELIGHTS

42 Layer Marney Tower, Essex. England's tallest Tudor gatehouse
43 Ty Penlan, Llandeilo, Dyfed. A village schoolhouse
44 Leez Priory, Essex. Priory with tower and medieval gatehouse
45 Little Thakeham, West Sussex. Lutyens manor house
46 Groombridge Place, Kent. *Draughtsman's Contract* filmed here
47 Tullie House Museum, Carlisle. Roman connections
48 Lord Crewe Arms, County Durham. Medieval abbot's house
49 Merchant Taylors Hall, York. Medieval guildhall

MUNICIPAL MARVELS

50 The Pump Room, Bath. Historic Roman baths
51 Liverpool Town Hall. Stunning Victorian architecture

52 Margam Park Orangery, West Glamorgan. Longest orangery in Britain

53 Chester Town Hall. Sweeping staircase and stained glass

54 Pittville Pump Room, Cheltenham. Regency spa

55 Pump House, Battersea Park, London. Former pumping station

56 Guildhall of St Mary, Coventry. Medieval guildhall

57 Under the Clock Tower, Wakefield. Held first ever new-style wedding

58 St Andrew's and Blackfriars' Halls, Norwich

59 Highbury, Birmingham. Former home of Joseph Chamberlain

A VERY CIVIL SERVICE (Unusual register offices outside London)

60 Sandwell. Georgian buildings

61 Dudley. A grand Victorian gatehouse in parkland

62 John Ray House, Braintree, Essex. Victorian gymnasium

63 Winchester. A converted pub

64 Coventry. Medieval house

65 St Austell. Former magistrates court

66 Chester. A modern suite of rooms

AT THE WATER'S EDGE

67 Phyllis Court Club, Henley-on-Thames. Victorian pavilion

68 Curdon Mill, Williton, Somerset

69 Oakley Court Hotel. On the Thames near Windsor

70 Ravens Ait. An island on the Thames at Surbiton

71 Hambleton Hall, overlooking Rutland Water

72 Close House Mansion, Newcastle. By the Tyne

73 Monkey Island Hotel. On the Thames at Bray

74 Swan at Bibury, Gloucestershire. Cotswolds riverside hotel

75 Armathwaite Hall, Lake District. Wedding room overlooks lake

76 The Priory, Ware, Hertfordshire. Medieval priory on the River Lea

A CAPITAL WEDDING (The best in London)

77 Trafalgar Tavern, Greenwich. Pub on the water

78 Cannizaro House. Country house in Wimbledon
79 Sutton House, Hackney. Urban stately home
80 Havering Register Office. Georgian house with its own lake
81 Templeton House, Roehampton. Churchill stayed here
82 The Ritz. London's most famous hotel
83 Westminster Register Office. Where the famous get wed
84 Waltham Forest Register Office. Old Victorian vicarage
85 Roof Gardens, Kensington High Street
86 Wandsworth Register Office. Market leaders in new-style weddings
87 Brent Register Office. Great gardens in the city
88 Searcy's. Elegant Georgian town house in Knightsbridge
89 Greenwich Register Office. Miniature Victorian town hall
90 Le Gothique. Restaurant in old orphanage in Wandsworth
91 Burgh House, Hampstead. A Queen Anne house
92 Chelsea Football Club
93 Heathrow Hilton Hotel

A COUNTRY WEDDING

94 Tewin Bury Farm Hotel, near Welwyn, Hertfordshire
95 Preston Priory Barn, Suffolk. On a working farm
96 Lythe Hill Hotel, Haslemere, Surrey. Tudor wedding room
97 The Manor, Guildford. Country house hotel
98 The Barn at Lainston House Hotel, Winchester
99 Chiseldon House, Wiltshire. Small country house hotel
100 Marshall Meadows Country House Hotel, Berwick-upon-Tweed. Northernmost wedding venue

The numbers on the following maps (of eastern England, western England and Wales, and northern England) refer to the list of venues arranged by theme.

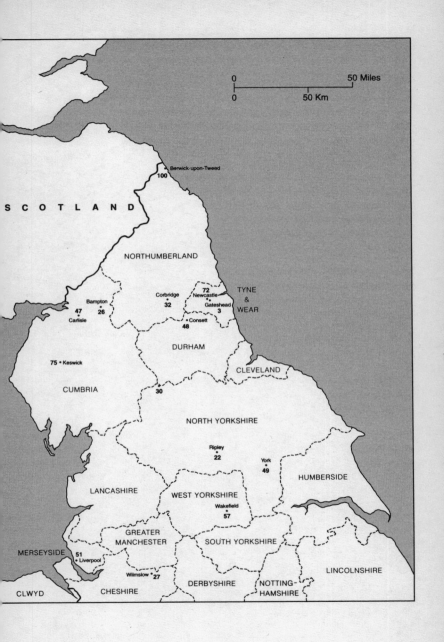

CHAPTER 7

The Venues listed by theme

SHIPS AND THE SEA

Come live with me, and be my love,
And we will some new pleasures prove
Of golden sands and crystal brooks,
With silken lines, and silver hooks.

JOHN DONNE

If you just love messing about in boats or simply being close to the water one of these places is bound to appeal. We have included boats in this section as well as glorious hotels with grounds which slope gently down to the water's edge. Probably the best known and best loved of all of these is Burgh Island which if you are an art deco freak has to be the number one choice for a romantic wedding. The setting is truly superb. The hotel is situated on its very own island which can only be reached at certain times of the day – for incurable romantics there could be nothing better than a wedding looking out to sea followed by a reception in the fabulous Palm Court and the rest of the weekend just exploring the island and swimming in the mild waters off the Devon coast. Perfect.

Name: Burgh Island
Address: Bigbury-on-Sea, South Devon TQ7 4BG
Tel: 01548 810514

Burgh Island is certainly a wedding venue with a difference. Firstly it is a real island which means when the tide is up twice a day it is totally inaccessible except by an eccentric mode of transport called a sea tractor. And secondly the hotel itself is probably one of the most extraordinary examples of genuine art deco architecture still surviving.

During the First World War the island was used by the army but in 1927 Archibald Nettlefold bought it and hired Matthew Dawson, the architect, to build a 'Great White Palace' for the enjoyment of himself and his friends who were members of the twenties jet set.

These friends included Agatha Christie who wrote *And Then There were None* and *Evil Under the Sun* at Burgh Island as well as Edward Prince of Wales who brought Wallis Simpson here to escape the glare of publicity surrounding their affair.

One of the main attractions was the Ganges Room, named after the famous ship believed to be the last sailing vessel that was a Flagship of the Royal Navy. When the ship was broken up in Plymouth in 1930, Nettlefold bought the Captain's Cabin

and stuck it on the front of the building. It survives to this day and is one of the rooms where you can have your wedding.

The hotel is now run by Tony Porter and his wife Beatrice who were almost pipped at the post when they put up their bid for the island in 1985. A snooker federation, a gay liberation group and a pop star were all much better placed financially to take on the building which had fallen into sorry disrepair.

When they bought it the place had been used for many years as holiday flats and had been sadly neglected. The fabulous peacock dome which now graces the Palm Court was broken and let the rain in all over the spectacular parquet flooring. The many priceless pieces of art deco furniture had been burned in a huge bonfire on the beach – the owner simply had not realized their true worth.

For Tony and Beatrice restoring the hotel has been a labour of love. They clearly are complete art decophiles and happily they have returned this gorgeous hotel to its former glory. There are two wedding rooms. The first is the Ganges Room which is light and airy and done out in black, white and green.

Every window has spectacular views out to sea and the bride and groom could have their preparatory talk with the registrar in the Captain's Cabin and then emerge as if by magic to walk up the aisle. After the ceremony guests can spill out into the Palm Court for drinks and photographs.

The second is in the huge Ballroom with its sprung dance floor and pale peach decor. Everywhere you look there are art deco artefacts including a beautiful fire surround. We felt the best wedding would be in the Ganges Room with up to 50 guests followed by drinks in the Palm Court and then a big bash in the Ballroom.

Couples can also take over the whole hotel for the weekend at a total cost of £7,160. That covers 36 people staying for bed, breakfast and evening meal and the wedding thrown in. Tony wants to discourage smaller groups from having weddings here. He is keen not to disrupt other guests who are staying – although a tiny hideaway wedding just for two could be arranged and you would be charged a fee of £150 plus VAT for the wedding room of your choice.

There are 14 suites of rooms all done out in original art deco furniture and all with magnificent sea views. The Noel Coward Suite is the honeymoon room – a corner room with its own balcony and sea views from every angle. Tony can organize anything from a jazz band to a duo who play music from the era, called Pennies from Devon.

The setting is absolutely idyllic for a glorious summer wedding on an island of your very own. Just bear in mind the timing for the wedding is quite important because it has to fit in with the tides!

Contact: Tony Porter
Main road: A38
Station: Totnes/Plymouth
Disabled access: Yes but limited
Parking: Car park in Bigbury-on-Sea
Registrar tel no: 01548 852682
Bedrooms: 14 suites
Wedding only: Yes

Name: **Carlyon Bay Hotel**
Address: **St Austell, Cornwall PL25 3RD**
Tel: **01726 812304**

The Carlyon Bay Hotel is reached via a private road which meanders through an opulent housing estate. The owners of these houses are clearly not short of a bob or two. Fabulous white thirties mansions perch perilously on the cliffs overlooking Carlyon Bay – part of the so-called Cornish Riviera.

The hotel itself is not overtly beautiful. Although it was built in the thirties and could be construed as art deco, it is painted a rather dull grey which does not add to its attractiveness. However once inside you can see why people love to come and stay at this particular beauty spot.

The hotel is set in 250 acres of grounds including its very own championship golf course. When we were there it was incredibly sunny and hot and it was hard not to be bowled over by the breathtaking views from the grounds. Standing on the edge of the cliffs with the seagulls swooping overhead made for a very romantic location.

One of the outstanding features of the hotel is that it positively welcomes childen – which may be important for second-time-arounders. A high energy entertainment programme keeps older children amused and there is a crèche with a fully trained nanny to take the younger ones off your hands.

All the rooms on the ground floor have been licensed to hold weddings. The first is the Green Room – a large and airy room done out in green and apricot with a terrace leading on to the lawn. Golfing prints adorn the walls which are decorated with dark green regency paper. The hotel caters for all sorts of sporting enthusiasts with its two swimming-pools, health suite and croquet lawn.

The best room by far for the wedding is the Cocktail Lounge with its huge window looking out to sea. In fact the first wedding ceremony to be held at the Carlyon was arranged on a sea theme. The bride wore a sea green frock with a crown to represent Lady Neptune. The operatic society sang sea songs and there were iced dolphins and a shark in the buffet to complete the effect! The room also has a fully sprung dance floor for after the wedding breakfast.

The Carlyon boasts all sorts of famous connections including Edward and Mrs Simpson. It was built in 1929 and then rebuilt in 1932 after it was destroyed by a fire. The nobility used to come and play at the golf club which is now owned by the hotel. They would often bring their servants who were provided with special quarters.

The Carlyon does not do evening functions as they have their resident guests to consider. For a finger buffet here you will pay between £14 and £23 but for an average bash including wine you are looking at around £25 a head.

An ideal wedding at the Carlyon would be in the Cocktail Lounge for the ceremony followed by a thirties tea dance or small reception in the Green Room and then on to one of the nearby hotels for a disco or barn dance in the evening. You may want to return to the hotel to stay in one of their superb suites or hire the penthouse. Outside the season the bride and groom get a honeymoon suite free of charge.

Contact: Peter Brennan
Main road: M5/A39
Station: St Austell
Disabled access: Yes
Parking: Ample
Registrar tel no: 01726 68974
Bedrooms: 72
Wedding only: Negotiable

Name: The *Tuxedo Royale*
Address: Hillgate Quay, Tyne Bridge, Gateshead NE8 2QS
Tel: 0191 477 8899

When Thelma Barnes supervised the couple having their wedding photographs taken, she was just a little puzzled that they insisted on having a shot with a lifeboat behind. 'I suggested that they might move a few yards so that they could have the Tyne Bridge as a backdrop,' recalled Thelma, who came to the venue that boasts 'one of Europe's most sensational night spots' from a career in advertising. The newly-weds were insistent however. 'That's where he proposed to me, you see,' explained the bride.

'The whole place is about boy meets girl – that's what the nightclub industry is all about,' says Thelma who can point to at least 4 wedding receptions in 6 years at which the bride and groom first met on board the place they call simply 'The Boat'. The Boat – *Tuxedo Royale* if we're being formal – is Newcastle night life writ large.

At the heart of the riverside area, a short stroll across the historic Swing Bridge to the Gateshead bank of the river, you will find the *Tuxedo Royale*, lying at anchor beneath the magnificent bowspring arch of the Tyne Bridge as it has done since December 1989.

Once The Boat plied the Irish Sea from Stranraer to Larne. More exotically it helped in the evacuations during the Middle East crisis in the 1960s and served as a passenger ferry in the Aegean. Now this boat is going nowhere and any sense of movement that the visitor experiences stems either from the seething mass of humanity that swarms through its many bars and cafés or from too much drink.

'We are licensed to take 1,760 people and we are very often full to capacity,' says Thelma. The wedding room is licensed for 100 guests and is a relatively unprepossessing, if reasonably smart, room on what was once The Boat's car deck. Here, the bride can walk down a central aisle to music of her choice. 'I have a couple getting married soon who have chosen Simply Red,' says Thelma. 'The registrar has said that you can't have the "Wedding March", but a suitable piece of classical music is fine.'

Thelma regards this addition to her reception-organizing role as bringing new interest to the job. 'I hope that if ever I get married, someone will take as much time and trouble as I do – you only get one go and it's got to be right.'

For the reception, The Boat offers a choice of rooms capable of holding up to 500, while smaller rooms are available for more intimate parties. You could even opt for a barbecue on deck if you could pretend that the towering developers' cranes which fringe the north bank of the Tyne were, say, Caribbean palm trees.

Other services The Boat can offer include flowers, photographs, a jazz duo, and a nearby helicopter landing pad. Prices per head range from £3.95 to £15.50 for a buffet, or £13 to £15.50 for a full wedding breakfast. Drinks packages range from £3 to £5 per head, while there is no specific charge for the hire of the wedding room itself. You could stage a real economy wedding aboard The Boat for around 50 people for as little as £350.

There is no accommodation on

The Boat, but the Waterside Hotel is only a short walk away and offers double rooms at weekend rates of £45. Other city centre hotels in the Quayside area include the Copthorne and the Vermont.

A wedding on The Boat would be ideal for any couple who first met on its renowned revolving dance floor. But it would also suit anyone who fancies a really modern wedding or, for that matter, a really good bash! But romantics shouldn't rule out tying the knot in nautical style. The Tyne riverbanks are a far cry from a few years ago and with the Tyne Bridge under floodlight, the five other bridges that span the gorge behind, and the city lights shimmering on one of the country's cleanest urban waterways, this can be a truly romantic setting.

Contact: Thelma Barnes
Main road: A1 (M)
Station: Newcastle Central
Disabled access: No
Parking: Ample
Registrar tel no: 0191 477 1011
Bedrooms: 0
Wedding only: Negotiable

**Name: SS *Great Britain*
Address: Great Western Dock, Bristol BS1 6TY
Tel: 01179 225737**

Bristol Docks are presently going through a period of change. Once a working port they are fast becoming a tourist and recreational area. Wandering around you come across small boats being restored by cou-

ples for a round-the-world-trip sitting alongside tour boats and outdoor cafés. In the middle of all this, in a dry dock, lies the SS *Great Britain*.

She is a huge iron ship designed by the legendary Isambard Kingdom Brunel and built in 1843 as a transatlantic passenger liner. She was the first iron propeller-driven steam ship and made regular trips to America and Australia. However as with many great old liners she fell on hard times and eventually ended her days in the Falklands. But in 1970 the SS *Great Britain* was brought back to Bristol for restoration in the very dock where she was originally built.

Today couples can get married in a piece of maritime history and relive some of the glory and style of those early travellers. However, the emphasis has to be on the word some. The ship is in the early stages of restoration and does not yet look as pristine as HMS *Victory* or the *Cutty Sark*. In many areas there are all the signs of the extensive restoration needed to return her to her former glory. Having said that, the wedding rooms are both charming and, in different ways, fabulous places to tie the knot.

The first wedding room is the original First Class Dining Saloon, 40 feet wide and 120 feet long with three rows of marbled columns. It has been fully restored with pale green walls and gorgeous brass hanging oil lamps. Built into the stern are several boxed settles which look rather like church pews. The burgundy and pink carpet is an exact replica of the original. Couples can get married next to the 'Campaign Table' which was originally used for displaying the ship's charts. A small Victorian piano can provide the music and there is disabled access.

The second wedding area is on the promenade deck at the stern of the ship. This is much more boaty. The walls are the iron hull of the ship painted white with plenty of rivets on view. There are windows looking out through the stern to the dockside. In the ceiling a large circular skylight means the guests can look up to the ship's wheel. There is a wooden floor and on either side two steep staircases lead down from the deck. The bride can walk up the aisle past the old passenger cabins and the couple can take their vows in among all the nautical paraphernalia. Both wedding areas can easily accommodate over 100 people.

After the ceremony drinks and photos can be taken on the main deck giving everyone the opportunity to look across the docks to the Georgian splendour of Clifton and the Cabot Tower in the trees beyond. The wedding party can then have a full reception downstairs in the Dining Saloon.

Guests who arrive early can browse around the souvenir shop or have a sandwich in the tea rooms. Late arrivals can buy last minute presents from the Bristol Blue Glass maker on the site. There is no accommodation on the ship although there is a small room where the bride can get changed. There are numerous hotels in Bristol city centre.

Weddings on the SS *Great Britain* are not expensive. Hire of the wedding room for the ceremony is £295. Special deals for receptions work out at around £30 per head. However, the ship is open to the public so timing the ceremony is important. If you are just having a wedding they will do their best to keep the public away from the wedding room while the ceremony takes place. They do, of course, have to allow access to any potential objectors. If you are having a reception it is best to have the ceremony at the end of the day so that the public have left by the time the feasting begins.

The SS *Great Britain* is an ideal spot for a medium-sized wedding for a couple who want to have something really different in the very heart of one of Britain's most important seaports.

Contact: Carol Wilkins
Main road: M32
Station: Bristol Templemeads
Disabled access: Some
Parking: Nearby
Registrar tel no: 0117 929246
Bedrooms: 0
Wedding only: Yes

Name: HMS *Warrior*
Address: Victory Gate, HM Naval Base, Portsmouth PQI 3QX
Tel: 01705 291379

HMS *Warrior* is certainly the grandest of the ships featured in this book. She was the first ocean-going iron-hulled armoured battleship in the world and was the largest and most powerful ship of her time. Launched in 1860, she was powered by a combination of steam and sail. Apparently her awesome firepower terrified the French so much that the guns were never actually used in combat.

After active service she suffered a sad decline, ending up as a floating oil jetty at Milford Haven. But now she has been fully restored to her former glory and is located in the Portsmouth Historic Dockyard close to HMS *Victory*.

Weddings are held in the Captain's Cabin, a beautiful room with white panelled walls picked out in gold. At one end there is a formal dining table set with cut glass and illuminated by oil lamps. In the middle of the room there is an enamel stove, an antique occasional table and some chairs. At the other end is a small sleeping area with the captain's cot which would have doubled up as a coffin should he have had the misfortune to die at sea.

The Captain's Cabin is at the stern of the ship but, unlike the *Victory*, it does not have windows looking out on to the water. Unfortunately the technology of the day put a propeller well in the way.

Weddings are conducted from the dining table. They have to be small affairs as only 20 other people are allowed in the room. HMS *Warrior* is a historic monument and Mrs Mitchell, who is responsible for

weddings, stresses that the room and all its historic artefacts must stay the same for the service. She can however arrange for a harpist or flautist to provide music for the ceremony.

The bride and groom will meet the registrar in the Commander's Cabin, a small room with a little oak desk and an open-backed chesterfield settee. It houses the ship's visitors' book, so take the opportunity to look out for some of the Royal visitors who have been here before.

There is a choice of areas for the reception. Small groups can have a dinner in the Wardroom which was originally the ship's officers' dining room. It can seat up to 18 and is sumptuously laid out with hanging oil lamps, fine linen, cut glass and delicate flower arrangements.

Larger receptions can be held on the Officers' Half Deck or on the Gun Deck. Here up to 200 people can be fed and watered at heavy pine mess tables set between huge broadside guns complete with all their fighting accessories and a selection of small arms. All sorts of music can be provided including a variety of military bands and a group performing traditional sea songs.

Mrs Mitchell organizes the weddings from her base in what was the ship's chaplain's office. She is from a nautical background and is extremely enthusiastic about weddings on board HMS *Warrior*. However, she does point out that there are some limitations that couples will have to consider before making a booking.

The ship is open to the public during the day. While the ceremony takes place a quartermaster will be posted at the door of the Captain's Cabin to maintain privacy and to allow anyone with a genuine interest to come and say their piece.

Receptions have to be held after the ship has closed to the public so timing is crucial. The ideal arrangement would be a late afternoon wedding followed by photos on the deck and a reception in the early evening. Couples who do not want to have a reception on board can have a wedding at any time of day subject to the needs of the ship. Mrs Mitchell will advise on the best time of day and try to ensure that the wedding does not coincide with a visit by hundreds of schoolchildren.

Weddings in the Captain's Cabin cost £500 and charges for the reception rooms start at £600. Catering is provided by two local firms and a good meal with drinks is likely to cost £25–30 per head. There is no accommodation on HMS *Warrior* but there are numerous hotels in Portsmouth. Disabled access is restricted to certain areas.

Portsmouth Harbour Station is just next to the entrance to the historic dockyard. So if money is no object hire the *Orient Express*, bring all the guests down from London for a slap-up reception and then take them back without having to worry about drinking and driving.

On HMS *Warrior* the emphasis is very much on dignified weddings in keeping with the surroundings. If you roll up and ask Mrs Mitchell for a Treasure Island theme wedding complete with parrots and a 'yo-ho-ho-and-a-bottle-of-rum' reception do not be surprised if you are quietly but firmly shown the door. If, however, you want to have a very special event with a maritime flavour in stunning surroundings this is definitely the place.

Contact: Mrs Sorel Mitchell
Main road: M275
Station: Portsmouth Harbour
Disabled access: Restricted
Parking: By arrangement
Registrar tel no: 01705 829041
Bedrooms: 0
Wedding only: Yes

Name: Polhawn Fort
Address: Military Road, Rame, Torpoint, Cornwall PL10 1LL
Tel: 01752 822864

If you fancy a themed wedding in dramatic surroundings in a place where you can do what you want, stay with all your friends and have a house party then Polhawn Fort could be the answer to your prayer.

Polhawn is an original Napoleonic fort set in the hillside on a cliff overlooking the sea 12 miles west of Plymouth. You approach it along a narrow cliff road high up on Whitsand Bay passing hundreds of holiday homes on the way.

At this point you may begin to think that this is not the sort of place for a posh wedding, but persevere and all will be revealed. The views from the cliffs are truly spectacular. Turn off the road and follow a drive down the cliff for half a mile. Even then the fort is still hidden from view in the cliff below. Walk over a small drawbridge and you are on the roof of the fort and a magnificent vista of the sea comes into view. The cliffs and the seashore curve away for miles on either side.

To reach the wedding room you go through a small doorway and descend a spiral staircase into a huge room. Just like Alice going down the rabbit hole, it appears you are in a series of vast interconnected vaulted rooms. The walls are of bare limestone several feet thick and the ceilings and arches are brick.

On one side there is a row of small windows looking out to sea. On closer inspection it is clear these are no ordinary windows. They are the gun emplacements, embrasures for the technically-minded, which used to hold the cannon which would defend England from the dreaded French. A semi-circular iron rail set in the floor allowed the gun to swivel round to face the imaginary foe. On the other side the windows look on to the cliff draped in a thick layer of greenery.

This gigantic room has been licensed to hold weddings and is over 80 feet long and 28 feet wide. It has arches each containing a gun emplacement but the guns have long since gone. There are small fireplaces in each section but the centrepiece is the big fireplace at the far end which can be stoked up to give the room a real medieval atmosphere – all that is needed is a small suckling pig roasting quietly in the fire to complete the effect.

Beyond the main room is a large catering-style kitchen and a total of 8 bedrooms. One of the larger suites is also licensed as a wedding room. It measures 28 by 17 feet and has a cannon embrasure for the window. It would be ideal if you wanted to have a small wedding before all the rest of your friends arrived for a big party.

The fort would certainly be a fabulous place to spend your wedding night. All the bedrooms face the sea and most of them have en-suite facilities. The fort can normally sleep 20 but it is possible to squeeze in a few more on special occasions.

Outside there is a sheltered private lawn with dramatic sea views. In one corner steps lead down to your very own stretch of Cornish beach complete with a small sandy bay and rock pools at low tide.

Polhawn Fort is not a hotel or guest house. Rather it is a sort of gigantic holiday cottage. It is only possible to book the whole building for use by groups. So you can have it for a weekend or for the week from Monday to Friday. Once it is booked you can make your own arrangements and do whatever you like. You can do your own catering or get outside caterers to come in and do all the work. For those staying a few days a local shop will send in supplies.

Polhawn is an ideal venue for a couple who really want to go to town and organize a truly exotic themed wedding. Some groups have already held medieval events there and decorated the walls with armour and flags. Others have brought a van load of flowers from Covent Garden and filled the room with scent and colour. On a winter's day it would be possible to have a very atmospheric wedding with a blazing log fire and lots of candles. The wedding rooms can hold up to 120 people but it feels more comfortable with 70 or 80.

The owner, John Wicksteed, can recommend caterers including one to do the roast pig but he is equally happy for couples to organize their own. That means you can bring your own drink, so why not persuade a kindly relative to do a wine run across to France to guarantee some really special celebrations?

Booking Polhawn Fort costs between £1,925 and £2,950 according to the length of stay and the time of year. It sounds a lot but when you consider that you are getting a fabulous venue and accommodation for 20 guests then the price begins to look quite reasonable. The fort is heavily booked in the summer so you will need to plan your wedding some time in advance. If, on the other hand, you want to have a mid-week winter wedding booking will be much easier and you might even be able to do a deal on the price with John.

We thought this was an absolutely stunning place for a couple who wanted to have an adventurous wedding with a lot of old friends in attendance. Ideal perhaps for some theatrical types getting married second time round.

Contact: John Wicksteed
Main road: A38
Station: Plymouth (12 miles)
Disabled access: Difficult
Parking: Ample
Registrar tel no: 01752 842624
Bedrooms: 8
Wedding only: Yes

Name: Trevigue Farm
Address: Crackington Haven, Bude, Cornwall EX23 0LQ

Crackington Haven is a magical place. A tiny Cornish fishing village which looks just like all those picture postcards you have seen of Cornwall − sun, sand, sea and a wild and rugged coastline.

Walking up the steep hill from the beach to Trevigue Farm there is a sense of timelessness here. For a city dweller it is disturbingly quiet. The occasional rustle in the bushes − usually a baby rabbit popping its nose out to see what's going on − is the only sound to break the silence.

The farm itself is a family-run dairy and beef farm and great emphasis is placed on conservation. The farm abounds with wildlife − badgers, foxes, many species of birds and of course beautiful wild flowers.

This fortified farmhouse, with its sturdy granite outhouses which form a defensive ring around a cobbled courtyard, dates back to the 16th century. Staddle stones, once used to deter rats from the grain stores, stand like huge mushroom-shaped sculptures around the building.

Trevigue's 500 acres stretch along the spectacular Cornish cliffs as far as the eye can see. It has kept its coastline entirely to itself and breathtaking views from the clifftops are a few minutes' stroll from the house. A steep donkey track winds precariously down to lonely Strangles Beach, 650 feet below, where Thomas Hardy walked with his first wife Emma. It is a wonderful place and one of the best spots for truly romantic wedding photographs.

Inside, the farmhouse is warm and cosy with massive fireplaces and oak beams. The cool slate-floored hall with its mullioned windows leads into a comfortable sitting room with deep sofas and a log-burning fire. There are two rooms which have been licensed. The first is the old hall in the farmhouse which is suitable for a small wedding of around 20 people. With its flagstone floors covered in loose rugs it has a lovely rustic atmosphere. The place is perfectly preserved without being chintzy.

The other is in a beautifully converted barn with a high, beamed ceiling. The barn has a stone floor and at one end there are steps up to a platform where the bride and groom could take their vows. Down a little staircase is the restaurant which used to be the old 'shippen' or milking parlour. The pine tables and dressers make it feel very much like a farmhouse kitchen.

Janet Crocker and her soon-to-be daughter-in-law Gayle run the place together and a more formidable team you could not hope to find. They clearly love making your stay as pleasant as possible and specialize in a very personal service. Janet believes the farm is ideal for those seeking a very private, away-from-it-all wedding.

For our money the best bet would be a small wedding in the old hall at lunchtime with just a few close family members. Then an afternoon reception in the restaurant with around 30 guests. Trevigue does not organize music or dancing but is happy to recommend the nearby pub in Crackington Haven who will provide a disco for evening revellers.

The farm has accommodation for up to 12 people. A special honeymoon suite within a separate cottage overlooks the glorious Cornish countryside. It has a swimming-pool and newly-weds could do worse than stay a few extra days just relaxing and enjoying the walks around the area. Bed and breakfast is £60 for a double room.

Catering is good wholesome farmhouse fare. A simple finger buffet will cost you around £15 a head plus wine at £6–7 a head. A full four-course meal will set you back around £25 a head. For a small romantic wedding in the idyllic setting of a genuine working farm we could not fault Trevigue.

Contact: Janet Crocker
Main road: A30
Station: Bodmin, Exeter, Plymouth
Disabled access: Yes
Parking: Ample

Registrar tel no: 01726 68974
Bedrooms: 6, and a cottage
Wedding only: Yes at a negotiated fee

SOMEWHERE SPECIAL – SOMEWHERE SPORTY

There's nothing worse than solitude, growing old without a shoulder to lean on. Marry, marry – even if he's fat and boring!

GABRIELLE CHANEL

We almost called this section wild and wacky but in fact it is really for anyone who is looking for something slightly different. These places are definitely not run of the mill. Here you will find anything from a football club to a zoo. Just because we have listed these particular venues under this title does not mean you will not find other places that will let you be as wacky as you like – and that includes register offices! The ones that we chose were all slightly eccentric, or different enough not to be everyone's cup of tea. They are also places in which you could really let your imagination run riot. What better, for example, than to have the wedding of your dreams in the place where they make dreams come true, on celluloid at least – Pinewood Studios.

Name: Pinewood Film Studios
Address: Pinewood Road, Iver,
Bucks SL0 0NH
Tel: 01753 656953

If you have ever had a secret hankering to be a film star even just for a day then Pinewood could make your dreams come true. Pinewood Studios has been host to over 600 feature films as well as a range of television series such as *Jeeves and Wooster* and *The Camomile Lawn*.

The 19th-century manor house was originally built as a private home with 39 bedrooms, 11 bathrooms, an indoor swimming-pool, a squash court, Turkish bath and a ballroom. All sorts of different people have lived in the house but in 1934 it was bought by J. Arthur Rank who wanted to turn the area into a feature film studio to rival Hollywood. In 1936 he realized his dream and Pinewood Studios was born.

Weddings take place in the opulent Gatsby Room which was built especially for the film *The Great Gatsby*. It was never meant to last for ever and you can still see some of the joins. Nevertheless the setting is quite superb. Every window overlooks the grounds which are laid out with lawns and cedar trees. There is a lake and formal gardens and a maze. In fact each part of the garden looks like a set from a film you have probably seen at some time or another. While we were there we stumbled upon the set for *Treasure Island*, the new Ken Russell movie. If you had got married on that day you could have had your photos taken against a backdrop of palm trees, sand and fake boulders.

Off the Gatsby Room is the Green Room – a beautiful sea green reception room done out in thirties style. It leads on to a terrace with stone balustrades and steps down to the garden. When we visited, it was set up for a twenties themed wedding.

For receptions you can hire the huge oak panelled Ballroom which is used during the week as a restaurant and featured as the library in *Fierce Creatures* starring John Cleese. Starstruck couples should visit before the wedding for a meal to discuss the arrangements just to see who they might end up sitting next to! Vivian who showed us around is still reeling from the fact she sat next to Pierce Brosnan the week before!

Off the Ballroom is what is affectionately called the Theatre but was in fact originally built as an indoor swimming-pool. This has a huge stage for anyone who wants to make a performance of taking their vows, a balcony leading to a small recess with an eccentric fountain in the middle and film posters all around the walls.

The Theatre is the most flexible of all the rooms and can be effectively turned into a nightclub. The staff at Pinewood can handle anything from a medieval banquet to a wild west party. They are thoroughly used to arranging themed wedding receptions including a fifties event complete with pink Cadillacs.

A basic wedding here including red carpet arrival, bucks fizz reception and wine with your meal will cost you around £38.50 a head and a top-of-the-range bash using all the facilities will set you back around £65 a head. Pinewood offers a variety of options from sparkling drinks on a sun-lit terrace to spicy mulled wine in front of a roaring log fire. The surroundings adapt themselves to any season.

This is definitely the place to come if you want a truly spectacular wedding arranged by people who really know their business. The staff are used to creating dreams here and are happy to help you make yours come true. But don't expect frills like glorious posh powder rooms. The Ladies' looks a little like those old school loos – all green paint and stone floors!

Contact: Michael Stone
Main road: M40/M4/M25
Station: Slough
Disabled access: Yes
Parking: Ample
Registrar tel no: 01753 520485
Bedrooms: 0
Wedding only: No

Name: 007 Bond Street
Address: Bond Gate, Nuneaton,
Warwickshire CV11 4DA
Tel: 01203 347563

If you want a fun wedding with a difference, 007 Bond Street is the place to go. It is a James Bond theme pub in a one-way system on the edge of Nuneaton town centre and now it calls itself '007 – Licensed to Wed'. The ground floor is a large music bar with a few places to prop up your drinks. Pictures of James Bond actors decorate the walls. The music pumps out at full volume from a disco in the corner shaped to look like James Bond's original Aston Martin. There are hardly any tables or chairs. This is a place to see, be seen, do a bit of chatting up and have a really good time.

Weddings take place upstairs in Moneypenny's Nightclub. In the daytime it is surprisingly light with a large bar, dance floor and some seating at the side. The pink and green room holds 300 people and looks lovely decorated with flowers and with the tables all set for a traditional reception. The club will roll out a red carpet right down the stairs for the couple. The nightclub is fully air-conditioned so it is cool even on the hottest summer day.

After the ceremony the couple can have their photos taken in the theme pub or outside on a terrace which overlooks a small river. The bushes on the river bank obscure the car park on the other side so it is almost possible to forget that you are in the middle of the town. Nuneaton Council has kindly agreed to plant some extra shrubs and flowers so that couples can have really good photos.

If you are going to get married in a nightclub you might as well have a party and 007 is just the place. A local balloon company will decorate the room and make a wedding arch or a palm tree out of balloons to give the room a party feel. After the ceremony and photos the club can pull down the blinds, turn on the disco lights and get the music going.

Lara Watson, who deals with the weddings, is keen to make sure that 007 weddings are carried out in style. She previously worked for Club 18–30 so she knows all about organizing a good time. She will make all the arrangements so that couples have a wedding with a difference. You can have a band playing in the evening and the DJs will play the music of your choice.

It is possible just to book the room for £100 but we thought that would defeat the object. Lara has a number of very reasonable package deals on offer which include room hire, arrival drinks, a buffet or meal and sparkling wine for the toast. These start at around £15 per head.

An evening buffet without drinks starts at £4 per head. There is no disabled access to the upstairs nightclub. Guests can stay in local hotels and there is a large car park opposite.

Finally, if you want to go off in style they can arrange for a James Bond Aston Martin with an 007 number plate which can be hired as the wedding car. Moneypenny would surely have approved!

Contact: Lara Watson or Heather Clelland
Main road: M1

Station: Nuneaton
Disabled access: No
Parking: Ample
Registrar tel no: 01203 348948
Bedrooms: 0
Wedding only: Yes

Name: Heritage Park Hotel
Address: Coed Cae Road, Trehafod, near Pontypridd, Mid Glamorgan CF37 2NP
Tel: **01443 687057**

Thanks to a recent injection of European cash the Rhondda Valley, once famed for its mining communities, now has its very own heritage park. Visitors to the park can take the 'journey of a lifetime' to discover the hardship and joys of life in the Lewis Merthyr Colliery in the 1950s. In the lamp room your very own miner will show you what preparations are needed before going underground. You are supplied with safety helmets and you ride in the cage to the pit bottom.

For over 150 years the Rhondda and the other valleys which radiate from their hub at Pontypridd formed an industrial dynamo which transformed Wales. During the 1920s the two narrow Rhondda valleys alone held nearly 170,000 people, brought there to contribute their manual efforts to produce nearly 10 million tons of Welsh coal.

Today the old pithead is still silhouetted against the skyline as a sombre reminder of the thriving industry which once employed thousands of local men. There is something rather poignant about the fact that the only jobs left for the men now are the ones where they dress up in the clothes they once wore so proudly to show American tourists round their heritage.

If you have mining roots or simply love the valleys you can now get married in the Heritage Park Hotel which is noteworthy simply because it stands bang next to the heritage park. It looks a little like an old Welsh church school on the outside but we were assured it never was.

The wedding room is the Conservatory with an outlook over some of the most green and pleasant valleys you will ever see. The bride enters the room through huge tall Georgian-style french windows and walks up an aisle to the main window where the registrar will sit.

After the ceremony the reception can take place in the Rhondda Suite – a light and airy function room with massive windows and a pitched pine ceiling with deep-set modern lighting. The whole room has a Scandinavian feel to it with plenty of pale sherry-coloured wood and vast areas of glass.

There is a balcony which could happily hold a brass band or Welsh male voice choir but is more likely to house the disco later on in the evening.

A sprung dance floor completes the effect making the room ideal for a huge bash of up to 250 people. For a smaller wedding you can still marry in the Conservatory but for the reception you can retire to the Loft Room Restaurant which has the appearance of an old granary. You get to it up some little stairs which lead you to a galleried room all done out with Welsh pine dressers and corn dollies. The room holds around 50 for a sit-down meal. Finally, you could also get married in the Lewis Merthyr Suite which holds up to 120 guests.

The bedrooms are well furnished but this is not the sort of place for four-posters and jacuzzis. Many overlook the car park and a rather unattractive slag heap. But do not worry. The council is due to camouflage it later in the year with grass. All in all the rooms are comfortable and adequate and very inexpensive. A honeymoon suite will set you back £55.

Simple finger buffets including wine will cost you around £8–20 and a sit-down meal with wine between £13 and £25. All in all we thought the deal was good value and the service very friendly.

We felt that anyone who has Welsh or mining connections may like to get married in the Rhondda Valley. As a base to explore this part of Wales it is second to none.

Contact: Mark Hutton
Main road: M4/A470
Station: Trehafod
Disabled access: Yes
Parking: Plenty
Registrar tel no: 01443 486869
Bedrooms: 50
Wedding only: No

Name: **Finchcocks Musical Museum**
Address: **Finchcocks, Goudhurst,
Kent TN17 1HH**
Tel: **01580 211702**

If you drive 10 miles south of Tunbridge Wells to the village of Goudhurst and then another half-mile
down a tiny country lane, you come
up over a rise in the road and see a
huge brick-built Georgian baroque
pile.

Finchcocks, a massive manor
house, was built in 1725 and has
remained in private hands ever
since. In 1970 it was acquired by
concert pianist Richard Burnett. He
lives there with his wife Katrina
together with their collection of
over 80 historical keyboard instruments. These include chamber
organs, harpsichords, virginals, spin-
ets and early pianos. Most of them
have been carefully restored and are
in full working order and several
could even be played during your
wedding.

Ceremonies for up to 100 take
place in what was the main entrance
hall to the house. It is normally the
Piano Museum and guests will be
surrounded by antique pianos of all
shapes and sizes. Although the
house looks huge from the front,
the building has no depth. This
gives the oak-panelled wedding
room rather strange proportions. It
is very tall and rather narrow with
a large staircase where the bride
can make a dramatic entrance to
the sound of early piano music or
perhaps a trio.

Weddings normally have the run

of the whole house so guests will be
able to wander around upstairs
looking at all the early musical
instruments including the piano
used in the soundtrack of the film
Amadeus. Richard Burnett used to
run a business making harpsichords
and there are also some fine examples of his firm's work.

Receptions can be held in the
Cellar Restaurant or outside in a
marquee. The vaulted cellar holds
about 100 people and classical
music buffs will recognize the simi-
larity to the Footstool Restaurant
in the basement of St John's Smith
Square in London. Hardly surprising as they were both designed by
the same architect. The cellar in
Finchcocks is painted white giving
it a rather Spanish atmosphere.
You can have a disco so that guests
can really let their hair down after
all that classical music at the
wedding.

Outside there is a large lawn and
space for a marquee which accommodates around 200 guests. Smaller
parties can use the delightful walled
garden. Originally it was the
vegetable garden. Now it is a haven
of peace and quiet with a small
goldfish pond and several pergolas
with benches. A small marquee can
be erected in the garden for buffets
and drinks. Linda the gardener will
be happy to do all the flower
arrangements.

The catering is done in-house and
ranges from a finger buffet with
wine for £10 per head to sit-down
meals at around £20 per head.

Finchcocks does not let out rooms
but the old children's quarters at the

top of the house can be used by the bridal party for their preparations. The rooms are largely unrestored and have a slightly battered look but they really do give a feel of what life was like at Finchcocks in the old days. Guests can stay at hotels in Goudhurst and Tunbridge Wells or in local bed and breakfast.

The Burnetts are keen that the house and its musical instruments should be used to the full. Richard gives regular performances to visitors and Katrina writes plays so they are very willing to help out with theatrical themed weddings. They have a supply of 18th-century costumes and their staff are willing to dress up for your event. The only real restrictions are that because of the antique floors stiletto heels are not allowed and for fire reasons there is no smoking in the main building.

To hire the wedding room will cost you £300 plus VAT. The whole building with all facilities can be hired at a range of rates starting from £600 plus VAT. Receptions will be costed according to individual needs.

Finchcocks is an extraordinary place run by a delightfully eccentric couple. It is an ideal venue for classical music buffs and a great opportunity to hold a themed wedding in original surroundings.

Contact: Katrina Burnett
Main road: A262
Station: Paddock Wood (8 miles), Tunbridge Wells (10 miles)
Disabled access: No
Parking: Plenty

Registrar tel no: 01892 527332
Bedrooms: 0
Wedding only: Yes

Name: Bentley Wildfowl Park and Motor Museum
Address: Halland, Lewes, East Sussex BN8 5AF
Tel: 01825 840573

In 1937 a young man discovered the property he had been searching for so that he could take up farming. Bentley was it. Within a few years he fell in love and married Mary and thanks to their skills the old farmhouse was lovingly restored and converted into the spectacular building it is today. Two Palladian rooms were then added on each end of the house.

In 1962 Gerald Askew returned from a trip and announced he had ordered 20 pairs of waterfowl and asked his wife Mary where should he put them. Mary could have been forgiven for telling him in no uncertain terms but she simply smiled and ordered a bulldozer to excavate a pond in one of the fields. And so Bentley opened as a wildfowl park in 1966 and today more than 100 different species of wildfowl can be seen there.

The work of this extraordinary couple was only brought to an end with Gerald's death in 1970. Sadly he died before he had a chance to enjoy the renovated house, particularly the Bird Room which features his collection of wildfowl paintings by local Sussex artist Philip Rickman.

For eight years Mary ran the place herself but as they had no immediate family and she wanted local people to be able to appreciate the place she gave the estate to East Sussex County Council to manage. She still lives in part of the building.

Barry Sutherland is the jolly chap who runs the estate and has the job of organizing weddings. He is also charged with the task of trying to make Bentley more commercial while preserving its very special identity.

If you want fireworks or loud rock music, Bentley is not the place to hold your wedding. However the house itself is truly delightful. The Philip Rickman Gallery is where weddings are held. It is decorated in bold colours of yellow and white and furnished with amazing oriental furniture. The floor is black and white chequered marble. In the centre of the room stands a circular marble table set on a pedestal of carved swans. The whole effect is truly exotic and is set off by the extraordinary formal gardens which are a delight to wander through. After the wedding a reception can be held in a marquee on the lawn outside.

Bentley is also known for one of the finest collections of veteran, Edwardian and vintage cars and motorcycles in the country. They are housed in a converted barn near the house. All are privately owned and many are used on the road. It is possible to hire one of the vehicles, with prior consent of its owner, for a really unique form of transport to the wedding!

Couples should bear in mind that Bentley is open to the public and there may be people in the grounds while the wedding is going on. However the wedding room itself will be shut so there is no danger of anyone wandering in uninvited.

The place would appeal to young couples who are environmentally conscious and want that reflected in some way. Or it may simply appeal to anyone who wants something which will give them a real day to remember.

There are no other usable rooms at Bentley but on-site catering can be provided. There are several local bed and breakfasts. Background music can be arranged as long as it is in keeping with the building, not necessarily what you want! '"A Whiter Shade of Pale" would be fine and low key but heavy metal might not go down so well,' says Barry. 'We can cater for wacky weddings as long as they are not too outrageous and it doesn't interfere with what we are doing here. We've got the cars on tap, contacts for flowers and any sort of music from a jazz band to a string quartet can be arranged.'

For our money the best bet would be a small wedding with about 50 guests followed by an open-air picnic (weather permitting) on the grassland around the building. The basic wedding ceremony will cost you £150 excluding the registrar. Catering ranges from £7.50 a head for a finger buffet with wine to £25 a head for a sit-down meal in a marquee which is also extra.

Contact: Barry Sutherland
Main road: M23/A26/A27
Station: Lewes/Uckfield
Disabled Access: Yes
Parking: Ample
Registrar tel no: 01892 653803
Bedrooms: 0
Wedding only: Yes

Name: **Rivers Nightclub and Boaters Restaurant**
Address: **I St Helen's Avenue, Benson, Oxon OX10 6RY**
Tel: **01491 838331**

To be honest, when you first see Rivers Nightclub and Boaters Restaurant – which incidentally are the same place – you may wonder why we included it in the 100 best places. The outside of the building looks like a large modern roadside pub. Persevere, looks can be deceptive – this is one of the country's most unusual wedding venues.

It was originally a thirties tea room used by day trippers coming up the river from Oxford. Later on it was a dinner and dance cabaret centre. Now it is a popular pub restaurant and nightclub. To get there you take a sharp right turn off the Oxford to Henley-on-Thames road at Benson.

Upstairs the wedding room is octagonal with rather wonderful stained-glass windows depicting exotic birds. The carpet throughout is woven with a design of boater hats. When it is not a wedding room it is part of Boaters Restaurant. It gives on to a roof terrace which does have superb views – unfortunately of the road rather than the river. Boaters can happily hold 75 guests either seated or standing for the ceremony and up to 100 guests for the reception.

Downstairs is Rivers Nightclub, at the time of writing, the only nightclub in the south east licensed for weddings. Apparently Rivers is immensely popular, with young people coming from a radius of about 100 miles. The club holds 500 people and is attractively laid out with tables along the edge and a huge dance floor in the middle.

Chris Price, who showed us around, originally had no intention of getting a wedding licence because he thought them prohibitively expensive in Oxford. But a couple who had met in the club and got engaged there, begged him to let them be married in the restaurant and have their reception in the nightclub. Being a bit of a soft touch he agreed and has since been deluged with requests for more of the same.

If you want to get married in style you could have a fantastic small wedding in the restaurant upstairs and then invite hundreds of friends for a real knees-up in the club downstairs. Or you could have a wedding downstairs in the nightclub for up to 400 guests, making it one of the biggest wedding venues for miles around. Once the ceremony was over and the food eaten everyone could dance till they dropped.

Food is inexpensive. A finger buffet will cost between £5 and £8 a head. A fork buffet will set you back between £10 and £15 and a full-scale sit-down meal will cost around £18. You can hire the place for a wedding only but it will cost you £175 for Boaters and £250 for Rivers. If you have a combined ceremony and reception the fees drop to £100 for Boaters and £150 for Rivers.

Although there is no accommodation at the venue there is a range of inexpensive hotels in the area. There is also extremely good accommodation at a little thatched pub at nearby Clifden Hamden.

Rivers Nightclub is definitely the place for a couple who are not traditionalists and want to have an unusual wedding followed by a great party with lots of their friends, without breaking the bank in the process.

Contact: Mike Allen
Main road: M40/A4074
Station: Didcot
Disabled access: Yes
Parking: Ample
Registrar tel no: 0867 74702
Bedrooms: 0
Wedding only: Yes

Name: Coombe Abbey
Address: Coombe Abbey Park, Brinklow Road, Binley, Coventry CV3 2AB
Tel: 01203 450450

Way back in 1150 Cistercian monks in the district of Smitham founded a monastery which became Coombe Abbey. According to the history books the monks expanded their empire by purchasing large tracts of local land. In the process they demolished the villages of Lower and Upper Smite which is how Smitham got its name. They finally got their come-uppance when Henry VIII enacted the dissolution of the monasteries in 1539.

Jumping a few centuries, the famous gardener Capability Brown was commissioned in 1771 to landscape the grounds creating the lakes and formal gardens which are still here today. In 1992 the council became involved in an imaginative venture with the private sector to turn the abbey's restored buildings into a hotel in the middle of a very popular country park which on a summer Sunday is filled with families out having picnics and walking their dogs. From the park you walk down a long drive, over a moat and into a courtyard to the hotel entrance. From the outside it looks like many other large country houses although here you can spot the difference between the old and restored parts of the building by the different colours of the stonework.

The inside is completely different from every other hotel that you might have ever visited. In fact the company which owns it is part of the 'No ordinary hotel' group which sums it up perfectly. There are no chintzy three-piece suites, no reproduction Chippendale chairs and no Laura Ashley curtains. Instead the interior is a gothic fantasy with dark oak furniture, stone-vaulted ceilings and bizarre sculptures of plants complete with tiny fairy lights. The hall is dimly lit and the whole effect is most strange, a cross between a church crypt and the set of a Hammer horror movie.

This over-the-top style is repeated in every part of the building. The corridors have heavy carved furniture and lots of thick carpets, ferns and ornamental lights. Each area is different but all are very unusual.

The main restaurant where wedding receptions are held has a large stone fireplace and three raised and enclosed dining areas which look down on the rest of the dining room. They are rather like those ornamental gazebos that are found hidden in the grounds of Victorian country estates. The bride, groom and close family could occupy these places of honour at the wedding breakfast.

The bridal suite is even more spectacular. It has the grandest four-poster bed you have ever seen, on a raised platform which is reached by steps decorated with an ornately carved balustrade. Another room is done out in the Chinese style and has a separate stage with a Victorian bath in the bedroom – great for couples who like a romantic champagne splash. Another is on split levels with sea green carpet, a sunken bath and steep steps up to the bed. A rather odd feature of many of the rooms is that the toilet is set in a carved surround and made to look like a throne. What would Freud have said of that?

By comparison the wedding rooms are rather low key. The De Camville Room holds about 20 people and is decorated in plain colours with mustard walls and a maroon carpet. There are no ornate carvings here, just a large window that fills the end of the room and a medieval spear-holder on the wall.

Bigger weddings are held in the Abbeygate, a larger hall in the old stable block which seats about 140. This has wooden pillars and a carved wooden stage with another raised area which looks rather like a pulpit. The room has been decorated in a medieval style with lots of shields on the walls and flags hanging from the ceiling.

The ornate gardens and lakes at the back of the hotel are part of the country park. There is an entrance into the gardens and drinks can be served there but the hotel does not have exclusive use of the grounds.

The De Camville Room and the Abbeygate can be hired for £100 and £200 respectively for weddings on the assumption that there will be a reception as well. The cost for food and wine at receptions ranges from £35 to £60 per head. Rooms vary from £95 a night up to £295 for the special suites. The hotel has exceptionally good disabled access including specially equipped disabled bedrooms. There is ample parking and more modestly priced rooms can be booked in several nearby hotels.

Coombe Abbey is very different

and you will either love it or hate it. It would be a great place for a medieval themed wedding and it is certainly somewhere to have a honeymoon night to remember.

Contact: Paul Gossage
Main road: M6/A46
Station: Coventry (5 miles)
Disabled access: Good
Parking: Ample
Registrar tel no: 01788 571233
Bedrooms: 63
Wedding only: Yes

Name: Coventry City Football Club
Address: Highfield Road Stadium, King Street, Coventry CV2 4FW
Tel: 01203 223535

Whoever thought that in England it would ever be possible to get married at a football club? Well it is, but as it is still England you can't tie the knot on the centre spot or in the goal mouth. Perhaps things will change eventually.

Fans of Coventry City can get married in the stadium, overlooking the pitch and even while a match is being played. As everybody knows the team is called the Sky Blues and you get to the stadium along the Sky Blue Way. Like many football stadiums it is surrounded by small streets of old terraced houses. These make the stadium look immense in comparison. But when you get inside, there are many wedding rooms which are on a more human scale. Anyone who has not been to a football match for a few years will be amazed at how clean and friendly the grounds look. No more bare concrete and draughty terraces. It is all fresh paint and comfortable seats now.

The Ladbroke Club is a large meeting room which is a restaurant on match days. To be honest it looks like a lot of other conference rooms and can hold up to 150 people. But when it is all set out for a wedding with arrangements of flowers it becomes a lot more homely.

Upstairs is the room where all real fans would like to take their vows. The Premier Club is the main restaurant and hospitality suite. Decked out in blue, it has huge windows giving panoramic views over the all-seater stadium. The room goes round a corner of the stand with seating along one side and a restaurant area on the other. Given the layout of the room you could have a wedding at one end followed by a reception at the other.

But by far the best wedding would surely be in the corner of the room with the registrar's table set up by the window. That way the couple and the guests could see the pitch during the ceremony. Bad luck for the registrar who would only have a view of the bar.

There are several other places in the grounds where weddings can take place including the Boardroom which holds 10 people, the Trophy Room and the Boxes. Couples cannot have their wedding on the pitch but Wendy O'Brien, venue sales manager, is happy to let them have their photos taken in the goal mouth. They can even have a few action shots with a football but she draws the line at all the guests getting out and having a full-scale match.

Wendy is a great fan of the new weddings. She is keen to give couples a real choice on their wedding day. If it is possible she will make it happen. Real fans can have blue cakes in the shape of the football pitch complete with a bride and groom. She can even arrange to show a video of Coventry City's 1987 FA Cup Winners match win against Tottenham at the reception. And believe it or not, it is far more likely to be the bride who wants her wedding at Coventry City. According to Wendy 75 per cent of enquiries come from the bride-to-be.

There is no charge for room hire for the wedding if it includes a reception. Food and wine packages start at about £25 per head although it would cost £70 a head on a match day. Music can be arranged for the ceremony and bands can be provided for dances in the evening.

Unfortunately the restaurant is out of bounds for weddings on match days unless you would like to have your reception alongside a lot of well-heeled fans. However the bride and groom who first met at a Coventry City football match should not give up hope. It would be possible to have a small wedding in one of the rooms at the ground and then have a slap-up champagne wedding breakfast while watching the match. But be warned, this would cost substantially more than getting married on other days. If money is no object, a couple with over £10,000 to burn could book a box for the whole season and then try to persuade the registrar to battle through the crowds and perform the ceremony at kick off.

Guests can stay at numerous local hotels and the club has some special deals which will give the couple a complimentary stay on their wedding night. The local papers have been quick to report the story using every cliché in the book. According to some, Coventry City is topping the venues league and is now the place to stage 'matches made in heaven'. OK, just make sure that the bride does not spoil the big day by turning up in a claret and blue dress, the colours of arch-rivals Aston Villa.

Contact: Wendy O'Brien
Main road: M6/A45
Station: Coventry
Disabled access: Yes
Parking: Ample
Registrar tel no: 01203 833141
Bedrooms: 0
Wedding only: Yes

Name: Wentworth Club
Address: Wentworth Drive, Virginia Water, Surrey GU25 4LS
Tel: 01344 842201

To reach Wentworth Club, which is set in over 700 acres of beautiful Surrey countryside, you turn off the

Old London Road through imposing wrought-iron gates and up a drive through a jungle of rhododendrons and evergreens. Virginia Water is the playground of the rich and famous. Pop stars and movie stars rub shoulders here and to own a mansion which backs on to one of the golf courses will set you back a bit.

Walter Hagen who won the Open Championship 4 years running once said: 'You are only here for a short visit. Don't hurry. Don't worry. And be sure to smell the flowers along the way.' The same is true today. Along the winding drive to the clubhouse signposts remind you to beware of golfers. So just as you are breathing in the scent of the flowers and looking out for someone stumbling after a misplaced ball the grand gothic-style clubhouse comes into view. The house itself was originally built in 1805 by someone who definitely believed that an Englishman's home is his castle. In fact it looks like a cross between a castle and a stately home, painted cream with turrets and castellated battlements. It was totally redeveloped and refurbished in 1993 at a cost of £10 million. It is a magical setting for a fairytale wedding.

In the main reception area golfers buzz to and fro. Some are just visiting the pro shop while others are sitting around having a refreshing drink in the Burma Bar after an exhilarating 18 holes.

Wentworth is one of the most prestigious and exclusive golf and country clubs in the world and as such you feel you are on hallowed ground. It has either initiated or hosted almost every major and international golfing event – the names on the Honours Board above the reception desk take your breath away – Ballesteros and Palmer to name just two.

However the granting of a licence to hold civil weddings here will mean a much broader catchment of clients. These days the club is keen to be seen as more of a country club in the American style and as such is a superb venue for a very special wedding.

The decor throughout the building is classy but discreet – plenty of polished wood panelling and wrought iron in the Burma Bar, slightly softened in the Club Lounge with deep and comfy floral printed sofas. There are rooms which have been nominated for marriage ceremonies but it is the sumptuous Ballroom with its wooden ceiling and elegant chandeliers which provides the sort of setting to die for.

This elegant room with cream-coloured walls hung with fake old masters can hold up to 180 guests. Huge ornate wall mirrors reflect the light beautifully. After the ceremony drinks could be taken in the adjoining suites while staff set up for the dining, drinking and dancing.

Smaller weddings can also be hosted in the historic Ryder Cup or Curtis Cup Rooms which give on to a private terrace overlooking stunning rhododendron gardens – a perfect setting for any size summer wedding.

The sporting and leisure facilities at Wentworth are second to none as you would expect. There are three 18-hole championship heathland courses, a 9-hole executive course and a driving range. In addition to two putting greens there are also 14 outdoor tennis courts, an outdoor heated 30-metre swimming-pool set within the rhododendron gardens and a fully equipped gym.

And, surprise surprise, you can stay overnight here. There are 4 single and 2 double bedrooms with ensuite bathrooms. There is also a 2-bedroomed suite with uninterrupted and stunning views.

The staff at Wentworth are keen to make your wedding a day to remember and will plan and advise on all aspects. Menus are created to suit individual requirements with buffet and dinner menus from £22.50 a head. Floral arrangements cost from £15 for a table arrangement to pedestals from £75.

Food and drink are subject to a 10 per cent service charge. Hire of the Ballroom for a wedding ceremony will set you back £1000 while the Ryder Cup Room costs £400 or the Curtis Cup Room is £200. Accommodation ranges from the Garden Suite at £225 per night to a double room at £55 per night. Karin Bidgood is on hand to provide an exhaustive list of contacts from vintage car hire and horse-drawn carriages to hot-air balloons and dance bands.

Contact: Karin Bidgood
Main road: A30/M4/M25

Station: Virginia Water
Disabled access: Yes
Parking: 3 car parks
Registrar tel no: 01483 62841
Bedrooms: 8
Wedding only: No

Name: The Fennes Estate
Address: Fennes, Bocking,
Braintree, Essex CM7 5PL
Tel: 01376 324555

Three miles north of Braintree stands Fennes – a square Georgian country house complete with a classical white pillared porch. It looks just like one of those country vicarages that you might drool over in the property pages of the Sunday papers. In fact it is a farmhouse that has been in the same family for generations. The owner is Edward Tabor whose ancestor Mr Tabor was 'something in the city' in the 1830s. He built the estate around a 250-acre farm and lived the life of a country gent.

Edward Tabor seems to have followed in the family tradition. He has moved with the times and turned his house and estate into a business providing corporate entertainment on the theme of country pursuits. Archery, shooting, fishing and even lessons in how to handle a 4-wheel drive are all on offer.

The house has been geared up for wedding receptions for some time and Edward has taken to the new marital law with some enthusiasm. The ceremony will be conducted in the formal drawing room of the house. Quite small and decorated in tasteful pinks and green the room has numerous antiques and comfortable armchairs. It can take up to 60 people but probably would be better with a smaller group. The couple will stand in front of the french windows which open out on to the garden with its ornamental pond. A piano can be used for the music. Because it is in daily use the room has a very homely atmosphere.

After the ceremony celebration drinks on the lawn would be nice while photos are taken by the lake or at the front of the house. Large receptions can be held in a state-of-the-art marquee tucked away at the back of the house. It seats 200, has purpose-built kitchens and its own garden. Smaller weddings can have a meal in the dining room which is decorated in deep blue. It can seat 35 around a formal dining table. At one end there is a large fireplace with a mirror above while at the other end there is a floor-to-ceiling window looking out towards a great oak tree.

The bride and groom can meet the registrar in the old library which is now used as a second sitting room. Fennes is not a hotel but the bride can prepare for the ceremony upstairs in a magnificent blue bedroom. On some occasions special arrangements can be made for the couple to stay at a number of hotels and bed and breakfasts in and around Braintree. There is disabled access to all the ground floor rooms. Edward keeps a list of local firms who can supply flowers, cars, musicians and horses and carriages.

Fennes does not normally charge for the use of the rooms for a wedding as long as there is a reception to follow. Catering is provided on site and a typical wedding package will cost around £35 per head although a smaller do with canapés and wine could be £20 or less.

Couples can have a big wedding at Fennes using the marquee but really the charm of the place is that it is essentially a family house. Fennes can, and regularly does, have weddings of over 100, but we thought it would be absolutely ideal for a small wedding in the sitting room followed by drinks in the garden and a slap-up meal in the dining room. And in the winter it would be possible to get the log fires burning and create the atmosphere of a real country houseparty.

Contact: Edward Tabor
Main road: M11/A12
Station: Braintree
Disabled access: Yes
Parking: Ample
Registrar tel no: 01376 23463
Bedrooms: 0
Wedding only: No

Name: Sandown Park Racecourse
Address: Portsmouth Road, Esher, Surrey KT10 9AJ
Tel: 01372 464790

Whatever your reasons for wanting to tie the knot at a racecourse you could not hope for a more attractive venue than Sandown Park in Esher. Set in acres of Surrey parkland it has spectacular views and is also the favourite racecourse of the Queen mum. Sandown Park is steeped in history and has seen some giants of the racing world grace its hallowed turf.

It has also been voted Racecourse of the Year 6 times in the last 10 due in part to the fact that it is one of the most modern and forward looking racecourses in the country. It has superb viewing from the 10,000 capacity grandstand, more than a dozen restaurants and bars, a state of the art betting shop and a professionally staffed crèche.

The first meet at Sandown Park was in 1875 when according to local diarists the enclosure was full of 'foulmouthed rednecks' and although the royal family and various London luminaries were often to be seen there, the Turf was rife with talk of doping, underhanded dealings and general 'skulduggery'. Once it set the trend as the first racecourse to be enclosed which meant people actually had to pay to get in, a 'day at the races' became a much more civilized experience altogether.

Nowadays £1000 prizes are commonplace and the Whitbread Gold Cup Meeting is one of the biggest and busiest held at Sandown Park. It was at this prestigious meeting that Georgia Sandown Cragg made her debut in the world by being born in the car park. Her parents had been en route to Kingston Hospital, realized they were not going to make it in time and turned into the car park. Georgia was duly granted a life membership of the racecourse and dad was presented with a bottle of champagne while onlookers cheered as mum and baby were transferred to an ambulance and taken on to Kingston.

Sandown Park has kept up its groundbreaking tradition by becoming the first racecourse in the country to offer a wedding ceremony. The first wedding room is the Director's Box which is a pretty special place. Not only do you have an uninterrupted view of the course but the surroundings are beautiful too. The room itself is quite large with huge windows on 3 sides. A wall which divides the room in two contains all the catering facilities you could possibly need.

Blues and beiges form the colour scheme here and there is a large and gloriously carved oak table at which you can take your vows whilst still overlooking the course. You could seat 60 people comfortably in this room.

The second room is the Ardross Suite which is pale blue and again extremely light with windows right across one wall. It holds up to 200 people and has a sprung dance floor for use later on in the evening.

Sandown Park also tried to get the Weighing Room licensed for the ceremony but came up against the red tape of the local register office just as Cheltenham Racecourse did. However they are currently negotiating licensing the Owners' & Trainers' Room next door to the

Weighing Room which would make a fabulous setting for a smaller wedding.

This room will seat about 50 people and has a much cosier feel altogether. There are french windows which open on to a terrace leading on to rolling lawns and to the right the Winners' Enclosure. It was a very sunny day when we visited and people were wandering about chinking champagne glasses and generally having a good time. The atmosphere is wonderful – a place where you feel a certain nostalgia for an era of gracious living.

Barbara Crow who will help you organize your wedding is a delight. She is very enthusiastic about the place and you can feel confident that she would advise you to make the right decisions about your special day.

Sandown Park has a fantastic selection of wedding packages which range from a light evening finger buffet at around £13 a head to a wide range of vegetarian dishes at £10 a head to the full works at £28 a head. They are very proud of their caterers who are exclusive to the racecourse and have been working in private catering for more than 300 years!

Contact: Barbara Crow
Main road: M3/A3
Station: Esher
Disabled access: Good
Parking: For 6000 cars
Registrar tel no: 01932 254360
Bedrooms: 21
Wedding only: Yes

Name: **London Zoo**
Address: **Regent's Park, The Outer Circle, London NW1 4RY**
Tel: **0171 586 3339**

London Zoo is situated right on the edge of one of London's most strikingly beautiful parks. Regent's Park was the centrepiece of John Nash's master streetplan for the Prince Regent. It is bordered by the fabulous Palladian mansions of Regent's Crescent and the Regent's Canal.

The Zoo was recently under threat of closure due to lack of funds but luckily it has been reprieved. Zoo buildings include some gems of modern architecture including the 1934 Penguin Pool and the world famous aviary designed by Lord Snowdon.

The Zoo was founded by Sir Stamford Raffles and the suite named after him is now one of the wedding rooms. On the ground floor, the room has cream walls, wooden floor and bamboo furniture. The ceiling fans complete the colonial effect. This room is not very light as there are few windows. There is an adjoining bar which is quite large with comfortable sofas. It would be nice in here for pre-reception drinks and is spacious enough for 120 people to have a sit-down meal in comfort.

The second wedding room is the large Regency Room situated on the first floor. It is a long room with windows across two walls. One overlooks Barclay Court where the gift shop and restaurant can be found. There is an attractive circular fountain in the middle of the court which is illuminated at night. The other overlooks a patio and lawn which can be used for photos and where you can have a temporary bar for your post-wedding drinks on fine days.

The Regency Room itself is very grand with a rich colour scheme of red and green. It is divided into 3 sections. The first is a reception area with a bar. The second has a fully sprung dance floor and the third is used for the ceremony. Each section can be divided by curtains. For a really big wedding of more than 200 the whole room can be used for a sit-down meal or a buffet and the Raffles Suite for the ceremony.

Although you can't see any animals from any of these suites, after 6.30 you can hire one of the animal houses for drinks and canapés. Why not have your drinks reception in the insect house for example, a dark hall with back-lit tanks which are home to poisonous spiders, rare snails and hissing cockroaches. Don't worry, the insects are safely contained behind glass and even the most dangerous are genuinely beautiful.

Or what about drinks on the lion terraces. This is a large open terrace area, ideal for summer barbecues or drinks receptions for up to 150 people. The viewing windows look on to some of the world's rarest animals, from Asian lions to Persian leopards. Reduced price tickets are also available if the function is held during opening hours.

There are no bedrooms here unless you fancy sharing a bed with a nice big tarantula in the insect house but the Zoo does have an arrangement with both the Langham Hilton and the White House Hotel so that you can book your honeymoon suite at one of their special prices.

The catering is very flexible with menus ranging from £15 for a buffet to £25 for a sit-down meal. That includes half a bottle of wine. To hire the Regency Suite will cost £765 and the Raffles Suite is £530.

We thought the Zoo was a very novel place for real animal lovers to tie the knot. There are plenty of opportunities to see some of the wildlife and the setting of Regent's Park is particularly lovely.

Contact: Nicky Elkington
Main road: M40
Station: Euston
Disabled access: Yes
Parking: Plenty
Registrar tel no: 0171 798 1162
Bedrooms: 0
Wedding only: No

FAIRYTALE CASTLES

It was so cold I almost got married!
SHELLEY WINTERS

If an Englishman's home is his castle what more romantic setting for a wedding could there possibly be than a historic castle? Maybe you can imagine yourself galloping up to the drawbridge on horseback to a fanfare of trumpets, rescuing a damsel in distress or two or waving to your knight in shining armour from a tower. It is a lovely dream and all the castles listed here are truly splendid and certainly steeped in history – but you need a big wedding to compete with such a setting. It can also be cold in a castle so be prepared to wear your winter long johns. So, if you want a huge no-holds-barred medieval-style bash with all the trimmings including lute-playing minstrels and serving wenches – go for this option!

Name: Herstmonceux
Address: International Study
Centre, Hailsham, East Sussex
BN27 1RP
Tel: 01323 834444

If you fancy yourself as a prince or princess for a day, Herstmonceux Castle has to be the place to get married. The castle was originally built as a country home in the mid 15th century and it combines the history of medieval England with the romance of renaissance Europe.

The road up to the castle is unprepossessing and gives little idea of what lies ahead. Through the gates and over the speed ramps you may be accosted at the gatehouse by an extremely genial chap who asks you your business. This is the castle's gatekeeper although from October onwards he is replaced by an automatic barrier!

Huge swaying poplars hide the castle from view until you round the final bend in the road. But when it eventually comes into view it is certainly worth the wait – you are immediately transported to a bygone era.

Magnificent and foreboding, the castle set in 500 acres of mature parkland stands proudly reflected in its own moat. It has a genuine portcullis and the towers were originally constructed as dovecotes. Under the south-east tower there is a dungeon where anyone sentenced to imprisonment could be dropped in through a trapdoor in the ceiling and left to rot.

Today the castle is owned by one of the larger Canadian universities and is used as an international centre by students from all over the world. But the students are not the only residents at the castle – like all good castles it has a resident ghost. The Grey Lady is reputed to walk the corridors late at night. The story goes she was starved to death in one of the towers by her wicked governess – who knows, but it certainly gives the castle an added sense of mystery!

There are 5 wedding rooms at Herstmonceux but only 2 were available the day we visited. The first is the Great Hall which is everything you'd expect a banqueting hall to be. Huge white stone walls loom up to a magnificent vaulted ceiling. Pretty lattice windows give on to the sanctuary of the inner courtyard.

A splendid Elizabethan- or medieval-style wedding could be held here – in fact the staff have already organized a medieval wedding reception at the castle. You can even hire a firm of local minstrels to pipe you through the portcullis and into the main courtyard.

The second room, the Dacre Room, is smaller and much less grand. At one time it was the old chapel although all signs of sacred images have been carefully disposed of. What is left is a rather austere shell with high white walls and a beautiful gallery from where guests could watch the ceremony. Hire this room for a small gathering of close family and then have a full-scale bash in the Great Hall afterwards.

You can hire the whole castle for a weekend which will cost you a mere £3,000. There are also very reasonably priced rooms at Herstmonceux. They are basic student-type rooms but they are quite comfortable. There are also one or two old-fashioned guest rooms within the castle itself which would suit the honeymoon couple but for family and guests a student room will only set them back around £17.50 a night.

To hire any one of the wedding rooms is £250, a simple finger buffet menu is around £18 a head exclusive of wine, and a carved buffet or a waitress-served menu for a minimum of 25 guests will set you back around £30 a head. Wine ranges from £9 to £25 a bottle.

Contact: Jo Brown or Sandy Montgomery
Main Road: A271/A27
Station: Polegate
Disabled Access: Yes
Parking: Excellent
Registrar tel no: 01323 41000
Bedrooms: 30 in Bader Hall, 2 in the castle
Wedding only: Yes

Name: Peckforton Castle
Address: Stonehouse Lane, Peckforton, near Tarporley, Cheshire CW6 9TN
Tel: 01829 260930

Just off the main A49 road from Warrington the silhouette of Peckforton Castle just above a wooded hilltop overlooking the Cheshire Plain can be seen for many miles. At one point you get slightly confused as on the other hill which forms the Sandstone Ridge stands Beeston Castle – but only Peckforton has the reputation of being the 'only fully deceptive of all the English 19th-century castles'.

As soon as you take the turning for the castle you realize that this is not going to be some huge National Trust moneyspinner. The driveway through a wild and spooky forest is definitely more suited to a horse and carriage than today's vehicles. Nevertheless the drive through bracken and forest is truly beautiful and eerily quiet.

At the top of the drive you approach the castle through a mighty drawbridge – quite a forbidding sight with its giant archway and broad battlements. The moat however has seen better days and appears rather forlorn. Just inside the gate is a chapel where couples can receive a blessing after the ceremony. To the left of the courtyard is the Coachhouse Bar which has been tastefully modernized and can cater for wedding receptions of up to 275 people.

There are 3 wedding rooms at Peckforton. The first is in the Great Hall itself with its impressive stone vaulted roof, ornate carved screen and minstrels gallery. The floor is paved with beautiful mosaic tiles and huge mock beacons light up the massive stone walls. Decorated with flowers and candles this room

would make a truly romantic setting for any budding Lancelot and
Guinevere.

During the day when the hall is
open to the public an animated wax-
work minstrel strums a lute and
acts as a guide but we are assured
he is switched off during weddings!

The second room is the octagonal
stone vaulted Dining Room. The
room was the scene of much activity
when Twentieth Century Fox spent
4 months here filming a production
of Robin Hood. In fact the huge
stone fireplace at the far end of the
room was built by them specially
for one scene. Although it looks
pretty real it is actually held there
by vacuum suction which is why no
flowers can be attached to it.

The Dining Room seats around
100 and is the most flexible of all
the rooms. The seats can either be
arranged theatre-style so the bride
and groom walk down an aisle to
the fireplace or guests can be seated
around the edge of the room leaving
the centre free for the couple to
take their vows. In fact some entertainers hired the room and had
tables around the outside and circus
acts performing in the centre between courses.

The third room is the Library
which is done out in rich tones of
deep red and royal blue. A recent
wedding had a scarlet theme which
would have been set off beautifully
in this room. With a log fire blazing
in the stone fireplace an idyllic cosy
winter wedding with around 30
guests would be ideal.

The castle was bought by former
hotelier Evelyn Graybill who had a
dream of turning it into a glorious
country house hotel. Unfortunately
the bank had other ideas and re-
fused her a loan. She has battled on
and turned the castle into an extra-
ordinarily successful business.
There are guided tours, a restaurant, a tea room serving cream teas.
Add to that lunches and hiring out
the rooms for weddings, balls, banquets and other functions and you
can see Peckforton is a pretty versatile place.

Mrs Graybill has even managed
to strike a deal with a local five-
star hotel, the Carden Park, to provide accommodation for wedding
guests for around £70 a night. And
for those on a really tight budget
you can bring a tent and stay at the
local ice-cream farm campsite!

And if you are in any doubt about
the sort of wedding you want she
has an album full of photographs
to help fire your imagination. She
has had a designer's wedding where
everything was black right down to
the place names at the high table
and the wedding cake which was
decorated with ivory-coloured
roses. She had a farmer's wedding
during harvest time with the Great
Hall decked out with sheaves of
corn and barley. The bride wore
antique cream lace with twists of
barley and corn in her hair.

'We can arrange anything from
fireworks to balloons. We even had
one event where the bride let loose
crates of white doves in the courtyard,' says Mrs Graybill. 'A castle
is a halfway house between church

and town hall. It is always here for you. Lots of people who have been married here come back to visit with their children. It is always their place.'

To hire the Great Hall with a music licence extension to 2 am will set you back £195. But the best thing to do is to hire the whole castle for 24 hours for just £1,500. A simple finger buffet comes to around £7 a head and a fully-fledged banquet works out at between £17.50 and £24.50 a head. Wine varies from £9 to £12 a bottle.

Contact: Mrs Evelyn Graybill
Main road: M6
Station: Chester
Disabled access: Good
Parking: No problem
Registrar tel no: 01270 505106
Bedrooms: None, use local hotels Carden Park, Wild Boar
Wedding only: Yes

Name: Ripley Castle
Address: Ripley, Harrogate, North Yorkshire HG3 3AY
Tel: 01423 770152

Once upon a time there was an eccentric gentleman who while visiting Alsace-Lorraine came upon a charming village and decided he would rather like one for himself. So on his return to England, he had his own estate village razed to the ground and rebuilt in the likeness of the French village. Which is why 170 years later there is – thanks to the endeavours of Sir William

Ancotts Ingilby – a little corner of Yorkshire that is forever France.

'Sir William was one of my more eccentric ancestors who was completely loopy by the age of 18,' confesses Sir Thomas Ingilby, present incumbent at Ripley Castle and the adjacent estate village. Had it not been for Sir William's bizarre indulgence, Ripley and its imposing Hôtel de Ville, would not be the idyllic spot it is today – and Sir Thomas might not be hosting wedding ceremonies at one of the North's grandest and most romantic venues.

The castle itself has been the Ingilby seat since the 1320s. But it owes much to the endeavours of Sir William who installed the Capability Brown landscaped lake, gardens and deer park, echoing nearby Studley Royal and Fountains Abbey.

If Ripley appears to have an air of familiarity to it, it may be because you have seen it in one of the many films and TV series that have been made here. The list is long, but take *Jane Eyre*, starring Susannah York and George C. Scott, or *Frankenstein*, starring Sir John Gielgud, Robert Powell and Carrie Fisher, for starters.

Sir Thomas produces a simple sheet explaining the 'dos and don'ts' of civil weddings. For some couples a wedding in the castle followed by a church blessing may be an attractive option. The local All Saints is a pleasant, airy church, no more than a stone's throw from the castle.

The wedding room is the Library – a majestic room, with views across the park. The bride and groom will take their vows beneath the watchful gaze of up to 40 guests and of Sir William's portrait on the wall between the bookshelves.

In decent weather, doors can be opened to give access to the terrace overlooking the lake and deer park. Another beautiful setting for photographs is the walled garden, where a planned conversion of the garden room will bring a potentially idyllic marriage venue into use in 1996.

For small receptions of up to 50, guests could then move upstairs to the Tower Room and tour the Knight's Chamber, with its original 16th-century panelling which only yielded the secret of its priest's hole in 1964. This was the hiding place for Francis Ingilby, Catholic seminary priest and martyr during the reign of Elizabeth I. Hung, drawn and quartered in York, he was beatified by Rome in 1989, making him the Blessed Francis.

The Morning Room, a lovely sunny south-facing room, will seat up to 66 guests for a meal prepared by the Castle's own full-time chefs. Other reception rooms are Cromwell's Restaurant in the grounds, seating up to 70 and offering the most economic option, with prices starting at just £8.50 per head for a 3-course meal. Alternatively, there's the Boar's Head Restaurant, at £27.50 per head. But for the wedding to end all weddings, the semi-permanent marquees in the castle courtyard will hold up to 800 guests, with prices ranging from £24 for a simple buffet to £48.75 for a

full meal, both prices including unlimited wine.

The hire of the Library costs £200, reduced to £100 if Ripley hosts the reception, while the special suite at the Boar's Head annexe across the road is free to the bride and groom, again if the reception is at Ripley. So a wedding here could set you back anything from £500 plus registrar's fees to £25,000!

Ripley would take a lot of beating for sheer romanticism and while it is an obvious choice for the real 'blockbuster', money-no-object wedding, a more intimate event would go down just as well. And, just for the record, marriage coordinator Harriet Crossley had her own reception here just a few years ago.

Contact: Harriet Crossley
Main road: A61/A1(M)
Station: Harrogate
Disabled access: Yes
Parking: Ample
Registrar tel no: 01423 569592
Bedrooms: 25
Wedding only: Yes

Name: Caerphilly Castle
Address: Cadw: Welsh Historic Monuments, Brunel House, 2 Fitzalan Road, Cardiff CF2 1UY
Tel: 01222 500261

Caerphilly Castle is by far the largest of all the Welsh castles, only overshadowed by the English castles of Windsor and Dover. Amazingly, this tremendous feat of engineering was achieved within two decades with most of the work taking place between 1268 and 1271.

The castle was originally built by 'Red Gilbert' de Clare, the Anglo-Norman lord of Glamorgan, to defend his territory against Llywelyn the Last, Prince of Wales. He flooded the valley to create a 30-acre lake and set his fortress on 3 artificial islands. One became a great fortified dam and one became a walled redoubt.

Often threatened but never taken, this fantastic multiple fortress has been carefully restored after centuries of neglect and its famous 'leaning tower' still remains. The castle is now administered by Cadw: Welsh Historic Monuments.

Caerphilly is outstanding because unlike so many other medieval castles it is not sited boldly against the skyline but is set in a hollow between hills, partly camouflaged by its construction in local coloured stone.

Now you can have a little piece of its history as part of your special day because the Great Hall has been licensed to hold weddings. It is a pretty impressive spot. The roof is the work of the third Marquess of Bute around 1870, and springs from 7 pairs of 14th-century wall columns.

Halfway down the hall on the courtyard side is a huge stone fireplace. When we saw it there was a wedding reception in full swing and the walls were festooned with flowers and balloons creating a lovely festive atmosphere. Two large banqueting tables were set out on each side of the hall with an aisle up the middle to the top table. Outside the little bridesmaids and pageboys were playing catch in and out of the old ruins in the courtyard.

The Great Hall holds around 200 people but 120 would be a good number. Unfortunately it can't be closed off to the public so anyone wanting a little privacy should not book here. There is no catering company based at the castle either so you have to book your own.

After 6.30 pm however you can have total privacy to hold a party and for just £500 plus VAT you can hire the Great Hall for a day. There is a drawbridge where you can have great wedding photos taken or better still at the back of the castle overlooking one of the 3 lakes surrounding it.

We felt the castle was very good value although it has a slightly municipal feel about it. It is quite exposed with people wandering through and peering in the door.

Contact: Phillip Stallard
Main road: A470/A469/M4
Station: Caerphilly
Disabled access: Yes
Parking: Off site (local authority)
Registrar tel no: 01685 723318
Bedrooms: 0
Wedding only: No

Name: Thornbury Castle
Address: Castle Street, Thornbury, near Bristol BS12 2HH
Tel: 01454 281182

Thornbury Castle is a rather confusing place, a castle that is a hotel where the bedrooms look more castle-like than the main building and where they have a vineyard in the gardens.

Apparently the castle was started in 1510 by Edward Stafford the third Duke of Buckingham when he received a licence from Henry VIII. Unfortunately for the Duke, he was accused of treason some 10 years later and ended up being topped by the executioner at Tower Hill on 17 May 1521. Henry VIII took advantage of the situation and appropriated the castle as a Royal Demesne, or estate. He visited it with Anne Boleyn for 10 days in 1535.

Today you can stay in the same castle and have a right royal wedding of your own, at a price. Situated just outside the town of Thornbury, 5 miles from the Severn Bridge and the junction of the M4 and M5, Thornbury Castle is now an upmarket country house hotel with 18 bedrooms, or bedchambers as they like to describe them.

Weddings take place in the Great Hall, the hotel's lounge. It is a long narrow room with a red beamed ceiling, pictures of Henry VIII and ancient tapestries depicting rural scenes. There is a large stone fireplace and an extremely unusual stone oriel window that runs from floor to ceiling. Instead of filling a bay it forms a star-shaped alcove. The ceremony will probably take place in the alcove by the window giving views out on to the garden with a castellated wall and a church beyond. The lounge can easily ac-commodate 70 people for the wedding.

Weddings for up to 12 could be held in the Library next door. It is a much smaller room with a stone fireplace surrounded by bookcases. Again there is an oriel window in an alcove but here it has a small raised platform making an ideal spot for the ceremony.

Couples will meet the registrar upstairs in the Chancellor's Room. It is small and square with windows overlooking both the vineyard and the garden. It is possible to have a wedding breakfast for up to 12 people here.

On most occasions the wedding party will have drinks outside in the gardens before returning to the dining room for the reception. Photos can be taken in the gardens with their privet hedges and in a secluded bower with its own seat. While they are in the garden guests can quiz each other about the architectural mysteries of Thornbury Castle. What do you call a tower with 7 sides and why does a stone castle have 2 Hampton Court-style redbrick chimneys that are older than the building itself?

Guests who stay in the bedrooms will find that they are the most interesting part of the building. Some are approached up a medieval spiral stone staircase and have bare stone walls, huge four-poster beds and intricate plaster ceilings. Others, on the ground floor, have narrow slit windows designed for use by archers. They may be old but they all have modern facilities such as ensuite bathrooms, televisions and trouser presses.

Themed weddings are no problem. The hotel is used to Tudor events and can even supply costumes and a seamstress to adjust them to fit anyone who has grown to Henry VIII proportions. The staff are happy to dress up in medieval gear and a local lute player can provide the music.

Thornbury Castle does not accept bookings for a wedding only. Couples who want to get married here will be charged £130 for the hire of the wedding room and will also have to have a reception. Prices start at around £18 per head for a buffet with wine while a sit-down meal with wine will cost anything from £35 per head. Double bedrooms range between £135 and £205. Couples who want to splash out can book the whole building for £5,500 which will cover dinner and continental breakfast for 34 guests. There would be additional charges for extras such as drinks. There is disabled access to the wedding rooms but no special toilet facilities. In normal circumstances the hotel does not offer facilities to children under 12 and gentlemen are required to wear a jacket and tie in the restaurant for dinner.

Thornbury is a very unusual building with particularly interesting bedrooms. It is quite expensive but if you have the money the best option would be to take over the whole place and have a themed medieval wedding.

Contact: Diane Crompton
Main road: M4/M5/A38
Station: Bristol Parkway
Disabled access: Restricted
Parking: Ample
Registrar tel no: 0117 9292461
Bedrooms: 18
Wedding only: No

Name: Amberley Castle
Address: Amberley, near Arundel, West Sussex BN18 9ND
Tel: 01798 831992

The village of Amberley is one of the prettiest of the Sussex downland villages with its ancient Saxon church, thatched country pubs and the quaint village shop. Sheep graze contentedly on the grass of Amberley Mount and you can see the historic South Downs Way which is so popular with walkers and horse riders.

Ever since the 12th century Amberley Castle has been a fortress against marauding intruders with its solid 60-foot-high walls and a portcullis which, once down, renders the castle impenetrable. Nowadays you are more likely to hear about high profile figures from the world of politics, industry or show business hiring the castle to escape the glare of Fleet Street paparazzi with their intrusive telephoto lenses.

The castle captures the imagination with its mighty battlements and the solid security of the oak portcullis. The lands of Amberley were given by the Saxon king Caedwalla to the first bishop of Selsey who converted the king to Christianity.

The reception area has huge flagstone floors and a grand piano in one corner at which is seated a large stuffed gorilla. No one explains why. Suits of armour lurch at crazy angles in many of the downstairs rooms and although the castle feels much like someone's own home there is still an almost tangible sense of history about it.

Weddings are conducted in the Great Room which can hold 50 people. It is the height of simplicity with great whitewashed walls and a barrel-vaulted ceiling. Huge tapestries, suits of armour and brass and iron candleholders adorn the walls. The furniture is dark polished wood. Nothing is overstated although King Arthur and Lady Guinevere would not look out of place seated at the great banqueting table. Hire of the room including floral table arrangements, red carpet and theatre-style seating will set you back £500.

Receptions are held in the restaurant, the 12th-century Queen's Room. The vaulted room is decorated in shades of cream and pale blue and has a seat of honour overlooking a stunning courtyard. It can cater for up to 40 guests. A typical lunch menu costs between £21.50 and £30 and a dinner works out at £25–£40 a head. House wine costs from £13.95 a bottle.

But the best idea is to hire the castle for exclusive use for 24 hours at a cost of £3,500 a day during the week and £5,000 on Friday or Satur-

day. Amberley Castle has 14 luxurious individually designed bedrooms each with ensuite jacuzzi bathrooms. The Arundel Room is just one of the honeymoon bedrooms. Somewhat bizarrely it has 2 full size four-poster beds and wonderful views from the leaded windows over the castle's inner garden and the South Downs beyond.

Naturally enough the hotel has its very own ghost. Emily, a local lass who was rumoured to have been taken advantage of by a lust-craved bishop, discovered she was having his child and when she was rejected by him, threw herself off one of the battlements. Now she wanders the turrets of the castle singing a melancholy song.

The hotel staff take delight in planning all sorts of wacky events from axe throwing and blunderbuss shooting to falconry and archery. So it would be a shame not to take advantage and go to town on a theme wedding of some sort. They can also arrange more mundane pursuits such as hot-air ballooning or riding. In fact one guest got so carried away by a spree in a hot-air balloon he proposed to his girlfriend in mid-flight!

Seating for the wedding is up to 50. The only way to hold a wedding in real style at Amberley is to hire the castle for the day or preferably a weekend so that guests can move freely around the whole place.

Contact: Emma Pearson
Main road: A24
Station: Amberley
Disabled access: Limited

Parking: Excellent
Registrar tel no: 01903 700080
Bedrooms: 14
Wedding only: No

Name: Naworth Castle
Address: Naworth, Brampton,
Cumbria CA8 2HF
Tel: 016977 3229

Naworth Castle stands in 2,000 acres of park and woodland. Pheasants wander across the lawns and there are becks and waterfalls only yards away. The first glimpse of the castle at the end of its long drive is quite breathtaking and unforgettable.

This former stronghold of the Wardens of the Marches stands in rugged and historic countryside. All around are relics of its turbulent history – Roman roads, walls and fortifications, echoes of Edward I's campaigns against the Scots – the Scottish border is visible from the rooftops. Much of the castle, approached through an impressive gatehouse, was destroyed by fire in the last century. Restoration was carried out by the distinguished Victorian architect Anthony Salvin.

The Howards were among the great territorial families of England, their seats included the famous Castle Howard in Yorkshire. In fact Naworth was once the family's second home, after Castle Howard itself. Naworth Castle was the family seat of the Earl of Carlisle for 700 years. The first structure, the Dacre Tower, was built by Sir Ranulph Dacre in 1335. It remained the family home until 18 months ago when Philip Howard, son of the 12th Earl of Carlisle who died in 1994, acquired it and began turning it into a leading function venue.

Naworth is a warren of wood-panelled rooms, towers, turrets and narrow spiral staircases. A tiny chapel is used for family christenings and secret passages burrow deep into the inner reaches of this magnificent building.

The historic Great Hall was built in 1513 and later restored after the disastrous fire in 1844. It has a timber beamed ceiling and vast inglenook fireplace and is licensed for weddings, as is the wood-panelled Library, with rows of books, huge leaded windows and galleries hung with paintings. The Library has been lovingly restored, and seats up to 75 for a wedding ceremony.

Hanging in the Great Hall of this impressive medieval castle are tapestries made for the marriage of Henry IV of France and Maria de' Medici in 1600. What could be a more romantic backdrop to a wedding than this? The 8 tapestries bought by the Howard family at the time of the French Revolution are a wonderful part of this magical castle which has you eagerly anticipating new delights round every corner.

The Great Hall is home to 4 great heraldic beasts. Either side of the fireplace are the red bull and the gryphon of the Dacres – once one of the most powerful families in the north of England – while at the far end of the room are the dolphin of the Greystokes and a mystery sheep which has never been identified.

The hall overlooks the castle's courtyard which in good weather can be used for wedding photographs and as an area to greet guests. The castle is not a hotel but it does have 10 double rooms for the use of wedding guests and a bridal suite in the tower – the 16th-century Lord William's bedchamber, complete with its own four-poster bed.

Staff guarantee a personal, tailor-made service and will cater for the bride and groom's every whim. If you want they will organize the entire wedding from the photographs and flowers to the car hire. Their caterers will discuss individual requirements from a formal silver service dinner to a simple shepherd's pie supper!

The owner Philip Howard, who lives close to the castle with his wife and young family, is proud of Naworth. It was his family home when he was a child, in fact one of the guest bedrooms is the room he slept in as a boy.

It will cost you £1,000 plus VAT for the use of the Great Hall by up to 100 guests, and of the bridal chamber, plus £250 for the Library for the ceremony. Catering is extra – expect to pay roughly £7.50 per head for a finger buffet to £20–£25 for a formal sit-down dinner.

Naworth is special and makes the ideal setting for any wedding whether large or small. It is a place where the bride and groom can put their individual stamp on their day. The castle is theirs for the duration of the celebrations so they can really be king and queen for a day.

Contact: Colleen Hall
Main road: A69
Station: Carlisle/Brampton
Disabled: No
Parking: Ample
Registrar tel no: 01228 23456
Bedrooms: 11
Wedding only: Yes

HOME FROM HOME

There is nothing nobler or more admirable than when two people who see eye to eye keep house as man and wife, confounding their enemies and delighting their friends.

HOMER

This section lists the places which are either still someone's home or feel like home. These are not places for huge grand weddings with hundreds of guests. They are places where you want to have a cosy and intimate wedding with a few close family members and friends. For example Finney Green Cottage is only licensed just for the wedding ceremony. But the room is perfectly charming and with a roaring log fire and a few well chosen friends present your day could be perfect. You can also have spectacular photos outside in the gardens but it is exactly like getting married at home. You have to go out for a meal after the ceremony and then you can return to stay the night. The owners jokingly call it wed, bed and breakfast. So if it's a little peace and tranquillity you are after – read on.

Name: Finney Green Cottage
Address: 134 Manchester Road,
Wilmslow, Cheshire SK9 2JW
Tel: 01625 533343

Not far from the market towns of
Knutsford and Wilmslow with their
exclusive shops, restaurants and
pubs stands Finney Green Cottage.
Situated on the Old Manchester
Road you would hardly imagine
such a delightful place was tucked
away just yards from the main
road.

Finney Green Cottage was originally built as a yeoman's house in the
early 16th century. A little timber-
framed house under a slate roof, it
has exposed purlins and wind-
braces in some of the bedrooms.

It looks just like all those tiny
cottages you used to read about in
fairytales – all whitewashed walls
and exposed timber beams. Roman
numerals cut into some of the principal timbers in the house show how
carpenters marked the joints in the
workshop before the house was
assembled on site.

Over the years the cottage has
been altered and extended in line
with increasing standards of comfort. When a fireplace was added
in the 17th century, a decorative
cast-iron fireback bearing King
Charles's initials was bought to
grace the hearth. It still survives to
this day.

Today the cottage is a delightful
period guesthouse offering the best
of modern comforts alongside good
old-fashioned charm. It is set in the
most wonderful leafy garden with
its own wishing well.

On arrival you are greeted by
Kay or Pat – two sisters who decided to take up the joint venture of
running the cottage. Both extend a
warm and hearty Cheshire welcome
and somehow immediately you feel
you are at home.

The wedding room doubles up as
the dining room and holds about 20
people at a push. The walls are
white and the latticed windows give
an attractive dappled light to the
room. The famous inglenook fireplace is where you will take your
vows.

Pat and Kay originally envisaged
that the cottage might be popular
with second- or even third-time-
arounders who would not expect a
grand do with a big reception. 'We
thought it would make a lovely setting for a couple who just wanted a
small wedding with maybe close
family and friends,' says Kay.

In fact if you want a wedding in
glorious surroundings the cottage is
idyllic and the garden perfect for
wedding photographs with its well
and ornamental pond and fountain.
Or for a winter wedding, photographs in one of the small sitting
rooms with a backdrop of a roaring
log fire would be lovely.

Although Finney Green does not
have catering facilities there is a
wide range of inexpensive restaurants in nearby Wilmslow. After
your meal you could return to
Finney Green to stay the night
before heading off to nearby Manchester Airport to catch a plane to

your honeymoon destination. The bedrooms are also steeped in history and one even boasts a resident ghost. 'You could say we do wed, bed and breakfast,' smiles Kay.

Contact: Kay or Pat
Main road: A34
Station: Wilmslow
Disabled access: Limited
Parking: 9 cars
Registrar tel no: 01625 423463
Bedrooms: 3
Wedding only: Yes

Name: **The Olde Stocks Restaurant**
Address: **Main Street, Grimston, near Melton Mowbray, Leicestershire LE14 3BZ**
Tel: **01664 812255**

Ten miles from Melton Mowbray, home of Leicestershire's genuine home-made pork pies, lies the tiny village of Grimston. The address of the Olde Stocks Restaurant may be Main Street but don't be fooled – Main Street comprises a village green and a pub. And of course the restaurant, a pretty white cottage set on the green with its very own spreading chestnut tree. The medieval stocks which give the building its name are some of the very few left in the country. They were used for nagging wives, bullies and general rowdies who were regularly pelted with rotten fruit and vegetables to teach them a lesson.

Penni and Jack Harrison have run the restaurant for 7 years and people come from miles around to eat here. Partly because the setting is so idyllic – Grimston lies in the heart of Quorn hunting country – and partly because the food is so good. Jack is the chef, Penni sorts out the weddings. An ancient Irish wolfhound called Bisto snores loudly in the corner while life goes on around her.

The restaurant has an interesting and slightly chequered past. During the sixties anyone worth their salt belonged to the Stocks Club as the restaurant was then called. But this was no sixties swingers bar – it was a private dining club run by a larger-than-life character called Robert Chatham. The Stocks Club was the place to be seen and the local glitterati frequented the restaurant to enjoy the food, atmosphere and above all – a drink or 3.

The wedding room is normally used as the bar. A small and cosy room with a semi-circular window-seat furnished with dusky pink velvet. The couple will take their vows in front of the little bow window which looks directly out over the green with its delightful spreading chestnut tree which was planted in 1897 to commemorate the Jubilee of Queen Victoria.

After the service guests can move through to the dining room which, by contrast, is decorated in bright creamy yellow. Somehow this room has the effect of always appearing sunny even when the weather is not so good. Cream-coloured rattan furniture and pale yellow tableware give the room a lovely light and airy atmosphere. Bride and groom should have pride of place at the table nicknamed the 'canoodling table' during its dining club days.

The restaurant can happily seat 40 people. Penni has also organized weddings of up to 150 in a marquee attached to the side of the restaurant and overlooking the rolling Leicestershire countryside beyond.

The Olde Stocks has a policy of closing whenever a wedding is on so that they can give their whole attention to the happy couple. A finger buffet will cost you around £10 a head and they charge £100 for the hire of the wedding room. You can also just have the ceremony there but we think the ideal would be a small wedding of around 20 people followed by a reception in the restaurant and a jazz band and dancing later on.

You get the feeling nothing would be a problem for Penni and Jack to arrange. Penni worked in marketing so she has a good idea of what people want and is happy to work hard to make your day special. She has also given the place her own seal of approval – she and Jack had their own reception there when they got married. You can't get much more of a recommendation than that!

Parking is no problem – they have an arrangement with a local landowner to borrow their paddock where there is room for 200 cars.

Contact: Penni Harrison
Main road: M1/A46
Station: Melton Mowbray
Disabled access: Limited
Parking: Excellent

Registrar tel no: 01572 756547
Bedrooms: 0
Wedding only: Yes

Name: **Sandhole Farm**
Address: **Manchester Road, Hulme Coalfield, Congleton, Cheshire CW12 2JH**
Tel: **01260 224419**

Driving through the Cheshire countryside along the main A34 Wilmslow to Congleton road you could be forgiven for thinking you were in the Surrey stockbroker belt. In this particularly green part of Cheshire there are no signs of the recession. Rolling green fields give way to huge farmhouses and country estates with the occasional swimming-pool.

On the right hand side just past a jolly pub called the Wagon and Horses you will see a sign marked 'Bed and Breakfast' where you turn up a long driveway past cornfields and meadows full of cows, sheep and goats. You can see the house clearly from the drive – a 200-year-old redbrick farmhouse with an assortment of outbuildings and stables which have been converted into luxury ensuite accommodation.

Veronica Worth and her husband David greet you with a friendly smile and a warm welcome. They decided to diversify from farming 6 years ago and started taking in bed and breakfast guests. They began in a small way with just a few rooms but gradually expanded and are now completing their 18th room which will serve as the honeymoon suite for couples who choose this as a venue for their wedding.

There are 2 wedding rooms which are equally attractive. The first is the Conservatory on the back of the house which would be ideal for a summer wedding. The room is circular and is done out like a typical country farmhouse with lots of pine furniture. Although it only seats around 30 it would be possible for the wedding ceremony to be conducted within the Conservatory with the guests standing outside on the lawn – weather permitting. The views from the room are truly spectacular. It overlooks acres of rolling farmland and in fact on a good day, according to David, you can see Snowdon.

The second wedding room is the Barn which has been tastefully converted and also overlooks farmland. This room would be perfect for either a summer or winter wedding. Decorated in pale pinks and creams there are huge pine beams supporting the pitched roof and massive patio doors on to a terrace with the fields beyond. There is a piano in one corner and Veronica has local connections with musicians so you could have either a pianist or a small band playing at the ceremony.

The room can happily hold 35 people. For larger gatherings a marquee on the lawn could accommodate up to 300 people. Overnight accommodation can be provided for up to 36 guests. There is ample parking and disabled access.

Veronica used to be a deputy registrar so really understands why couples are so keen to have more choice in where they get married. 'People who previously had no choice about where to wed can now do it in more attractive surroundings. Register offices are usually in the centre of towns or cities but now couples who do not want a church wedding can still get married in a picturesque setting which they will remember for ever,' she says.

To hire either of the wedding rooms costs £100 and to stay at the farm overnight will set you back £43 for a double and £33 for a single. The honeymoon suite will cost £53. Flowers can be provided by Veronica.

Catering is extremely good value. The local caterer is a local farmer's wife who specializes in 'good wholesome farmhouse fare' ranging from poached salmon and honeyroast ham to Waldorf salads and cucumber and grapes in mint jelly. She is extremely reasonable by our reckoning, with prices ranging from £6 a head for a finger buffet to a sit-down meal for around £13 a head.

For a couple who love the countryside and favour a rural setting, a small summer wedding in the Barn with drinks outside afterwards would be ideal. They could follow that up with a reception for about 30 in the Conservatory overlooking the fields full of gambolling lambs. The couple could stay overnight and take advantage of the walks around the Cheshire countryside before flying off to sunnier climes from nearby Manchester Airport.

Contact: Veronica Worth
Main road: A34
Station: Macclesfield
Disabled access: Quite good
Parking: Ample
Registrar tel no: 01270 505106
Bedrooms: 18
Wedding only: No

Name: Tan Hill Inn
Address: Keld, near Richmond,
North Yorkshire DL11 6ED
Tel: 01833 628246

Alex and Margaret Baines took over Britain's highest inn back in 1985 and their leaflet proclaims that it 'takes a special kind of person' to live up here, 1,732 feet above sea level, astride the Pennine Way on the very roof of England.

Indeed, you could count on the fingers of one hand the number of post-war landlords or landladies who have stood the rigours of Tan Hill for anything approaching the length of time since sheep farmers Alex and Margaret splashed £82,500 to clinch ownership of the Inn at a bizarre auction in the bar.

You have to go right back to the turn of the century, when one Susan Peacock was licensee for nigh on 40 years, witnessing in that time the demise of 600 years of coal mining, and with it much of her regular trade.

In 1947 Harry Earnshaw was first wished happy new year by a shepherd who wandered in at the end of March, while in the infamous winter of 1963, David Clifferd melted snow to fend for his family as the beer froze and frost shattered the whisky bottles.

Ten years later, Colin Kellett gave up the job when he was injured in a gas explosion that started a serious fire. And Neil Hanson, the then editor of the *Good Beer Guide*, was forced to put the place up for sale after a winter in the place wrecked his marriage.

Now let not that be a bad omen. Although former licensee Patrick Lisle insisted at the auction that 'the place is jinxed', and although that famous Everest double-glazing advert featuring Ted Moult was followed not so long afterwards by his suicide, Margaret and Alex Baines came in as self-professed eccentrics and set about stamping their own individuality on the place.

Today you will find fewer more welcoming or cosy bars than Tan Hill's. Nor will you find more wholesome fare (remember, many of those calling here are walkers who haven't eaten in miles of Pennine Way!). And whether you have your head in the clouds or your feet on the not-so terra firma that is the peaty moorland stretching for miles, you certainly won't find anywhere else to wed that is simply so HIGH above sea level.

Alex and Margaret are Yorkshire folk and so stubbornly proud of it that one of their first actions after taking over was to campaign for the shifting of the county boundary so that the pub was back in its original Yorkshire from which it had been removed (albeit by only a few yards) by local government re-organization in 1974.

Now, the registrar will come from Richmond, North Yorkshire, even if the local telephone exchange is in County Durham, letters bear a postmark from that county, and the nearest station is at Kirkby Stephen, Cumbria, on the celebrated Settle and Carlisle Railway.

Clearly, a Tan Hill wedding would be right up the street of anyone wanting to be just that little bit off-beat – perhaps even a couple who, like Ian Cooper and Carolyn Richardson from Derbyshire, first met at the pub. Ian and Carolyn brushed aside the superstitious nonsense to become the first couple to tie the knot in a pub on 17 June 1995.

Others who might fancy a Tan Hill wedding could include motorcycle or bicycle fans, both of whom congregate en masse at Tan Hill at weekends or anyone with a taste for the sense of freedom conferred by the vast open moorland.

Alex and Margaret even suggest the idea of stopping for a quick wedding while doing the Pennine Way, then walking off into the sunset.

The room licensed for marriages is the lounge/dining room, with views to the west, seats for 30 'with unlimited standing room'. The hire fee is £75. After the ceremony, the happy couple can be toasted with Theakston's Best, before all tuck in to a wedding breakfast from a princely £3.95 per head (for sand-wiches and salad) to £6.50 for the biggest buffet. Size constraints make a full sit-down reception impractical.

Contact: Maureen Keating
Main road: A66 (5 miles)
Station: Kirkby Stephen (12 miles)
Disabled access: Yes
Parking: Unlimited
Registrar tel no: 01748 823008
Bedrooms: 7
Wedding only: Yes, but no outside caterers, please

Name: Boughton Monchelsea Place
**Address: Near Maidstone, Kent
ME17 4BU**
Tel: 01622 743120

Just south of Maidstone and only a mile from the A229, Boughton Monchelsea Place is a small Elizabethan manor house set in its own grounds with spectacular views across the Kent Weald.

A small building, 3 storeys high and built out of grey Kentish Rag-stone, it has an intimate atmosphere rather than the imposing grandeur associated with many stately homes. Although it is open to the public it is still privately owned so it is full of the paraphernalia which one family can accumulate over several generations.

Charlie Gooch was the son of the chauffeur at Boughton Monchelsea. The owner made Charles his godson and left him the house in his will. Which just goes to show that the meek sometimes do inherit the earth. However, inheritance does not pay for upkeep. So Charles opens the house up to the public and allows you to step into his home for a fabulous wedding.

Although the original building is Elizabethan, much of the interior was redesigned in Regency times. Wedding ceremonies are conducted in the Entrance Hall of the house. This is a small, but beautifully proportioned, square room. The ceiling is held up by 4 wooden pillars and there is an intricate wood-block floor. A nautical oil painting adorns one wall and an ornate French clock another.

The room gets the sun until mid-afternoon, bathing the buttermilk walls with a warm light. Guests can come straight in from the gardens and the bride will be able to make a grand entrance down the main staircase into the wedding room. The room will take 60 people at a squeeze. Any more and they would be standing in the garden peeking through the windows.

Recorded music can be provided but it would be much better to have a single musician, perhaps a harpist or flute player. The Kent music school is based in nearby Maidstone and students are often willing to perform at weddings for a small fee.

There are 2 rooms on either side of the hall, a drawing room to the left and a dining room to the right. After the wedding, guests can have drinks out in the gardens or, if the weather is bad, use the drawing room. From there they can venture through the french windows into the gardens. The drawing room is crammed with a wonderful array of antique furniture including a magnificent lacquered cabinet, a Chinese Chippendale-style gilded mirror and assorted antique settees. These antiques are not fenced off so guests can really make themselves at home.

A marquee on the lawn can provide for up to 500 guests. While they are eating they can look at the deer in the ancient deer park below and across the Weald of Kent. Smaller weddings can have a wedding breakfast in Boughton Monchelsea's dining room. This is a quite extraordinary room painted a deep red with a huge tapestry on the far wall depicting a Greek mythological landscape. It can seat up to 50 people but 30 is the ideal number. The silver candlesticks can be lit for a genuine candlelight supper. After the meal guests could retire to the library for a quiet chat and a brandy.

Jill Harris runs the house and is responsible for organizing weddings. She is an engaging and down-to-earth woman who is keen to help couples make the most of their wedding day. If it is at all possible she will organize it. Florists can be booked locally, horses and carriages can be arranged and even the vicar from the church next door can be roped in to give a blessing once the formal civil wedding is over. As it is essentially a private house caterers have to be brought in but Jill can suggest local firms who will do a good job starting at around £17 per head.

To hire the wedding room on its

own will cost £250 plus VAT or you can have all the rooms to yourself for the whole day for £900 plus VAT. There is no overnight accommodation but the wedding party can stay in the nearby Tanyard Hotel or in numerous local bed and breakfasts. The bride can use one of the upstairs rooms to prepare for the wedding. Normally it is on display as an Edwardian lady's bedroom complete with period bed linen and assorted nightdresses.

One of the joys of weddings in private houses is that the owners sometimes have little quirks. Jill says Charlie Gooch is particularly keen on fireworks. So if you want to finish off the day in style she can arrange a spectacular display for around £250, and no doubt he will be sneaking a look out of one of the upstairs windows.

Boughton Monchelsea Place can handle big weddings but the best arrangement would probably be to take over the house with about 40 people. You could have a lovely wedding followed by a great meal in the dining room and finish off the evening with fireworks. It is also ideal for winter weddings, with log fires and a crisp walk between the ceremony and the wedding breakfast.

Contact: Jill Harris
Main road: M20/A229
Station: Maidstone
Disabled access: Yes
Parking: Plenty
Registrar tel no: 01622 752891
Bedrooms: 0
Wedding only: Yes

Name: **Ramblers Restaurant**
Address: **Farnley, Corbridge, Northumberland NE45 5RN**
Tel: **01434 632424**

Being one of the few restaurants in the country to boast a wedding licence, Ramblers prides itself on its cuisine which has a reputation locally second to none.

Lovers of good food from miles around – and some, like the former King and Queen of Romania, from rather further afield – have dined at Ramblers. It is set in its own gardens, just across the Tyne from historic Corbridge.

Corbridge with its Roman bridge and the nearby fort of Corstopitum is a picturesque town in Newcastle's Tyne valley 'stockbroker belt'. It is an affluent, attractive area surrounded by the rolling Northumbrian hills.

Celebrities who have visited Ramblers include best-selling Northumbrian author Catherine Cookson, who apparently rates it as her favourite restaurant, and co-median Rowan Atkinson, a former student of Newcastle University.

Owners Jennifer and Heini Herrmann have 20 years' experience of hosting wedding receptions to draw on as they take on this new venture of opening up their restaurant for civil marriage ceremonies.

The 19th-century building, Cliffe House, has been carefully developed into a friendly, comfortable eating establishment by the couple. All the staff are friends and family, including Jennifer and Heini's two eldest sons Christopher and Richard. There is a cosy, intimate feel about the elegantly furnished dining rooms and lounges.

Jennifer has the ability to make visitors feel instantly at ease with her bubbly, friendly personality. She takes an obvious delight in helping couples plan their wedding and is more than happy to throw open the doors of Ramblers – a place she plainly cherishes – for the 'big day'.

There are 5 wedding rooms which can cater for parties of between 15 and 90. Most rooms open on to the garden and one boasts a grand piano which can be used at weddings.

Jennifer, a native of Sunderland, met and married Heini in Bermuda. Over the years, the couple have built up a reputation for fine food. Jennifer is quick to put the restaurant's undoubted success down to chef Heini's culinary flair – he has been in catering since he left school at 15 to undergo a strict training in southern Germany, before moving to Switzerland.

While Heini reigns supreme in the kitchen, it is Jennifer who provides the welcoming face to the guests. She is a superb hostess and can be spotted flitting about the restaurant checking that diners are enjoying their meal. Jennifer's charisma fills the restaurant and she has embraced this latest venture with eager enthusiasm believing that the surroundings of Ramblers are a perfect alternative to a register office for anyone wanting a civil wedding.

Couples tying the knot at Ramblers can hand over the arrangements to Jennifer with confidence. She will run right through the wedding day with the couple from the actual ceremony to the photographs and reception. As well as offering a wide choice of menus, Heini is ready to take on board the couple's own suggestions when he prepares the food.

Wedding room hire ranges between £50 and £100. As a rough guide, a sit-down meal with wine starts at around £17 a head but as Jennifer points out each wedding is individually planned and priced according to the couple's own wishes. There is no accommodation at Ramblers but there are plenty of local hotels and bed and breakfasts.

Ramblers is the ideal venue for couples wanting an intimate wedding in stylish surroundings with the emphasis on wonderful food.

Contact: Jennifer Herrmann
Main road: A68/A69
Station: Corbridge
Disabled access: Yes
Parking: Yes
Registrar tel no: 01434 602355
Bedrooms: 0
Wedding only: Yes

Name: The Lawn
Address: Hall Road, Rochford, Essex SS4 1DL
Tel: 01702 203 701

Most Londoners head off down the A13 to Southend either to give their

Ford Escort XR3i a good thrashing or to visit the quiet cockle sheds set in the marshes at Leigh-on-Sea. However if you drive on to the A127 and turn off at Rayleigh you find rural Essex – a very different place.

The Lawn is at the end of a quiet country road which runs through grazing land filled with horses. It is a square Georgian country house painted white with green shutters. Until recently it was used as a family home but now it is solely used for functions.

The wedding room which must have once been the drawing room is on the ground floor and has doors out on to the gardens. It has thick carpet, cream and beige walls, lots of decorative china, old family furniture and a grand mirror reflecting the light from the garden. The room will hold 60 people sitting in easy chairs, settees and some formal seats. The ceremony will be conducted from a small antique table and suitable wedding music can be played.

Before the wedding, couples meet the registrar in the old dining room. It now has a bar so the bride or groom could take one last drink to steady their nerves!

Receptions are held in the main hall of the house, a tall square room with a large sweeping staircase and a gallery above on all sides. Musicians can play from the gallery. The fireplace in the hall once graced the home of prime minister Disraeli and for some unexplained reason the chandelier came from Stowe House.

The bride can make her grand entrance down the staircase to the reception.

Guests who slip out of the reception to use the facilities will find that the ladies' loo is an original twenties bathroom complete with green tiles and a working servants' bell.

Outside there is a lovely terrace with 6 columns supporting an ornate balcony above. Guests can have post-wedding drinks here and will be guaranteed to keep dry should it rain. There is a large lawn and to the right an archway leads to an old rose garden with box hedges and even some mistletoe growing in an apple tree.

The horses from the surrounding fields are naturally curious and nearly always come to see what is going on. Quite often some unknown Dobbin ends up starring in the wedding photos. Standing in its grounds The Lawn takes on a quite different look. The low building with its cream walls, colonnaded porch and horses at the fence looks rather like one of those southern mansions in *Gone With the Wind*.

There is no accommodation here but the bride can make final preparations in a bedroom which has a balcony overlooking the garden. It can also be used by the photographer to take a group shot of all the guests. Guests can stay at the nearby Moat House Hotel.

Hiring the house for the whole day depends on the time and size of the wedding. Catering is supplied by a number of external firms and meals start at about £13 per head. It is possible to have a small wedding at The Lawn without a reception but with some drinks. Then the room hire would be about £250 with the drinks and canapés costed on top.

We think The Lawn would be ideal for a themed wedding complete with a carriage and all those southern bonnets and crinoline dresses. Just hope the groom does not stamp off saying, 'quite frankly my dear, I don't give a damn!'

Contact: Mrs Keddie
Main road: A127
Station: Rochford
Disabled access: Yes
Parking: Ample
Registrar tel no: 01702 343728
Bedrooms: 0
Wedding only: Yes

Name: Langtry Manor Hotel
Address: Derby Road, Eastcliff, Bournemouth BH1 3QB
Tel: 01202 553887

Bournemouth has hundreds of hotels but none quite like the Langtry Manor. From the outside it looks just like a medium-sized family hotel set in one of Bournemouth's tree-lined streets. But when you get into the wedding room you realize that it is rather unusual – not many small family hotels have such a large hall with stained-glass windows and a minstrels gallery.

The Langtry Manor was originally built as a home for Lillie Langtry, the mistress of Edward VII. It is said that it was to provide a permanent rendezvous for Lillie and the Prince of Wales. You can still see signs of Lillie's handiwork and there is definitely an atmosphere of secret liaisons.

The wedding room was originally a dining hall which doubled up as a small bedroom. It can hold up to 100 people for the ceremony. A large stained-glass window backs on to the garden and features entwined swans, and an inglenook fireplace dominates the middle of the room. It has a wood surround with Lillie's initials carved on it. The minstrels gallery runs across the back of the room and is inscribed with the motto 'They say – What say they – Let them say'. Freely translated it means 'I don't give a damn what they say, I'll do whatever I like'. The remaining wall is covered with two medieval wall hangings which have faded to a rather gloomy brown colour. High up in the corner of the room, almost in the ceiling, is a small hatch. Apparently the king used it to check who was at the ball – if they looked a boring bunch he didn't bother to come and join them!

After the ceremony couples can have their pictures taken out in the small garden while the room is transformed into a dining area for the reception.

Upstairs the hotel looks very much like a private house. On the first-floor landing there is a small collection of 1877 memorabilia, the date when the house was built.

Next to it is the king's chair which guests are forbidden to sit in.

In this sort of building guests expect a standard sort of bedroom with a television on the wall and perhaps a small ensuite shower. But open the door to the King Edward VII Suite and you get a real surprise. The room is massive with a high beamed roof and a huge Jacobean four-poster bed. The inglenook fireplace is decorated with golden tiles depicting Shakespearean scenes. This must have been how it looked when Lillie had her amorous trysts with the king.

More adventurous couples may want to use the Langtry Suite which has a heart-shaped bath in the corner of the bedroom – ideal for a candle-lit bottle of champagne.

Tara Howard, the manager of the hotel, is a bundle of energy who is really keen to make a go of the new wedding law. Outside the hotel a sign proudly announces 'you can get married here'. She welcomes themed events and already runs Edwardian evenings – she will even get the staff to welcome the bride in servants' outfits complete with mobcaps.

Weddings at the Langtry Manor cost £200 if you do not have a reception and £100 if you do. Receptions start at about £20 per head. The hotel also does special arrangements for exclusive use, giving guests the chance to meet up with old friends the night before or after the big event. There is disabled access, including a ground-floor ensuite room. Tara can recommend local florists, car hire firms and musicians for the day.

The Langtry Manor is not the poshest of hotels but you can have an unusual wedding here without paying the earth for the privilege. Most important of all, Tara Howard will do everything possible to make it a special occasion.

Contact: Tara Howard
Main road: A338
Station: Bournemouth
Disabled access: Yes
Parking: Ample
Registrar tel no: 01202 551668
Bedrooms: 25
Wedding only: Yes

FIT FOR A KING

Love requires respect and friendship as well as passion. Because there comes a time when you have to get out of bed.

ERICA JONG

These venues are strictly out of bounds to shrinking violets. You simply cannot have a wedding in any of the following places which does not make some kind of statement. You have to compete with the surroundings you are in and for those who are extrovert and gregarious these venues are ideal. They are also exotic in the sense they have decor or certain rooms which are done out in an exotic style. Alexandra Palace for example has extraordinary trompe l'oeil murals while Rhinefield House Hotel has a fabulous Alhambra Room with mosaic floor and tiled walls decorated with Islamic patterns. And of course don't forget the Royal Pavilion in Brighton – you'd need a hell of a wedding to match that extraordinary mix of oriental and western designs!

Name: The Royal Pavilion
Address: Brighton BN1 1EE
Tel: 01273 603005

It is hard to imagine a more fairy-tale setting than one at the Royal Pavilion in Brighton. Apart from the fact that 'London by the Sea' has such a lot going for it in its own right, it has earned a reputation over the years as the place for lovers. In fact it was probably Brighton which inspired the first ever 'dirty weekend'!

The town itself is bustling with life. You can take a stroll on the promenade or wander along the famous Brighton Pier munching candy floss and somehow you feel all is well with the world. Bargain hunters can happily mooch around the myriad of backstreets known as the Lanes peering into all the interesting little shops selling everything from tacky tourist junk to some of the highest quality jewellery and antiques in the country.

But no one who visits Brighton can call it a visit unless they see the famous Pavilion. It began life as little more than a 'modest farm-house' for George, Prince of Wales who first began visiting the seaside town in 1783. Four years later he fell under the spell of the place and asked Henry Holland to create a classically-styled villa on the same site.

When he was exalted to the rank of Prince Regent he commissioned John Nash to enlarge the villa and it was transformed into the Pavilion as we know it today. It was his great love of India and the Orient which inspired the mishmash of architectural styles. Its silhouette is probably one of the most famous in the country – a sort of Taj Mahal meets seaside resort.

Nowadays the Pavilion is owned by Brighton Council who have spent a small fortune on returning it to its original splendour. Inside is a total fantasy world filled with mythical creatures, astonishing colours and superb craftsmanship including many original furnishings and decorations on loan from the Queen. Domed ceilings with gilded scallop-shaped shells, hand-knotted carpets and cast-iron palm trees are just a few of the delights which have all been painstakingly restored.

Weddings can now take place in the Red Drawing Room which doubles up as the mayor's parlour during the rest of the week. The decor is in Chinese style with red dragon wallpaper and reproduction Chinese watercolours. Huge bamboo-like pillars topped with palm leaves rise up to meet the carved ceiling and mythical dragons in the satinwood graining. It has direct access to the gardens where superb wedding photographs could be taken. The whole place provides a fantasy backdrop to almost any imaginative theme wedding a couple could come up with.

To hire the room which can take up to 40 people will set you back £450 but if you have your reception in the nearby William IV Room which holds 70 people a special inclusive price of £850 will be charged. The Queen Adelaide Suite with its balcony giving on to the newly restored gardens provides an alternative venue for the reception.

We think the setting of the Pavilion is truly spectacular but it is incredibly ornate and the bride may feel she is competing with her environment. A themed oriental or Georgian wedding would be fantastic followed by a fancy-dress reception in the Queen Adelaide Suite. There is no dance licence at the Pavilion so no loud discos or thumping dance music are allowed.

A finger buffet starts at around £5 a head with a stand-up buffet at between £12 and £15. A full sit-down meal will set you back around £20–£25 per person. There is no overnight accommodation at the Pavilion but Brighton is awash with hotels and bed and breakfasts, many with outstanding sea views.

Contact: Debbie Steel
Main road: M23
Station: Brighton
Disabled access: Yes
Parking: No
Registrar tel no: 01273 722795
Bedrooms: 0
Wedding only: Yes

Name: Alexandra Palace
Address: Alexandra Palace Way,
Wood Green, London N22 4AY
Tel: 0181 365 2121

Anyone who knows North London will recognize this entry. Ally Pally,

as it is known affectionately amongst locals, dominates the skyline for miles around. The People's Palace has had a long and chequered history but its story is one of survival against the odds. It has risen like a phoenix from the ashes out of two disastrous fires and has faced recurring crises and fluctuating prosperity in its lifetime. Today it is a flourishing exhibition centre and venue for conferences, banquets and now weddings.

The Palace was first opened in 1873 on Queen Victoria's birthday but was consumed by fire within a month. During the 16 days of its short life there were no less than 124,000 visitors. The directors decided to rebuild it immediately but the second palace was never really a commercial success. In 1900 an Act of Parliament was passed which effectively gave control over to local authorities and it became the Palace of the People.

In 1980 disaster again struck and the Palace was almost demolished by fire. In August 1983 work began on repairing the Great Hall, the Palm Court and the West Hall which had been most badly damaged. That work is now finished and the Great Hall is absolutely staggering with one uninterrupted area the size of a football pitch to accommodate exhibitions and leisure events.

The Palm Court has palm trees imported from Alexandria together with casts of sphinxes and lions' heads. In the restaurant the trompe l'oeil murals on the end walls provide a spectacular continuation of real space and in the west corridor scenes from the history of the People's Palace are depicted in the work of local Haringey artists.

What more splendid place for a wedding? There are two wedding rooms at Ally Pally. The Londesborough Room boasts dramatic Cinalli murals depicting the destructive prowess of Samson. Romanesque pillars complete the distinctly Italian Renaissance atmosphere. Large west-facing windows open on to the terrace. From here guests can take in the panoramic views of the Palace grounds and the city below while sipping their drinks. Receptions can also be held in this room – it has seating for 120 guests.

The famous Palm Court has also been licensed and is about four times the size of the Londesborough Room. This magnificent space has 2 fountains in the centre banked by palm trees. The high roof is made almost entirely of glass which is what gives the room its al fresco atmosphere. It is built like a large airy courtyard and you could almost be forgiven for thinking you were outside. Because the Palm Court is the main entrance to exhibitions in the West Hall, exclusive use may be difficult to arrange.

Catering here is all coordinated by the Palace staff who can provide a wide variety of meals, buffets and drinks. The menus range from the traditional to the exotic. It is not unknown for Ally Pally to cater for wedding receptions of up to 1000 people so nothing is going to faze them.

You can also book the Palace Restaurant which can seat anything from 130 to 250 guests in comfort. It has atmospheric low lighting and wonderful murals which give the illusion of an Italian courtyard. And the West Hall is also available for receptions. This can seat up to 1400 people. Marquees can be set up in the Palace grounds at a price. If you are considering holding your marriage ceremony in the Londesborough Room it will cost £195 plus VAT. Receptions on their own in that room will cost around £29.50 per person which includes room hire, service and VAT. Drinks packages start at around £10.50 per person. You are encouraged to arrange your own entertainment.

Ally Pally offers a quiet haven of beauty in the heart of a bustling metropolis which we felt is best suited for large summer weddings. If you were thinking of having a rather alcoholic and noisy bash then it would perhaps be better to avoid the tranquil parkland of Alexandra Palace. But the address does look wonderfully prestigious on wedding invitations.

Contact: Geoff Snell
Main road: A406
Station: Wood Green BR
Disabled access: Yes
Parking: 2000
Registrar tel no: 0181 528 0186
Bedrooms: None, but list of hotels available
Wedding only: Yes

Name: Clandon Park
Address: West Clandon, Guildford,
Surrey GU4 7RQ
Tel: 01483 222482

Shrinking violets need not apply to get married in the Marble Hall at Clandon Park near Guildford. We are talking serious splendour here and any wedding would have to match it for sheer magnificence. The house itself is a huge redbrick Georgian-style pile set in 10 acres of open parkland.

Before it acquired a licence for weddings, couples would marry in the nearby church and then meander a mile up the path to the great house for their reception. Now they can do the reverse and meander back down to the village for a blessing by the local vicar.

Clandon Park itself has been the home of the Onslow family since 1641. They have traditionally followed political careers and no less than 3 family members have been Speakers of the House of Commons.

Sir Richard Onslow tried to persuade Cromwell to accept the Crown and in 1651 he was directed to raise a regiment and join Cromwell for the Battle of Worcester. Unfortunately he arrived too late and incurred Cromwell's wrath who declared in the Commons afterwards that if the 'fox of Surrey' had arrived in time to do battle no one could be sure on which side he would have fought.

Two rooms have been licensed for weddings at Clandon Park. The Marble Hall is, as its name suggests, almost entirely decorated in marble. Huge marble pillars support an ornate balustrade with carvings in the style of Michelangelo. The relief sculptures on the chimney breast are works of art in themselves. One depicts Diana, the goddess of hunting – the other Bacchus, the god of having a good time. White walls are set off by fabulous paintings of birds and all around are wonderful antiques in muted colours. The overall effect is of opulence. But, be warned, the hall, being marble, is cold and best suited to a summer wedding.

Through the marble hall you reach the Saloon which is the less formal of the two rooms but just as ornate. The ceiling is decorated with gods and goddesses and the walls are in varying shades of blue and covered with the famous Mortlake tapestries. Enormous french windows give out on to the gardens and can be opened completely for a summer wedding.

There are two restaurants downstairs in the vaulted undercroft of the building. The main one can seat up to 180 guests but has the air of a school refectory, the ceiling low and slightly oppressive. The converted stable which seats around 30 is lighter and with its whitewashed walls and candlelit tables creates a rather Mediterranean feel.

The food is traditionally English although the banqueting manager is happy to discuss any other cuisine. The menus range from a lunch or dinner at £14 to £24 a head to a finger buffet starting at just £6.95. Additional space is available for larger weddings with a marquee on the lawn which can hold up to 300 people. A complete planning service is available including entertainment, wedding cake, flowers, photographers and toastmakers to ensure a perfect day.

The hire of the Marble Hall is not cheap at £850 for a full wedding ceremony and reception. But no one in their right mind would be considering a small intimate wedding here. Clandon Park is an imposing stately home and as such we think would make a superb venue for a large ornate summer wedding with all the trimmings. If you are planning a winter wedding better tell the guests to bring their thermal undies!

Contact: David Brock-Doyle
Main road: M25/A247
Station: Clandon
Disabled access: Limited but with electric stair-climber
Parking: Good
Registrar tel no: 01483 62841
Bedrooms: None, but plenty of local hotels and bed and breakfasts
Wedding only: Yes

Name: Tatton Park
Address: Knutsford, Cheshire WA16 6QN
Tel: 01565 654822

Set in 1000 acres of one of Britain's finest deer parks, Tatton Park has long been recognized as one of Cheshire's great historic houses. You enter Tatton Park through a sweeping tree-lined drive which seems to go on for ever. Herds of deer graze freely across the expansive parkland which embraces lakes, gardens, the mansion, a medieval hall and a working farm.

Tatton Park has been in the Egerton family since the 1500s but was never actually lived in until the mid-1600s when Thomas Egerton had a house built for him on the present site. The last Egerton to live at Tatton was Maurice who was dubbed 'the bachelor baron' by the press after he died in 1958.

In fact he was a shy man who loathed publicity and big social gatherings. He had a great sense of adventure though and often travelled abroad to British Columbia and India. In Africa he built a house modelled on Tatton in the middle of the Kenyan bush. During the war Tatton became a great centre of activity when Dunkirk troops, a tank regiment and RAF and American Army units pitched camp in the park and took over the stables. Parachutists practised descents into the park while commandos learned to detonate bombs.

After Maurice's death there was much speculation over the future of Tatton but doubts were all dispelled when his will was eventually made public and Tatton was handed over to the National Trust so that it could 'be permanently preserved for the benefit of the nation'.

Tatton Park has now been open to the public for more than 30 years and is financed, maintained and managed by Chesire County Council. Although it is home to one of the finest collections of paintings, porcelain and furniture in Britain there is a sense of fading glory about the house itself. Maintaining this property seems a hard task for the county council.

They are still doing a great job despite obvious financial constraints. The gardens are truly spectacular. They run to over 50 acres and feature a surprise at every turn. There are giant redwoods from America, a Victorian maze, an Italian terrace, a Japanese garden and the Orangery which has recently been restored to its former elegance. Inside the house the furnishings and decorations of each room have been arranged so that they seem to capture the very essence of the people who once lived here.

Although there are 4 areas which have been licensed for weddings there are 3 which really stand out as special. The first is the Entrance Hall which is more reminiscent of a Greek temple than an English country house. The marble floor and columns and ornate ceiling decorations reflected the revival of all things Greek which was a huge influence on architects of the time. Pale pink walls and grand oil paintings on the walls create a very formal atmosphere. This room would suit a formal and traditional white wedding. It holds around 80 people and costs £300.

The second is the Tenants Hall which can hold up to 400 people and costs £1,500 to hire. Maurice travelled worldwide and was frequently on safari in India and Africa where he shot many hunting trophies. The large showcases on the walls contain curios brought home by him and many are even labelled in his own handwriting. When the hall was built in the 1930s Maurice had a Willis electropneumatic organ installed which was restored in 1978. This is a massive room and needs to be festooned with decorations and balloons to look really spectacular.

But the jewel in Tatton's crown has to be Lord Egerton's Apartments which have been beautifully restored to provide 2 large reception rooms with huge Georgian windows leading out on to a stone balcony overlooking the Italianate garden below. You can really be master and mistress of all you survey as the view from here is absolutely stunning – on a clear day you can see right across Cheshire. The balcony accommodates 40 people for 'drinks with a view' whatever the weather and costs £200 to hire.

Just like any other stately home which is open to the public Tatton is not always available and you need to check when you can hire the rooms. There is no problem with the Tenants Hall and Lord Egerton's Apartments however which are available 10 am–4 pm Monday to Saturday. Hire charges include the opportunity for photographs to be taken in Tatton's entrance hall, staircase hall or gardens.

Contact: Sheila Wych
Main road: A537

Station: Knutsford
Disabled access: Good
Parking: Excellent, 3 car parks
Registrar tel no: 01244 602668
Bedrooms: 0
Wedding only: No

Name: Rhinefield House Hotel
Address: Rhinefield Road,
Brockenhurst, Hampshire SO42
7QB
Tel: 01590 622922

Rhinefield House Hotel is deep in the New Forest on the A35 Lyndhurst road towards Bournemouth. This is not the open heathland that most visitors see but rather ancient woodland covered in rhododendrons and Canadian redwood trees. The single-track road eventually reaches the entrance to the hotel grounds. A drive lined with copper beeches leads to a large mansion which has all the signs of a Victorian architect let loose on a drawing board. The grey stone building has a central clock tower complete with stone minarets and a drive-through arch. On one side is an arched walkway whilst on the other is a clump of Tudor-style chimney stacks.

The house was built in 1890 for Mrs Walker-Munro, a coal heiress. Apparently she was quite a woman and it certainly shows in her dramatic architectural taste. Inside the building a replica of the Great Hall at Westminster rubs shoulders with a moorish palace while outside a Greek amphitheatre mingles with Italianate gardens.

Weddings are held in the Orangery, a modern conservatory-style extension at the side of the house. It overlooks the gardens and a long ornamental pond. It is hard to tell now but apparently the pond started life as an open-air swimming-pool when Rhinefield was a school. Today, 50 people can sit in the Orangery among the palms and watch the bride and groom walking up the aisle. In the summer the doors could be opened for an almost al fresco wedding.

Winter weddings can be held in the Kings Room which is decorated with cream and blue wallpaper and has a large fireplace, and where the walls are covered with pictures of kings. It holds 75 people.

The real interest at Rhinefield House is in the wonderfully eccentric rooms that can be used for receptions. The Grand Hall has heavy oak panelling, carvings, a balcony and a large picture window. It seats up to 110 around a massive stone fireplace.

Smaller weddings can be followed by a candlelit dinner for 12 in the Alhambra Room. This extraordinary room is built in the style of the famous Alhambra Palace in Granada with its mosaic floor and tiled walls decorated with Islamic patterns and inscriptions. Onyx pillars support dramatically patterned arches in the ceiling. It would be a wonderfully exotic place to eat after a small wedding.

Between the wedding and the reception guests can have drinks on the terrace and wander round the gardens. These include ornamental lakes, a small maze, a herb garden and a grass amphitheatre.

Before the wedding the couple meet the registrar upstairs in the Oriel Room overlooked by cupids playing a lyre on the ornate ceiling. For couples who want to stay the night there is a bridal suite – a grand but simple room with a large bay window overlooking the gardens.

Other guests can stay at the hotel or in hotels and bed and breakfasts in nearby Brockenhurst. There is disabled access to the ground-floor wedding rooms but not to the bedrooms. There's an in-house florist and a long list of local cars, photographers and musicians. A horse and carriage can be arranged and a helicopter pad can be used.

There is a charge of £250 for the wedding ceremony and room hire charge for other function rooms. For receptions of over 60 the bride and groom have the complimentary use of a bedroom for their wedding night. Standard menus with drinks start at about £30 per head. A special deal gives guests the chance to stay for 2 nights at the hotel with meals for £120. In effect they can come to the wedding and stay for the whole weekend.

Rhinefield House is a very special hotel. To get the best out of it you really need to have a small wedding followed by a dinner in the Alhambra Room or a large wedding with a grand reception that will fill the whole of the Grand Hall.
Contact: Jan Hamon

Main road: A35
Station: Brockenhurst
Disabled access: Some
Parking: Ample
Registrar tel no: 01590 673547
Bedrooms: 34
Wedding only: Yes

Name: Lucknam Park
Address: Colerne, Wiltshire SN14 8AZ
Tel: 01225 742777

Lucknam Park is one of those places where the seriously rich go to rest and relax in discreet style. To get to it you have to drive through a mile-long avenue of beech trees. The road then opens out to reveal a perfectly proportioned Palladian mansion. A long low building, it has a central colonnaded porch and two wings on either side each finished off with a grand curved bay frontage. It was built in 1720 and remained in private hands until 1987 when it became one of England's most exclusive hotels.

The main entrance exactly reflects the Lucknam Park culture. The beautifully proportioned room is tastefully decorated in a soothing sand colour. It is furnished with comfy armchairs, antique furniture and old rugs. An assortment of prints of country dogs and oil paintings cover the walls. Occasionally a member of staff glides past noiselessly.

Weddings take place in the Drawing Room. A magnificent yellow room 40 feet by 20 feet, it has ornate plasterwork, lots of antiques and enough sofas to seat most of the guests in style. Old masters cover the walls. The couple will take their vows in front of the curved french windows which look directly down the avenue of beech trees. The other window looks out over the rose garden. In the summer the windows could be thrown wide open to bring the fragrance of the countryside right into the gathering. The room is licensed for 80 people but it would be a bit of a squeeze. However you could have 40 or 50 guests without any trouble at all.

After the ceremony the newly-weds will want to go outside and have their photos taken by the house or in front of the grand avenue. On a fine day drinks can be served on the lawn. If the weather is not so good they can be served in the wood-panelled Library with its rows of ancient leather-bound books and stag's head on the wall. The silence of the Library is only disturbed by the ticking of the clock. When grandfather goes missing towards the end of the reception you will probably find him dozing quietly in here.

The wedding breakfast is served in the Dining Room which has windows on all sides, a large fireplace and a sky mural on the ceiling complete with clouds. The best seats are in the bay window at the end. Smaller weddings can have a dinner in a private dining room.

The honeymoon suite has 3 large windows with spectacular views down the drive and across the grounds. As you would expect the bathroom is fitted out with enough marble to keep an Italian quarry in business for months.

Guests who make a weekend of it will have the opportunity to use the luxurious leisure spa and beauty salon.

The staff are far too discreet to mention any names but a careful study of the papers will tell you that Margaret Thatcher and Ruby Wax have stayed here. And, of course, Raine Spencer the Princess of Wales's stepmother had her own wedding reception at the house.

There is a £1,000 facility fee to hire the drawing room and restaurant for a wedding. Food and drink is likely to start at around £40 per head but the sky is the limit. Standard rooms start at £160 for 2 people going up to £450 for a couple in a suite. The hotel will normally have other guests present so you cannot have a loud band playing at the reception. But if you are prepared to pay for it, you can have the whole place for 24 hours, have a grand bash and let all the guests sleep it off before going home the next day.

There is ample parking, but if you don't want to look out of place bring the Range Rover or the Porsche and make sure you leave the fluffy dice behind. There is good disabled access to the wedding areas and to some of the bedrooms.

Lucknam Park is an ideal place for a stylish wedding in grand surroundings backed up by the highest quality service. But if you want to invite all your old friends for a noisy bash and get uproariously drunk go somewhere else.

Contact: Michelle Haynes
Main road: M4/A420
Station: Chippenham (7 miles)
Disabled access: Fair
Parking: Ample
Registrar tel no: 01249 654361
Bedrooms: 42
Wedding only: Yes

Name: The Lygon Arms
Address: Broadway, Worcestershire WR12 7DU
Tel: 01386 852255

If you want a small wedding with impeccable old-style service in a venue steeped in history then the Lygon Arms is just the ticket. Set deep in the Cotswolds in the ancient village of Broadway, the hotel was originally a coaching inn, built to cater to the prosperous merchants of the wool trade.

Wisteria covers the traditional honey-coloured stone building. Going in through the heavy oak front door you are immediately aware of the aroma of woodsmoke from the smouldering log fires which burn in the various cosy sitting rooms. It's the sort of place where wedding guests will love to curl up with a hot toddy and a good book after a long wedding eve walk in the Cotswold countryside.

Hotels and stately homes often boast of their connections with the Civil War but at the Lygon Arms you really can get married in the hotel where Oliver Cromwell slept in 1651 on the eve of the Battle of Worcester. You can spend the night in the very room where Charles I met his supporters.

Unfortunately, although there is no doubt that Charles I stayed at the hotel, he would not have used the marriage rooms as they are a later addition. But royal fans need not panic. They can get married in the Edinburgh Room which was opened in 1968 when Prince Philip lunched at the hotel. A tasteful room decorated in a traditional style it can seat 40 people for the ceremony.

Larger weddings can be held in the Torrington Room, a more modern but tastefully decorated function room at the back of the hotel. It can seat 70 people, has its own entrance and a small lobby that would be great for serving post-wedding drinks.

The ideal place for an intimate reception following a family wedding is the Cromwell Room. It is small but oozes the sort of atmosphere that can never be artificially created. The ceiling has heavily decorated plasterwork and the room is filled with serious period furniture. We are not talking reproductions here – 1669 and 1686 are 2 of the dates carved on the original pieces.

On their wedding night a couple with a sense of history should book into the Charles I Suite with its massive four-poster bed which you literally climb up on to and then sink blissfully into. The ensuite sitting room is where Charles I is supposed to have met his Cavaliers. Watching the log fire crackling in the hearth it is easy to transport yourself back to the days of the Civil War.

There is a mysterious latch in one of the oak panels – if you open it you can see a narrow staircase leading downstairs. According to legend it was used by the king's mistresses. If you are staying here the night before your wedding and are the slightest bit worried that your partner might have a change of heart it may be worthwhile asking the hotel to block the escape route!

Elsewhere the old part of the hotel is equally atmospheric with plenty of beams and authentic period furniture. The communal areas are all decorated with beautiful fresh floral displays painstakingly arranged by the hotel's own florist.

Small receptions can take place in a number of private dining rooms in the older part of the building. Bigger events can be held in the Great Hall – a vast vaulted room built in 1910 with its own minstrels gallery and an array of suits of armour ranged along the walls.

The hotel has a helipad which is useful if you need one but for guests who prefer to 'let the train take the strain' Evesham and Moreton-in-Marsh stations are close by. There is a pretty garden for wedding photos and disabled access to all areas.

General manager Kirk Ritchie prides himself on running the hotel in the old-fashioned way with high standards and good quality service. He first visited the hotel as a boy of 13 and vowed to become manager one day. He trained at the Savoy and 20 years ago returned to fulfil his childhood ambition.

But he is far from stuffy. He fondly remembers one Christmas party when the Great Hall was decorated as a wild west saloon and guests were amazed at the arrival of a cowboy on horseback complete with stetson and six-shooter.

Anyone who hankers after a wedding at the Lygon Arms should bear in mind the hotel is part of the Savoy Group which is reflected in the price. Unusually for this sort of establishment it has a swimming-pool and health suite – useful if the bride or groom want to pamper themselves with a full beauty treatment the day before the wedding.

Guests who can't afford to stay at the hotel can choose from around 60 bed and breakfasts in the area. There are also a number of smaller hotels and restaurants near Broadway.

The Lygon Arms can handle large and small weddings and we feel that couples should go for one or the other avoiding the middle ground. An intimate ceremony followed by dinner in the Cromwell Room would be fabulous. Otherwise go for a bigger wedding followed by a huge bash in the Great Hall. Whatever happens make sure you have a romantic night in the Charles I Suite.

A basic wedding costs from £2,500 based on 100 people having finger buffet, excluding wine. A top-of-the-range wedding using all facilities costs £4,000 based on 100 people and a set menu excluding drink. Accommodation runs from £98 plus VAT, special suites from £210 plus VAT.

Contact: James Partridge

Main road: M5/A44
Station: Moreton-in-Marsh/Evesham
Disabled access: Yes
Parking: Ample
Registrar tel no: 01386 443945
Bedrooms: 65
Wedding only: No

ARCHITECTURAL DELIGHTS

I nailed it, and I
will live in it until it kills me.
I can nail my left palm
to the left hand cross-piece but
I can't do everything myself.
I need a hand to nail the right,
a help, a love, a you, a wife.

ALAN DUGAN

Some of these venues are truly spectacular in their architectural design – but that does not mean many of the buildings in other sections are not just as beautiful. It is just that these are ones which have particular architectural significance. Little Thakeham, for example is one of the finest examples of a Sir Edwin Lutyens manor house in the country. Leez Priory is a superb example of a tower. So if you are looking for a particularly fine backdrop to your wedding photographs this may be the section for you.

Name: **Layer Marney Tower**
Address: **near Colchester, Essex
CO5 9US**
Tel: **01206 330784**

Layer Marney Tower describes itself as the tallest Tudor gatehouse in the country. It is set in 120 acres of farmland at the end of a quiet country lane some 6 miles south of Colchester. It is a truly enormous brick building with a main gatehouse flanked by twin towers each 8 storeys high. Layer Marney was built by Henry, the first Lord Marney, in the reign of Henry VIII. It was clearly designed to impress visitors and to vie with folk like Cardinal Wolsey who built Hampton Court Palace. It is still privately owned by Nicholas and Sheila Charrington who live in the house and run, among other things, a deer farm.

In spite of the building's size it is possible to have a very small and intimate wedding in the Entrance Hall which has been licensed. It is a narrow oak-panelled room with a wooden arch leading to the garden. There are stone archways leading off into the depths of the great house and a small gallery which would make an ideal spot for a single musician to play the 'Wedding March'. The room is decorated with 2 stuffed deer and a stuffed tiger. Don't ask. In the corner is an antique oak settle. The ceremony is conducted from a small round antique table with the garden as a backdrop. The hall can hold about 15 people.

Bigger weddings can be held in the brick-built Carpenter's Hall in the old servants' quarters. The room is dominated by a large chimney rising from the old bakehouse below. It is tall and airy, decorated with silk flowers and has plenty of exposed beams. It will easily seat 120 and there is space outside for post-wedding drinks. However, this part of the building has no disabled access.

Guests will be surprised when they come out of the wedding rooms to discover that the gardens are in what was originally the front of the house. Laid out in a formal style with box hedges, they look across a deer park to the Essex marshes and the Blackwater Estuary.

Receptions are held in the Long Gallery, a large brick building which was once a stable block. In 1910 it was turned into a magnificent hall with a sprung dance floor, a Jacobean fireplace and most important of all, 3 large windows with Kentish Ragstone surrounds. The hall is over 80 feet long and has huge pincer beams holding up the roof. One of the windows completely fills the west wall bathing the whole room in light from the Essex skies.

The Long Gallery can easily seat 120 and could accommodate more for a buffet and dance. In the evening it can be lit by candles from the iron candelabra that hang in the centre of the hall. It looks beautiful but the owner, Nicholas Charrington, warns you to watch out for wax dripping in the soup!

Nicholas can supply lists of local florists, car companies and musicians. He can also arrange fireworks and is happy for staff to dress up in all the gear if you want a Tudor wedding.

There is no accommodation at Layer Marney but there are 3 reasonable-sized hotels within 4 miles and several local bed and breakfasts.

The Charringtons have taken an imaginative approach to pricing their weddings. Before 1 pm you can have a wedding only without having to book a reception. This will cost a bargain £150 although the registrar's fee will cost at least another £120. If you wanted they could supply post-wedding drinks while photos are taken. A reception could then be held in a local pub.

Weddings that are held after 1 pm still cost £150 but you must also book the Long Gallery, which will cost £500 for 4 hours. Or for £1,000 you can have the Long Gallery for a reception and an evening party. Catering is provided by a local firm and will cost upwards of £14 a head for a 3-course meal.

Layer Marney Tower is ideally suited for an afternoon wedding and reception for 120 people. If yours is a second-time-round marriage and you fancy an intimate event Layer Marney is also very suitable. Without spending a lot you could have a morning wedding to remember followed by a slap-up meal in a local restaurant with a few friends.

Finally, if you have a head for heights see if you can persuade the Charringtons to show you the top of the tower. It has an amazing painted room with views across the Essex countryside.

Contact: Nicholas or Sheila Charrington
Main road: A12/B1022
Station: Kelvedon (4 miles), Colchester (7 miles)
Disabled access: Partial
Parking: Plenty
Registrar tel no: 01206 572926
Bedrooms: 0
Wedding only: Yes

Name: Ty Penlan
Address: The Old School, Carmarthen St, Llandeilo, Dyfed SA19 6AW
Tel: 01558 822644

If you have never been to the Brecon Beacons you would not believe the beauty of the countryside around the area. You can literally drive for miles through the most stunning countryside without seeing another soul. Having said that, the roads are good and the trip to Llandeilo is definitely worth making.

Llandeilo may look like any other Welsh town but there is more to it than meets the eye – it is home to the 1996 National Eisteddfod. Walk up the steep hill and you will come to Ty Penlan, which translated from the Welsh means the house at the top of the hill. The building looks like one of those old-fashioned church schools which used to have 'boys' and 'girls' over the entrances.

In fact that is exactly what Ty Penlan used to be – the village school.

Now it has been tastefully converted into a thriving restaurant and bar serving excellent home-cooked food. Going in through the old entrance you come into the bar which is nicely decorated in creams and greens. But the wedding room itself is the Restaurant which is quite exceptional.

The Restaurant was converted out of the two original classrooms. It has a very tall pitched roof with glorious stone mullioned windows almost like a church but with plain glass. There are large fireplaces at each end of the room and a balcony with 2 sets of stairs, one either side, so the bride could come down one side and the groom the other.

The room is extremely attractive with bare stonework walls, pine beams and pillars. Because it is broken up with these pillars the room has a cosy feel and you could imagine a lovely winter wedding here with roaring log fires at each end.

In the centre is a stripped pine dance floor where Noson Lawens, traditional Welsh clog dances, are frequently held. We were shown the box containing the clogs which is kept upstairs on the balcony so we know it's true!

It's easy to see how you could have a very lovely traditional Welsh wedding at Ty Penlan. While we were there a 'celtic moods' tape was playing, creating a very romantic atmosphere. You could even have a Welsh male voice choir belting out a few numbers from the balcony.

At the back is the old school playground which is going to be renovated so that they can erect a permanent marquee which would be reached via the Restaurant.

Owner Eleri Beckett is also planning to add a gate to the back wall which would lead directly to the open parkland behind. This is a truly beautiful spot to have your wedding photographs taken – there is a panoramic view of the Brecon Beacons to one side and the Black Mountains to the other. There is also a Victorian bandstand which would provide an attractive backdrop for the happy newly-weds.

Because Ty Penlan is a restaurant the catering is excellent and very reasonably priced. A sit-down meal will cost from £12.50 to £17.50 a head. Arrival drinks are £1 a head but they have a large wine list available if you would rather choose your own.

There is no accommodation but guests can use the local Cawdor Hotel and various bed and breakfasts. Flowers can be arranged and evening entertainment is no problem whether you want a disco or a live band. We thought an ideal wedding here would be for around 60 people followed by a typical Welsh knees-up with clog dancing and a proper Welsh band with a harp, piano, fiddle, guitar and accordion.

Contact: Eleri Beckett
Main road: A483
Station: Llandeilo

Disabled access: Yes
Parking: Ample
Registrar tel no: 01267 230875
Bedrooms: 0
Wedding only: Yes

Name: Leez Priory
Address: Hartford End, Great
Leighs, Chelmsford, Essex CM3 1JP
Tel: 01245 362555

Leez Priory is one of the few venues in the country that has managed to get round the legal restrictions on holding open-air wedding ceremonies. The entrance to the courtyard of this Tudor mansion is through a huge archway complete with ancient wooden doors at the front and back. The archway had to be big to allow a horse and carriage to get through.

The Essex registrars have sensibly said that the Carriageway constitutes a room and have licensed it for weddings. So it is now possible to have the doors wide open, the ceremony conducted under the archway and the guests sitting outside in the garden. Hey presto, an open-air wedding!

But there is much more to Leez Priory than an archway, once you have found it, and that is no mean feat. Arriving at Chelmsford you seem to go for ever round a one-way system. Just as you want to give up, a sign takes you off down narrow country lanes into the middle of nowhere. Eventually you turn sharp left through some gates and see why the journey was worth-

while – a perfectly preserved Tudor manor house in a hollow among the trees. The house was built in 1536 on the site of a priory that fell victim to the dissolution of the monasteries by Henry VIII.

Now it is privately owned and used solely for weddings and other functions. Weddings can be held in several rooms but the most interesting are the Carriageway and the Tower. A wedding in the Gatehouse could be a small affair with the doors open and the bride and groom framed by the views of the gardens outside. For a summer wedding the bride and groom could be just indoors and you could then have as many guests as you liked seated on the grass outside.

For a really unusual wedding the Tower takes some beating. Leez Priory is built around a square courtyard. In one corner there is a free-standing tower that was originally the inner gatehouse to a bigger building. The Tower is a square building over 60 feet high with octagonal turrets on each corner.

A tiny spiral staircase leads up to the wedding room on the first floor. The large square room appears to be completely untouched from medieval times. It has a plain wood floor, bare brick walls and very high ceiling. Overall the effect is rather austere. But fortunately the 2 large stone windows bring a bit of light and warmth into the room. There is a big fireplace so a real log fire would transform the atmosphere for winter weddings. The Tower can hold over 150 but there is no disabled access.

After the wedding, photos can be taken in the garden outside the Tower by a rather ancient stone well and you can have drinks on the courtyard lawn. Receptions for 120 or more can be held in the Great Hall – a huge banqueting room with oak-panelled walls, stone fireplace and an open beamed roof. Guests can also use the adjoining Gatehouse Room. If there are lots of children at the wedding they can have a special room on one side complete with a bouncy castle. And to finish off the day a 'Dungeon Disco' in a large vaulted cellar will make sure everyone stays cool however hot it is outside.

Guests have the complete run of the grounds which include 2 ancient fish ponds, one with a fountain and the other hidden among the trees with its own island. There are 5 bedrooms on site together with a separate cottage that holds up to 7 people. They are all original conversions so there are plenty of exposed beams and views across the grounds.

Prices at Leez Priory vary tremendously according to the time of year and the day of the week so it is extremely difficult to give a precise idea of what the wedding will cost. The charge for exclusive use could be anywhere between £500 and £2,500. Catering, which is provided in-house, and accommodation charges are all extra.

Leez Priory is an extremely beautiful and secluded venue. To get the most of it you really need to have a large wedding that will fill the grounds. The Tower and the Gatehouse would both be ideal for a themed medieval event complete with lute players.

Contact: Sue Morhall
Main road: A12/A120
Station: Chelmsford (6 miles), Braintree (6 miles)
Disabled access: Not for the Tower
Parking: Ample
Registrar tel no: 01245 430701
Bedrooms: 5, and a cottage
Wedding only: No

Name: Little Thakeham
Address: Merrywood Lane, Storrington, West Sussex RH20 3HE
Tel: 01903 744416

To get to Little Thakeham you take a sharp turn off the B2139 and find yourself on one of those windy little Sussex country roads with high hedgerows on either side. It reminds you of those places you used to read about as a child where everywhere there was a secret hideout.

The long approach to the house is lined with walnut trees and before you know it you are feasting your eyes on one of the country's most exquisite examples of a Sir Edwin Lutyens manor house.

The house is built of honey-coloured stone and is set in superb gardens which were created in the style of Gertrude Jekyll, the leading garden designer of the time. There are paved walks, a rose pergola, a whole array of flowering shrubs and specimen trees.

Inside the house, stone walls keep it cool in the summer but warm and cosy in winter. Little Thakeham was converted into a luxurious country house hotel quite recently but the character of the grand manor house has been retained with its antique furnishings, the unusual minstrels gallery and huge open log fires.

The wedding room is spectacular with a floor-to-ceiling latticed window giving on to the breathtaking terraced gardens. A polished wooden staircase leads to a mezzanine level minstrels gallery where you can have your wedding overlooking the guests below, to the accompaniment of a grand piano.

Alternatively, a simple wedding held at the far end of the room, or in the alcove created by the latticed window, would be lovely.

Pre-wedding drinks can be had in the sitting room which has its own bar and a large open fireplace. A winter wedding would be cosy here but a summer one which spilled out on to the many terraces leading off the main house would be just as delightful.

All the bedrooms are individually furnished and appropriately named. The Nursery for example was originally made for the children of the family and still has a tiny, child-high window which was specially designed for them to look out on to the gardens. The Mistress Suite has a huge queen-size bed decorated in striking black and white fabrics and again overlooks the gardens. A basic room costs £150 but honey-moon suites will set you back around £180.

The area around Little Thakeham is full of antique shops and collectors can make the short trip to Brighton and browse in the famous Lanes or the new antique centre at Petworth. For racing enthusiasts, Goodwood, Plumpton and Fontwell Park are all close by while polo at Cowdray Park is a regular local attraction.

The staff at Little Thakeham are incredibly friendly and willing to rise to any occasion. A recent Henry VIII-style banquet saw the female staff all dressed up as wenches serving wine out of pewter jugs while the bar staff dressed up in doublet and hose. Murder mystery weekends are quite popular but have caused a few near heart attacks. One guest neglected to tell his friends about the weekend so when one of the actors began choking at the dinner table a guest who was a nurse started to administer vigorous first aid – thumping the unsuspecting actor on the back!

The wedding room seats up to 50 and the dining room can seat 80 for the reception. To hire the house and gardens costs anything from £500 to £1,000. For a sit-down meal prices start from £25 a head and a finger buffet would cost around £15 a head. House wines start at £12.50 a bottle and house champagne is £32.50. These prices are only a guide as each wedding is individually catered for and priced accordingly.

Why not go for a summery

Romeo-and-Juliet-style wedding on the balcony accompanied by the piano, drinks out on the terrace followed by a sit-down meal for around 40 in the dining room? Guests could stay overnight and friends and family could round off the weekend with a visit to the races.

Contact: Fiona Watson
Main road: M25/M3
Station: Pulborough
Disabled access: Limited
Parking: Ample
Registrar tel no: 01903 700080
Bedrooms: 9, plus plenty of local bed and breakfasts
Wedding only: No

Name: Groombridge Place
Address: Groombridge, near Tunbridge Wells, Kent TN3 9QQ
Tel: 01892 861444

Anyone who saw the film *The Draughtsman's Contract* will remember the stunning gardens which were a central feature of the movie. It was shot at Groombridge Place, a small country house set deep in the Kent countryside. This is not just any country house. It is a place steeped in history with many of its original features preserved to this day. Although it dates back to the 13th century the present building was built in the 1660s by Philip Packer, a member of the king's court and a friend of the great architect Sir Christopher Wren.

The house is privately owned and is still used as a family home. It is a relatively small brick building with a moat, some giant redwood trees and fabulous gardens which are open to the public.

Weddings can be held in the Baronial Hall or the Wren Room. The Baronial Hall is next to the main house across a cobbled courtyard. It was originally the stables but was converted at the turn of the century to a fine oak-panelled hall complete with impressive stone fireplace, a minstrels gallery and assorted suits of armour. The stained-glass windows look across the moat to open fields. The Baronial Hall holds 65 people and would be a wonderful place for a winter wedding complete with holly, ivy and a roaring log fire.

The Wren Room is part of the main building. Guests cross over the moat, with its black swans, to the main entrance and go into the hall which has carved oak panelling, an antique piano and a harp. This is no stately home, but feels as if you are entering a private house. The Wren Room is on the left. It is not very big and will only hold 35 people. The walls have original 17th-century panelling, ornate gilt mirrors and a gilt plasterwork ceiling with an oval painting of the sky. A huge marble fireplace dominates the room. But the most interesting feature is the lighting. The Wren Room is completely lit by candles, there is no electric light and this creates a tremendous atmosphere.

After the ceremony guests walk

through an avenue of yew hedges called the 'twelve apostles' even though there are 13 of them. They pass the ornamental gardens that were laid out in the 17th century and lead to a purpose-built marquee with its own lawn.

Arthur Conan Doyle wrote *The Valley of Fear*, one of his Sherlock Holmes stories, while he stayed at the house. He described 'rows of ancient yew trees cut into strange designs'. Conan Doyle was a great believer in all matters spiritual and held seances in the house. He claimed to have been accompanied by a ghostly groom as he walked across the park. But as it was en route to the local pub the story has to be taken with a pinch of salt.

Unlike most wedding venues you only book the room and marquee. That means you can choose your own caterers or make your own arrangements. As it is in Kent it is quite possible to pop over to France to buy all the champagne the day before the big event.

Honey Wilson organizes all the weddings. She says that they have already had a Draughtsman's Contract Ball and enquiries about a Sherlock Holmes wedding, so themed events would be welcome.

It is possible to just have a wedding at Groombridge Place. Either room would cost £350 plus VAT. Hiring the marquee is more expensive at £1,700 plus VAT, but it does have a proper floor and purpose-built toilets nearby. There is reasonable disabled access to the wedding rooms and a disabled toilet in the shop. There is no accommodation at the house but guests can stay at the Ashdown Park Hotel in Whych Cross or have bed and breakfast at the Crown on the village green.

Groombridge Place is a lovely spot for a large summer wedding but real romantics will go for an atmospheric winter wedding in the Wren Room or the Baronial Hall.

Contact: Honey Wilson
Main road: A264
Station: Tunbridge Wells
Disabled access: Yes
Parking: Ample
Registrar tel no: 01892 527332
Bedrooms: 0
Wedding only: Yes

Name: **Tullie House Museum**
Address: **Castle Street, Carlisle CA3 8TP**
Tel: **01228 34781**

Tullie House is an award-winning museum and art gallery and is an ideal venue for a couple looking for a romantic wedding with a difference.

Steeped in history, Tullie House, which overlooks Carlisle's ancient castle, provides a fine backdrop for those who want to take a step back in time when they tie the knot. You can almost hear the ghostly echoes of the Roman centurions' footsteps as they marched through the grounds where archaeologists have found so many remains of Carlisle's chequered past.

Tullie House itself has an interesting if varied history. It first became a museum in 1890 when a scheme was put forward for the establishment of a permanent home for the arts and sciences in Carlisle. Together with other buildings in Castle Street, Tullie House was acquired by the city fathers for this purpose.

The old house was altered and a set of new buildings constructed following an extensive archaeological dig which uncovered the foundations of Roman buildings providing an insight into the origins of the city's layout. The Victorian extension housed a free library, picture galleries, lecture theatre, School of Art and Technical School while the old Tullie House was home for the museum.

In the 1950s the Technical School and School of Art moved into new premises, then in 1986 the library moved into its current home in the nearby Lanes shopping complex. The latest stage in its history was in 1991 when, after a £5 million redevelopment, the new Tullie House flagship museum and art gallery was opened by the Queen. It now attracts 200,000 visitors a year and has won awards from tourist authorities as well as for its disabled facilities and architectural interpretation.

Couples with an eye for history and tradition will be charmed by the place hidden away in a quiet corner of the 'Great Border City', which has both Hadrian's Wall and the Lake District at its front and back doorsteps.

Unfortunately, the museum's original plan to hold civil marriages over the Roman altar had to be abandoned because of the registrar's interpretation of the legislative requirements. Wedding rooms are not allowed to have any religious connotations. Nor can weddings be performed in the museum's galleries which are packed with works depicting Carlisle's turbulent border history.

Instead, weddings take place in the Victorian Function Suite of this former Jacobean mansion which was built in 1689 as a family residence. The wedding room itself is the original museum lecture theatre and has tiered seating for 100 guests. Adjoining it are the function room and restaurant where catering can be specifically tailored for each wedding.

Prices vary according to what people want – the choice is theirs from a simple, quiet affair to a large, formal wedding. The Function Room with its Victorian fireplace and original features has french windows which open on to the museum's splendid gardens, ideal for photographs and for summer weddings using the outdoor seating and tables.

Close to the terrace is the museum's secluded herb garden, complete with sundial. On a warm summer's evening the scent of exotic herbs wafts through the gardens – what could be more romantic!

As one would imagine Tullie House doesn't have accommodation but, situated in the heart of the city, it is close to an excellent choice of hotels, guest houses and bed and breakfasts. There are a number of council-run car parks nearby and the main line rail station is just a few minutes' walk through the city centre.

Museum director Nick Winterbotham and his team of enthusiastic staff are justly proud of Tullie House and are looking forward to the next era in its history. They are eager to see the museum – with its tales of people's lives full of romanticism and significance – playing its part in the future by hosting weddings.

Contact: Mary Robinson
Main road: M6/A6
Station: Carlisle
Disabled access: Yes
Parking: Ample nearby
Registrar tel no: 01228 23456
Bedrooms: 0
Wedding only: Yes

Name: **The Lord Crewe Arms Hotel**
Address: **Blanchland, near Consett, County Durham DH8 9SP**
Tel: **01434 675251**

Blanchland's Durham postal address is a little confusing as this is in fact one of neighbouring Northumberland's best-loved and most picturesque villages. Although only 15 miles or so from Newcastle, this village at the head of the lonely Derwent reservoir is in another world.

Reached by quiet and undulating roads that cross endless moorland, Blanchland's extraordinary Italianate L-shaped 'piazza' stands more than 800 feet above sea level and was at one time regularly cut off by snow.

Almost as well known as the village itself is the Lord Crewe Arms Hotel and the ghost of Dorothy Forster who reputedly haunts it. The Lord Crewe Arms, just like the village that surrounds it, is steeped in history and was originally the abbot's house, attached to the adjacent abbey. After its dissolution in 1539, the abbey fell into disrepair, along with the church and the village.

Today's village rose, quite literally, out of the ruins in the 18th century, and was built from what remained of the abbey. It has remained essentially unchanged since then, thanks to the Lord Crewe Trustees who still hold the freehold of all the properties.

The hotel itself is one of these properties and boasts 5-foot-thick medieval walls and a tower dating from 1160. Partners Alex Todd, Peter Gingell and chef Ian Press moved from London and acquired the hotel in 1987.

The Lord Crewe title dates from the 1699 marriage of another Dorothy Forster to Lord Crewe, the then Bishop of Durham and a devotee of the Stuart cause. He went on to buy the estates from the Forsters in 1704.

Thomas Forster, Lady Crewe's nephew – although neither a Scot nor a Catholic – was military commander of the first Jacobite uprising of 1715, but surrendered to government troops without a fight. He was imprisoned in London but escaped to France with the aid of his sister, also called Dorothy Forster. It is this Dorothy who is the hotel's most famous ghost, reputedly asking anyone who will listen to take a message to Thomas telling him that the coast is now clear for his return to England!

One of the hotel's cavernous fireplaces was used as a priest hole where Thomas was hidden en route to France. This hiding place is off the Hilyard Room, one of two licensed for marriage, the other being the large Restaurant in the tower, with its views across the courtyard to the rear of the hotel and open moorland beyond.

Bedrooms at the Lord Crewe include the 2 'haunted' rooms, the Bamburgh, where Dorothy Forster makes her occasional appearances, and the Radcliffe. Some of the 20 bedrooms are in a newly converted ground-floor wing, while others, including arguably the best Honeymoon Suite, are in a separate building across the piazza.

The Lord Crewe has traditionally been a wedding reception venue for people in the area. Sit-down meals start at a reasonable £16.75, not including wine. With function room hire, flowers and table decorations, a reception for 20 in a private dining room could be expected to come to £500 upwards.

There is no specific parking, but the village can absorb a reasonable number of cars. A wedding at the Lord Crewe should suit romantics (particularly ghost-loving ones) who may be able to enjoy a blessing in the local church afterwards. In winter, the blazing fires in those huge fireplaces can create a lovely cosy feel as it can get pretty cold in these parts.

Contact: Wendy Hart
Main road: A68/A69
Station: Hexham (10 miles)
Disabled access: No
Parking: In village
Registrar tel no: 01434 602355
Bedrooms: 20
Wedding only: No

Name: Merchant Taylors Hall
Address: Aldwark, York YO1 2BX
Tel: 01904 624889

Merchant Taylors Hall is a truly historic venue at the heart of perhaps Britain's finest medieval city. It has 2 main rooms, the Great Hall and the Little Hall. The late 14th-century hall's history is intrinsically wrapped up with that of the ancient craft guild that gives it its name and which still meets to this day. The tradition of the hall's usage for social and other events extends even further back than the incorporation of the Company of Merchant Taylors by Charles II in 1662. The records show events going as far back as 1454.

The building is a little austere and would not suit a couple set on a small, intimate gathering of close friends (although the Little Hall accommodates 45, rather than the 150 of the Great Hall itself). If, however, you want to dine off the Company's finest china and cut the cake with the silver service beneath the light of the chandeliers, then this could be the venue for you.

The internal fabric of both halls survives today remarkably intact, albeit within brick exteriors of the late 17th and early 18th centuries. The Great Hall is the older of the two and measures 30 by 60 feet and 30 feet from floor to the original 14th-century arch-braced ceiling, modified and reinforced at some later date. Other original features include parts of the half-timbered exterior and the outer doorway.

The hall is dark oak panelled for more than half its height and features a vast fireplace and minstrels gallery. It owes its present condition to a general revival in interest in the guild that has underpinned restoration work since the last war.

The Little Hall has Tudor origins and is dominated by 2 heraldic stained-glass windows. On the walls are such dignified and important documents as the guild's Roll of Masters, while a moveable screen allows access to a small bar area. There are separate, modern rooms in which bride and groom can prepare themselves.

Today, guild membership retains close links with the textile trade. Merchant Taylors Hall has a more religious 'feel' to it than most buildings sanctioned for the marriage ceremony and this can be traced in part to the distinctly religious leanings of the tailors' craft from the 14th century, when it played a formative role in the formation of the fraternity of St John the Baptist. The hall itself was apparently built by the fraternity and was known as St John the Baptist's Hall until the late 16th century.

Receptions at the hall are arranged by the Taylors' exclusive caterers who enjoy the right to use the hall for that purpose.

The hall is one of two, along with the Merchant Adventurers, in the city that offer the opportunity for a ceremony in truly medieval surroundings. The Merchant Taylors, however, boast good car parking. There is no accommodation at the hall but there are many hotels and bed and breakfasts within easy walking distance.

A wedding at Merchant Taylors Hall certainly won't cost you the earth. Wedding room hire starts at £50 and catering prices start with wedding breakfasts at £15 per head including wine. Considering the historic surroundings this is remarkable value.

A wedding here would give the opportunity to marry in the heart of a romantic city, awash with street entertainment, cosy pubs, fine eating houses, river boats and a host of places to visit. Reception guests would have little trouble finding accommodation within reasonable distance, except perhaps at the height of summer.

Contact: Ian and Caroline Woodcock
Main road: A19/A64

Station: York

Disabled access: Yes

Parking: Adequate

Registrar tel no: 01904 654477

Bedrooms: 0

Wedding only: No

MUNICIPAL MARVELS

To be sure not, Sir. I believe marriages would in general be as happy, and often more so, if they were all made by the Lord Chancellor, upon a due consideration of the characters and circumstances, without the parties having any choice in the matter.

SAMUEL JOHNSON

We could not possibly miss out the fact that there are so many municipal buildings which by hook or by crook the local authorities have managed to maintain in some style. Many of these glorious venues are exceedingly cheap simply because they *are* municipal. It is certainly worth bearing in mind that if you want to get married in a fabulous place it does not have to cost an arm and a leg. Margam Park Orangery is a shining example. Owned by West Glamorgan Council it is set in beautiful surroundings just off the M4 and yet you can hire the whole place for a fraction of the cost of a country house hotel. Or what about Liverpool Town Hall which knocks the spots off most stately homes in terms of grandeur and good value. Or if you are looking for a sense of history and some style it is hard to beat the Pump Room at Bath.

Name: **The Pump Room and Roman Baths**
Address: **Stall Street, Bath BA1 1LZ**
Tel: **01225 477783**

Bath has a surfeit of extraordinary rooms for weddings. They are run by the council and are all reasonably priced. They can also be mixed and matched according to the size of the wedding or the reception. There are 3 separate complexes, the Pump Room, the Assembly Rooms and the Guildhall, each reflecting different periods in Bath's history.

The Pump Room complex is the most dramatic. It consists of the magnificent Georgian Pump Room, the Concert Room, Drawing Room, Smoking Room, Terrace Room and the famous Roman Baths.

Weddings are held in the Drawing or Smoking Rooms. The Drawing Room is long, narrow and quite small. Decorated in cream and beige it will hold 40 people seated in Chippendale-style chairs. The room is not very special but the windows have glorious views out on to Bath cathedral. The Smoking Room is the same sort of size and also has views of the abbey. But it has the added benefit of doors that open out on to the terrace which is directly above the bath.

The terrace is a truly magical place. Guests can stroll around and look down on the baths below or across the courtyard to the abbey. At night the baths are lit with flares set into the walls. Small parties can have a reception on the terrace while bigger ones can use it for drinks before going into one of the larger rooms for a meal.

Guests can also go down to the edge of the bath for drinks and canapés. The bath itself is full of limpid green water and is open to the sky. It is surrounded by stone arches and pillars supporting the terrace above. The floor has ancient flagstones and even some of the original Roman lead piping. The edge of the bath makes a wonderful spot for wedding photos.

Large receptions can be held in the Pump Room – a rather grand Georgian tea room with a stage in an alcove at one end with a balcony above. On one side it looks over the water and on the other there are views over the abbey churchyard and the floodlit abbey beyond.

A cupola with a fountain dispenses the famous Bath spa waters. You can have a drink but be warned, the water is warm and tastes disgusting. The room has a lovely light oak floor and a large 18th-century chandelier. In the daytime it is a rather grand tea place, so engaged couples can go and plan their wedding reception over a cup of Earl Grey and a Bath bun. After tea they could wander through to the Concert Room which is also used for receptions. It is a Victorian addition with a spectacular dome and a minstrels gallery all in carved oak held up by marble pillars.

The Assembly Rooms are a short walk away up through the city centre. The entrance is down a marble pillared corridor complete with a red carpet and chandeliers. The wedding rooms are in typical Georgian style. The Ballroom, a massive barn of a hall, can easily hold 500 people. Decorated in light blue with white plasterwork friezes, it has huge chandeliers and a balcony set under a cupola. The windows are all rather high up so there are no views out – presumably the Georgians were more interested in looking at each other than the riff-raff outside.

Smaller weddings for 80 people can be held in the Octagon Room. As you would expect it has 8 sides but unusually it has 4 fireplaces and 4 doors out into other rooms. The yellow and white room is extremely tall, again with windows at first floor level. The overall effect is rather church-like, particularly as the bride can walk into the room down the red carpeted corridor.

The third wedding location is the Tea Room. This holds 250 people and is a more manageable size with its elegant pillared gallery complete with 3 chandeliers. The various rooms can also be used for drinks and receptions according to the size of the event.

Most couples will find all this choice a bit overwhelming. Fortunately Christina Scott who organizes weddings is on hand to offer advice and assistance. A dynamic Scot, she is certainly not your average local government officer. She takes great pride in the facilities at Bath and will be determined to help you sort out a perfect wedding.

There is no problem with themed weddings. They have already had Roman evenings in the Baths complete with roast sucking pigs. The caterers, Milburns, will even rise to the occasion by providing themed food such as gold sprayed pineapples and the staff serve the food dressed up in togas.

However couples do need to remember that the Pump Room and Baths are open to the public. Consequently weddings generally have to be held at the end of the day so that the reception can start just as the building closes to the public. Weddings in the Assembly Rooms do not have these restrictions. It is also possible to have weddings without receptions in some of the rooms.

The buildings are all in the centre of town which has literally hundreds of local hotels and bed and breakfasts. There is town centre parking nearby. Couples should talk to Christina about disabled access to the various rooms.

Prices are remarkably low given the quality and grandeur of the buildings. Some rooms start at £20–£50 per hour and the Pump Room can be booked for £110 an hour. For £500 you could probably book a range of rooms for a late afternoon wedding and early evening reception. Food prices vary but with drink are likely to range somewhere between £25 and £40 per head.

With so much choice it is hard to make a recommendation about the best sort of wedding to have in Bath. But here goes. For a small event try a wedding in the Drawing Room followed by drinks at the

edge of the Roman Bath and a meal on the terrace. A bigger event could have the wedding in the Octagon Room at the Assembly Hall followed by a gentle stroll through the town for drinks and a reception in the Roman Bath and Pump Room.
Contact: Christina Scott
Main road: M4/M5/A46
Station: Bath Spa
Disabled access: Varies
Parking: Nearby
Registrar tel no: 01225 312032
Bedrooms: 0
Wedding only: Yes

Name: **Liverpool Town Hall**
Address: **High Street, Liverpool L2 3SW**
Tel: **0151 707 2391**

Liverpool is famous for music, ferries and politics. The wedding law prevents you from getting married on the ferry across the Mersey. The Cavern Club were thinking about getting a licence but at the time of writing had not decided whether to go ahead. But do not give up hope. You can get married at Liverpool Town Hall, traditional seat of Liverpool politics and one of the country's most magnificent Victorian buildings.

The Town Hall was built at a time when the city was immensely wealthy and the city fathers wanted to show everyone just how important the city had become. They did not mess about. It is a truly stunning building with chandeliers, a staircase worthy of a stately home and a ballroom fit for royalty.

The building is in the centre of the city's old Victorian business district. Approached from the side on the road down from the station it does not look particularly impressive. But cross over into Castle Street and the building takes on a completely different perspective. It has a magnificent high dome with a gold statue of Minerva on top. Minerva was the goddess of wisdom which should be an encouragement to all couples who enter the building for their wedding. Most people will remember it as a backdrop for the film *Chariots of Fire* or will have seen Liverpool or Everton footballers holding up a winners' cup to hundreds of fans.

Once inside, Victorian lavishness abounds. The foyer has a Flemish carved wood fireplace. A marble floor, marble statues, marble columns and ornate plasterwork set the scene. The centrepiece is the grand staircase complete with red carpet and brass stair rods. Do not be surprised if half the guests develop a crick in the neck. It just means that they have been straining to look up at the domed ceiling, surely one of the most impressive in the country.

The wedding ceremony and reception take place in the suite of rooms at the top of this staircase so whatever happens the bride is going to have the opportunity for some fabulous photos on the stairs.

There are two wedding rooms, the West Reception Room and the Small Ballroom. The West Reception Room seats 70 people. It is a finely decorated state room with a grand marble fireplace, a crystal chandelier and original oil paintings depicting 19th-century Liverpool landscapes. It has a green carpet and terracotta walls with lots of inlaid gold leaf.

The registrar will conduct the ceremony from a genuine Louis XIV mahogany table complete with brass inlays. The guests watch from fine leather state dining-room chairs. All in all a very grand scene.

Bigger weddings are held in the Small Ballroom which holds 150 people. It's only small because there is an even bigger one next door. It is 56 feet long and 27 wide and boasts 3 chandeliers, 2 marble fireplaces and some oil paintings of former Lord Mayors of Liverpool. At one end are 2 minstrels galleries. They are recessed in the walls and about 3 feet off the ground making an ideal spot for a string quartet to play. Again the walls are terracotta with some fancy gold leaf on the plasterwork.

Smaller weddings will probably be held in the West Reception Room followed by a reception in the Small Ballroom. Bigger weddings would start off in the Small Ballroom and could then have a really big reception in the other larger ballroom. This is a truly huge room, with 3 of Europe's largest chandeliers, and massive mirrors at each end. The mirrors are slightly concave so that the reflections seem to go on to infinity. Again there is elaborate gold leaf on the plasterwork. In fact, according to the hall's manager, Simon Osborne, there is enough gold leaf in Liverpool Town Hall to cover two hockey pitches. A fact that could be noted for the after-dinner speeches.

Unlike most venues, the Town Hall offers couples a choice of 8 recommended caterers. Prices range from buffets with wine at £18 a head and seated meals with wine at around £27 a head. Hire charges vary according to the room and the time spent for the event. As a guide the small room for a wedding only would cost about £150 while a big wedding with a separate reception in the ballroom could end up costing around £1,000. The council is quite happy for couples to hire a room for a wedding without a reception.

There is no accommodation at the Town Hall but the council has arranged preferential rates with the nearby Atlantic Tower Thistle Hotel. The wedding rooms have full disabled access and there is a car park close by.

Liverpool Town Hall is an ideal venue for a stylish wedding. And when it's all over why not take a short walk to the Pierhead for photos by the Mersey ferry or take the last remaining guests down to the Cavern Club to boogie the night away.

Contact: Simon Osborne
Main road: M62
Station: Lime Street
Disabled access: Good
Parking: Nearby
Registrar tel no: 0151 2252343
Bedrooms: 0
Wedding only: Yes

Name: **Margam Park Orangery**
Address: **Margam Park, Port Talbot,**
West Glamorgan SA13 2TJ
Tel: **01639 881635**

If you have ever made the journey along the M4 from Bristol to Cardiff you may remember an awful smell somewhere near junction 38. And if you have ever bothered to look over towards the left you will see just what causes it – the massive Port Talbot steel works.

However, if you got off the motorway at junction 38 you might mysteriously find yourself in Margam Park, 800 acres of some of the most beautiful and peaceful parkland in the country. Wandering around the grounds you are likely to spot foxes, badgers, rabbits and squirrels. If you sit under a tree for a picnic you can simply waste away the hours watching the deer graze contentedly by the side of the track.

Margam Park was acquired by West Glamorgan County Council in April 1974. Originally it was a country estate but has evidence of human occupation dating back some 5,000 years. Now all that is left is an Iron Age hill fort mound, the remains of a Cistercian abbey and a fully restored 18th-century Orangery – a magnificent building built in 1786 for the sole purpose of housing a great collection of orange, lemon and other citrus trees. It is the largest of its kind in Britain and is licensed to hold weddings.

The origins of the collection of citrus trees at Margam remain something of a mystery although it had been in existence for many years when Thomas Mansel Talbot inherited the estate in 1787. In 1727 Lord Mansel's gardener recorded 60 large and small citron, bergamot, lemon, china orange and Seville orange trees 'in perfect health and frught and bewtyfull in thear leavs'.

Inside the Orangery the walls are painted stark white and there are 29 Georgian-style windows overlooking the circular fountains and ornamental gardens at the front. A huge glass wall separates one end from the other. One end, the Grove, has stone floors and classical statues and houses the orange trees. The other is carpeted with curtains at the windows and a large stage at one end.

At the far end of the building is the West Pavilion, a green room with Wedgwood motifs worked into the ornate plasterwork. A large door opens on to parkland and gardens with an ornamental glasshouse to one side and sculptures of all types dotted around the garden.

If you hanker after a small wedding with a big do afterwards, Margam could be the place. The ceremony could be conducted in the West Pavilion with just a few close family around. You could then be joined by however many friends and relations you wanted. The sky is the limit as far as catering and entertainment go because the main hall of the Orangery can hold up to 500 people.

For a really stylish wedding hold the ceremony in the Grove but make sure the bride and groom are dressed to match the surroundings.

To hire the Orangery up to midnight will cost you £250 during the week. On a weekend it goes up to £380. Finger buffets start at around £4.25 a head but for around £20 a head you can have the full works. Monday to Saturday the council has a licence for music and dancing until 2 am and the staff are happy to recommend a first class disc jockey or band for the party.

You cannot stay at Margam but they have a list of local hotels, guesthouses and self-catering accommodation available in nearby Port Talbot. To get the best out of the Orangery have a big do with around 100 to 250 guests. The room would swamp any smaller group.

Contact: Ian Cadogan
Main road: M4
Station: Port Talbot
Disabled access: Yes
Parking: Plenty
Registrar tel no: 01639 643696
Bedrooms: 0
Wedding only: No

Name: **Chester Town Hall**
Address: **Northgate Street, Chester CH1 2HS**
Tel: **01244 402350**

Chester is still one of the most popular tourist destinations for UK and international visitors. It was originally a Roman fortress but it is famous for its unique Chester Rows, or medieval two-tier shopping galleries – not to mention its 900-year-old cathedral, encircling Roman walls and over 700 listed buildings which give it its elegant and fascinating appeal.

Set right in the very heart of the historic city, Chester Town Hall is arguably one of the most stunning of all those buildings. Walking through the entrance your eye is immediately drawn upwards to the arched stained-glass windows and cupola which pour coloured light downwards into the hall. From the centre of the hallway there is a magnificent curving staircase with highly polished wooden balustrades.

The hallway itself is pretty spectacular. Made of stone with mullioned stained-glass windows, the arches which lead off it create the feeling of a church.

There are 2 wedding rooms which are both equally beautiful in their own way. The first is actually the Council Chamber which has a tall vaulted ceiling with impressive oak beams as well as wood panelling throughout. The walls are adorned with splendid carvings in wood and stone. A huge wrought-iron chandelier hangs in the centre of the room and there is a large carved stone fireplace at one end. Although the room is large enough to hold 180 guests it has a feeling of warmth and intimacy.

The second is the Assembly Room on the ground floor of the building. This is a huge stately hall with an amazingly ornate ceiling, panelled walls and very high arched windows. The highly polished wooden floor is ideal for dancing after the ceremony and can cater for up to 300 guests at a buffet, 280 for a formal meal or 240 at a dinner dance.

For a really memorable wedding a ceremony in the Council Chamber followed by a tremendous bash complete with discotheque in the Assembly Room would be pretty spectacular. Once again this is not a venue for a bride who wants a low-key affair in a Chanel two-piece. For maximum effect any bride worth her salt is going to want her picture taken on the sweeping staircase in the entrance hall – so a long dress preferably with a train is *de rigueur*.

Anne Kedney had the right idea. She was the first bride to have her wedding at the Town Hall and was escorted there by 6 outriders on classic motorcycles. 'Chester City Council are very switched on about the new marriage laws. They introduced afternoon weddings and original words and music to add to the ceremony, before anyone else. The Town Hall is such a lovely building that we decided to go for it,' she said.

The staff at the Town Hall will bend over backwards to make your day one to remember. They can provide table plans to suit most combinations. Bar facilities can be arranged if needed but they do not have their own caterers. Couples can make their own catering arrangements or use one of several recommended firms.

Prices are very reasonable for such a splendid venue. A wedding only costs £150. To hire the rooms for a wedding and reception will cost £500–£600 and you can keep on partying until 2 am.

Contact: Linda Clements
Main road: M56
Station: Chester
Disabled access: Poor
Parking: Nearby
Registrar tel no: 01244 603938
Bedrooms: 0
Wedding only: Yes

Name: Pittville Pump Room
Address: Pittville Park, Cheltenham, Gloucestershire GL2 3JE
Tel: 01242 523852

Pittville Pump Room is on the outskirts of Cheltenham – not far from Cheltenham racecourse. In keeping with the town's regency traditions the Pump Room is a splendid piece of over-the-top architecture, an ideal place for a grand wedding bash but without having to pay through the nose.

The Pump Room was built between 1825 and 1830 as part of the estate of Joseph Pitt, a wealthy landowner, entrepreneur and politician. In its heyday it was the place to be seen drinking the health-giving Cheltenham spa waters. Apparently visitors would take the waters and promenade around listening to the musicians playing on the balcony. Joseph Pitt was not a man troubled by modesty. He wanted to build a new town on the estate called Pittville.

The estate is now owned by Cheltenham Council. It is part of a large public park and is approached through the Cheltenham suburbs. There is plenty of parking out of sight at the back of the Pump Room. The public entrance is at the side and couples need to go round the front to see the building in all its splendour. It is a truly grand building with a colonnaded terrace across the whole of the front. There is another floor above with a large green dome on top. On wedding days a red carpet is laid up the steps to the main entrance.

Inside is a huge hall with Greek columns supporting an ornate plaster ceiling. The centrepiece of the room is a central gallery with a tall dome above. Guests should prepare to get a crick in the neck taking it all in.

The hall can be laid out with tables and chairs for a reception of over 100 and still have plenty of room for a dance floor and a band on the stage at the far end of the room. It is decorated in cream with blue curtains and there are wonderful views out over the park to a lake.

The ceremony can take place in the apse which is just off the main hall. On one side is the large marble fountain that dispenses the spa water. It is an ornate marble affair over 15 feet high with assorted carvings. Couples can get married and exchange their rings next to the fountain with the guests seated in a semicircle around them. The newly-weds can finish off the ceremony in true regency style by taking the waters which are still supposed to cure all ills. The water is cold and salty and the Pump Room manager gives absolutely no guarantees as to any aphrodisiac qualities.

After the wedding everyone can go outside for a drink on the terrace. Photos can be taken in front of the building, down by the lake or in a particularly picturesque bandstand which is close to the building. There may be members of the public in the park but they tend to keep well away from the weddings.

Receptions in the Pump Room can go on until the early hours of the morning. It is fully licensed for music and dancing so it is possible to book a band and have a really good bash. As everything is on one level there is good disabled access and there is a disabled toilet. There's no accommodation at the Pump Room but there are loads of hotels and bed and breakfasts in Cheltenham.

A wedding in the Pump Room can be surprisingly cheap. Couples who want to book the room for a wedding only can do so for just £100. To book the building for a wedding and reception will cost between £250 and £350 depending on how late the reception finishes. It is closed to the public whenever a wedding is taking place. Catering is supplied by the council's own caterers and menus with wine start at around £25 per head.

You could have a small wedding

at the Pump Room but it would be rather overwhelmed by the grandeur of the building. Instead it is an ideal venue for a wedding of about 80–150 people followed by a reception and a live band to boogie the night away.

Contact: Chris Aldred
Main road: M5
Station: Cheltenham Spa
Disabled access: Good
Parking: Ample
Registrar tel no: 01242 532455
Bedrooms: 0
Wedding only: Yes

Name: **Battersea Pump House**
Address: **Battersea Park, London SW11 4WJ**
Tel: **0171 350 0523**

Battersea Pump House had been left unused and lay derelict for years and became known as the 'Haunted House' before it was returned to its former splendour in 1992. The building itself is a rectangular tower with a pitched roof. Originally built in 1861 to pump water into the nearby lake, it was restored as a joint venture between Wandsworth Council and English Heritage.

You approach the building through the park down a path between 2 lakes. Two long windows stretch down the whole height of the brick-built structure and the front entrance is through a little porch which is attached to the main building. There are lovely arched windows and the interior walls are all of natural brick. The whole effect is of plenty of light and space.

There is one room on each of the 4 floors. The ground-floor room has no windows but there are large double doors in the front wall which stretch right up to the first-floor room. These can be opened wide and a marquee attached for a reception of up to 150 people. The 2 rooms on the third and fourth floors are presently used as a gallery. They are also connected by a balcony which would make a great place to have pre-wedding drinks.

The upper 3 rooms all have wooden floors with white walls and open brickwork. The simple decor gives the bride and groom a chance to be quite creative. Flowers twisted around the banisters, flags and banners have all been used to liven up the space.

There is no getting away from it, the Pump House is a small venue but you could have a wedding for up to 100 people if you took over the whole building. The location is absolutely stunning with lakes on either side.

There is no inside caterer so you have plenty of freedom in your choice of food. Flowers, music and other extras can all be arranged. If you are after just a small wedding with a large reception afterwards there are plenty of larger venues within the park. The Riverside and Grandvista are just 2 which they recommend. They have facilities for lasers and fireworks for a really memorable do. You can arrive by horse and carriage or even by boat.

There are plenty of scenic backdrops for your wedding photos too. The Grandvista has a series of fountains which may not look very special in the day but at night look amazing. There are 2 rectangular fountain pools at the end of which is another large pool. Fireworks reflected in the water would really set off any reception.

The Peace pagoda is another prominent feature in the park and is illuminated in turquoise and gold at night. Lights are hung between the lamp-posts along the river and the Chelsea and Albert Bridges are all lit up. Night time is definitely the time for your reception here so you could have a fabulous afternoon wedding at the Pump House followed by a meal at the Grandvista and photographs taken in the evening in front of the Pagoda.

Battersea Park and the Pump House offer facilities for a range of budgets. The cost of hiring the whole Pump House at the weekend or after 9 pm on weekdays is £60 an hour. This is obviously the most expensive rate and they do offer cheaper deals. The Pump House is really the place for people who want to organize everything themselves and be creative about their wedding day.

Contact: Kristene Fedewa
Main road: A3/M3
Station: Battersea Park BR
Disabled access: Ground floor only
Parking: Plenty
Registrar tel no: 0181 871 6120
Bedrooms: 0
Wedding only: Yes

Name: **Guildhall of St Mary**
Address: **Bayley Lane, Coventry CV8 3AG**
Tel: **01203 833327**

Coventry's most famous landmark is its cathedral – rising up from the shell of its war-damaged predecessor. In its shadow lies one of Coventry's other great buildings, the Guildhall of St Mary, originally built in 1342 as a meeting place for the merchants of the town. The building was enlarged in the 15th century and has been substantially preserved.

It is approached from a small street at the side of the cathedral. Visitors enter a courtyard of modest timber-framed buildings. But don't be deceived by its simple exterior – like some ancient Tardis the building seems much bigger on the inside.

Several rooms have been licensed to hold weddings and receptions. The Drapers Room is the most popular room for a wedding ceremony. Up some stairs and to the side of the main hall it holds about 40 people. It is a medium-sized room with pale green carpet and an unusual Tudor ceiling. A stone fireplace has a niche holding a statue of Lady Godiva who made her name by riding naked on a horse through the town in protest at high taxes. On one side is a huge stained-glass window and on the other a window overlooks the cathedral ruins.

The Great Hall is the place for

your reception although it is also licensed for larger wedding ceremonies. It was originally built as a banqueting hall for the Merchants Guild at a time when Coventry was awash with money generated by the cloth trade. It is a large oblong room, 30 feet wide by 80 long. The high ceiling is over 30 feet from the floor. At one end is a low stage which is ideal for the ceremony or the top table at the reception. A tapestry covers the whole of one wall. Made in 1500, it was hanging in the same place when Henry VII and Queen Elizabeth visited the hall.

Above the tapestry stained-glass windows depict kings of England and Emperor Constantine, the only Englishman ever to have been a Roman Emperor. The other end of the room has a timber-framed wall with a minstrels gallery and is decorated with period armour. Lady Godiva obviously was quite an influence on the citizens of Coventry – in a little niche at the side of a bay window is yet another statue of her.

More intimate weddings can be held in the Mercers Room which holds about 12 people – it is a wood-panelled affair with a carved frieze. While you are waiting for the bride to arrive instead of looking at the order of the ceremony see if you can spot the crowned green man among the carvings.

Prices at the Guildhall range from £50 to £180 to hire the rooms just for a ceremony. But the building is absolutely ideal for a combined wedding and reception. There are lots of choices on food and wine. As a guide, a meal with wine can be had from about £20 per head.

At present disabled access is not good but the council is looking at ways of making improvements without altering the listed building. There is no accommodation but there are numerous hotels within a short walking distance. The Guildhall staff will be delighted to help you arrange overnight accommodation. There is no parking at the Guildhall but arrangements are normally made to use the university car park just around the corner.

With several different rooms St Mary's Guildhall is a surprisingly flexible venue. It is possible to have a beautiful wedding in grand surroundings without having to spend a small fortune. The truly adventurous who want a wedding with a difference will go for a ceremony in the crypt. This stone room has fabulous star vaulting supported by 3 central pillars. It holds 80 people and would be ideal for a medieval themed wedding – but no Lady Godivas please!

Contact: Roma Stone
Main road: M6
Station: Coventry
Disabled access: Difficult, may change soon
Parking: Nearby
Registrar tel no: 01203 833137
Bedrooms: 0
Wedding only: Yes

Name: Under the Clock Tower
Address: Town Hall, Wood Street,
Wakefield WF1 2HQ
Tel: 01924 295121

You could not walk through the town of Wakefield and fail to notice the huge Victorian building which dominates the skyline – the old Town Hall. Impressive it certainly is, but not half as impressive as the people who run it. Not only were they quick enough off the mark to be the first venue in the country to get their licence to hold weddings, but when we said we might have problems visiting they agreed to show us around by video conference!

Wakefield is an ancient cathedral city which was once an inland grain and cloth port. The old town is built on a hill overlooking the River Calder whilst the centre is dominated by the Cathedral of All Saints. A church has stood on the same site since Roman times and its 500-year-old spire is said to be the tallest in Yorkshire at 247 feet.

Wakefield boasts a bustling market which is one of the largest and liveliest in the country and for those who prefer more modern pursuits the Ridings Centre was recently acclaimed as one of Europe's finest shopping complexes.

But this was not the main reason which prompted Robert Edwards and Sharon Hinchcliffe to be the first couple to take advantage of the new marriage law. They chose the Town Hall because of its obvious architectural merits and so they could have a 'quiet and informal do', never realizing half the country's press would descend on them to record their day for posterity!

Sharon said later, 'We were very surprised when we found out we'd be the first in the country to marry under the new law. I thought it would be some very grand couple, not someone normal like us!'

Robert who admits to being quite shy persuaded Sharon to marry in the Town Hall because he did not want the fuss of a church or a register office wedding. 'It didn't quite work out as I had planned. I never thought we'd get all this attention,' he said.

The wedding took place in the Old Court Room, just one of 11 rooms the council has had registered. It used to be Wakefield City Magistrates Court but was closed more than 15 years ago when the new court complex was built.

The room has spectacular carved wooden panelling and deep red carpet. The chairs were arranged theatre-style to allow Sharon and Robert to come up the aisle to the tune of the 'Trumpet Voluntary'. Before the service Sharon's brother played a piano version of one of Sharon's favourite songs by Diana Ross, 'When you tell me that you love me'. He was followed by Sharon's best friend who read a poem by W. H. Auden entitled 'Tell me the Truth about Love'.

The couple chose traditional dress and sat throughout the ceremony. During the piano recital

Robert had to wipe a tear away surreptitiously. After the wedding, bride, groom and guests milled around to watch the signing of the register and then trooped off for a reception in the Kingswood Suite, a rather regal room with highly polished wood panelling, ornate plasterwork and golden chandeliers.

Smaller groups could have a meal in the Clock Tower Restaurant with its panoramic views of the city. It was formerly the councillors' dining room and still retains the original oak panelling and carved plasterwork which makes the room so distinctive. The Clock Tower itself stands a further 194 feet above the building and it is even possible to have a trip up to take a bird's eye view of the city if you have a real head for heights!

The staff can organize any kind of entertainment from disc jockeys to organ music. There is also a wedding package. For up to 80 guests a budget menu will cost around £15.50 a head while deluxe will cost you £30. Drinks will be an additional £5 a head and to hire the evening buffet and disco a further £4 a head is charged.

We thought Under the Clock Tower was very good value. The venue has been tastefully restored to its former Victorian glory. Sharon and Robert probably chose the best sort of do — a small ceremony with close family and friends followed by a big reception, although the Clock Tower Restaurant takes some beating for the views. There is no accommodation here but they have tie-ups with local hotels and can offer very competitive deals for the bride and groom.

Contact: Lesley Grogan
Main road: M1/M62
Station: Wakefield
Disabled access: Yes
Parking: Local
Registrar tel no: 01924 305293
Bedrooms: 0
Wedding only: No

Name: **St Andrew's and Blackfriars' Halls**
Address: **St Andrew's Plain, Norwich NR3 1AU**
Tel: **01603 628477**

St Andrew's and Blackfriars' Halls are a true municipal marvel. They were originally the nave and choir of the convent church of Norwich's Dominican friars, more commonly known as the Black friars. The Black friars were an order who carried out pastoral works in poor areas. When they came to Norwich in the 13th century the city was a relatively poor outpost of the country. However, shortly after their arrival it experienced a boom as it became a centre for the cloth trade and the main market town in a rapidly growing area. The Dominicans grew as well and were able to build a large friary in the centre of the ancient city in the 1400s.

But why is it a municipal marvel? In 1535 Henry VIII dissolved the monasteries. In most places they were knocked down and the stone used for building materials. But in

Norwich the mayor had other ideas. He wanted to turn the friary into a free school and so he wrote to Henry offering to buy the building for £81. Henry agreed and so Norwich Council became the proud owners. They have looked after it ever since and that is why you can now get married in the country's best preserved friary complex.

The 2 halls are next to each other on the same site. Both are impressive spaces retaining all the atmosphere that can only come from a building that has watched the world go by for hundreds of years.

Blackfriars' Hall is a tall room over 80 feet long and 30 feet wide. It has oak panelling on the lower half of the walls and cream painted stonework above. There are a series of paintings of the famous sons of Norwich including a picture of Lord Nelson, the local boy who made good. A number of very large medieval stone mullioned windows allow light to stream into the room.

At one end there is a fixed platform where ceremonies are held. It also makes an ideal place for a string quartet to entertain the guests. The room holds up to 400 people and, because of its size, it is perfectly possible to have a wedding at one end and the reception at the other.

St Andrew's Hall is even larger, seating up to 900 people. This truly massive room has a main aisle with 2 rows of stone columns soaring up to the original hammerbeam roof. A modern strip maple floor provides a pleasant contrast lightening the whole space. At the far end of the hall is an orchestra platform and choir stall so if you really wanted to go to town you could have a spectacular musical accompaniment to the wedding, provided of course that it had no religious connotations. How about 200 people singing 'Ode to Joy' or a brass band doing a version of 'Summertime'?

Behind the concert platform is a licensed bar and a well-equipped kitchen so there is no problem feeding and watering the 900. After the ceremony photos can be taken outside below the trees in the cloisters. Some couples prefer to have their photos taken in front of the buildings' many architecturally interesting nooks and crannies such as stone doorways or beneath a particularly nice archway. Some even go outside to nearby Elm Hill, a cobbled street of medieval half-timbered buildings.

Blackfriars' and St Andrew's may be fabulous buildings but they do not charge fabulous prices. In fact a wedding here is remarkably good value. If you do not want to have a reception it is possible to have a wedding only for about £50. If you hire either hall for a wedding and reception the charge starts at £170. If you have a really big bash and use several of the rooms you will still probably spend less than £400.

Couples can have their own caterers or use one of a number recommended by the council. Buffets with wine start at around £6 and full meals with wine can be had for about £16. The halls have excellent disabled access, an induction loop system for the hard of hearing and even baby-changing facilities. There is access for bridal cars and the cars of principal guests. Other guests will have to park in the multi-storey nearby. There is no accommodation on the site but there are plenty of hotels and bed and breakfasts in Norwich.

Blackfriars' and St Andrew's Halls are truly magnificent venues which would not be there if the local city had not taken the initiative all those years ago. They are ideally suited to a couple who want to have a grand wedding. If you are using the St Andrew's Hall you really do need to dress in style to match the building. A wedding dress with a 20-foot train followed by 6 bridesmaids and page boys would seem to be the order of the day. And couples who want a romantic departure can leave the halls, walk down Elm Street to the River Wensum and take a boat off to their honeymoon.

Contact: Tim Aldous
Main road: A11/A47
Station: Norwich
Disabled access: Yes
Parking: Limited
Registrar tel no: 01603 767600
Bedrooms: 0
Wedding only: Yes

Name: Highbury
Address: 4 Yew Tree Road,
Moseley, Birmingham B13 8QD
Tel: 0121 449 6549

Highbury is the former home of Joseph Chamberlain, Birmingham's great politician and statesman. Built in 1878, it is a large brick and stone mansion in the Moseley district of the city. Then it was described as his country retreat. Today when you turn off Yew Tree Road into the grounds it is easy to see what it was like in his day. There are still acres of grounds with many ancient yew bushes and there is a sense of tranquillity amidst the hubbub of the city.

Now Highbury is run by Birmingham City Council and is used for conferences, functions and weddings. The house itself is as grand as you will find without moving up into the major stately homes league. But it is also slightly odd. The main entrance is generally closed. You have to ring a bell which has a sign warning you to wait several minutes to give the staff time to get to the door. Eventually someone emerges from the inner recesses of the house to let you into the main hall which actually serves as the main room of the house.

The hall is two storeys high and occupies the whole of the central area of the building. There is a balcony around the first floor with a huge oak roof above. The walls are decorated with unusual marquetry panels. These combined with the dark roof and the fact that most of the light comes from above gives the room a rather oppressive atmosphere. Somewhat ahead of its time the hall was designed to be a multipurpose space. In the daytime it was furnished with comfortable tables and chairs. In the evening these could be cleared away to make space for entertaining.

The weddings take place in the Drawing Room off the main hall which seats 98 people. It is square with a large bay window looking out over the grounds. The blue wallpaper is offset by the beautiful ceiling of inlaid walnut and satinwood. There is an ornate marble fireplace with family portraits above. In the far corner are some old photos of Highbury which show that not a lot has changed over the years. The registrar can conduct the wedding from the bay window with the couple and the guests looking on to the gardens.

After the wedding, couples can have photos taken in the grounds and the guests can have drinks outside before going into the main hall for the reception.

Highbury is not a hotel and does not have any accommodation for general use. However it does have a very impressive room which is normally used by the most important guests of the city council which can be booked by the bride and groom as a Honeymoon Suite for £150. The bedroom overlooks the grounds and seems to be as big as a football pitch. It has a four-poster bed but bring your binoculars if you want to see the television in the far corner of the room. The down side is that the ground floor of the building is alarmed at night so once you are in the Honeymoon Suite you cannot escape!

It costs £150 to book Highbury for a wedding and there is an hourly rate of £38 plus VAT for hire of the whole of the ground floor for receptions. Food prices range from a buffet with wine at £17 per head to sit-down meals with wine at £25 per head. Guests can stay at nearby hotels and there is ample parking in the grounds. There is disabled access to the ground floor but not to the Honeymoon Suite.

Highbury is a historic building in beautiful grounds but it lacks warmth. It feels like a museum without the bustling atmosphere of a stately home. You would need to fill the place with decorations, flowers, balloons and music to give it some atmosphere.

Contact: Janette Morley
Main road: M42
Station: Birmingham New Street
Disabled access: Partial
Parking: Ample
Registrar tel no: 0121 235 3421
Bedrooms: 1
Wedding only: No

A VERY CIVIL SERVICE

Listen flowers, birds, winds, worlds,
tell all today that I married
more than a white girl in the barley
for today I took to my human bed
flower and bird and wind and world,
and all the living and all the dead.

DANNIE ABSE

Register offices have had a bit of a bad press of late. Partly because many of them are not particularly aesthetic and partly because they suffer from an unfair association with bureaucracy. In fact we found several register offices struggling to keep up appearances against huge financial hardship.

For those situated in a Town Hall where other municipal functions are going on all the time they are battling against terrible odds. It is very difficult to create a romantic ambience when the wedding guests have to walk past the latest literature on Income Support or leaflets on how to get a rent rebate!

The register offices we have listed here however are really on the ball. Many, like Chester, were instrumental in the implementation of the new law and are setting the pace for the more commercial premises. Others are in very unusual buildings. Whoever would have thought that you could get married in a former magistrates court, a Victorian gymnasium or a converted pub.

For people who do not want a lot of pomp and circumstance but just a low-key marriage a register office will always remain the best option. And don't forget that register offices still charge a standard fee wherever you go. So even on a shoestring budget, you can still have a reasonably priced wedding in a glorious setting.

London register offices are listed under the Capital Wedding section.

Name: Sandwell Register Office
Address: Highfields, High Street,
West Bromwich B70 8RJ
Tel: 0121 569 2480

Chris Street is the proud superintendent registrar at Highfields, Sandwell's old but recently refurbished register office. The building is just off the main Sandwell shopping centre but feels a million miles away.

Highfields originally consisted of 4 separate Georgian houses which were owned by a succession of wealthy families including coal masters and businessmen, doctors and solicitors. In the 1930s the houses were nearly demolished to make way for new council houses. The war intervened and saved them. By the 1980s they had gone into some decline and their future was again threatened. This time English Heritage stepped in and listed the buildings forcing the council to take action. Which is why Chris Street is such a happy man. The council decided to spend some money and turn Highfields into a new register office. Chris worked closely with the architects to restore the building to its former glory and at the same time make it into a modern register office.

The Sandwell Suite at one end of the building is the main marriage room. It is rather long and thin but it has 9 beautiful Georgian windows making it really light and airy. It is tastefully decorated with antique desks, maroon seats and colour co-ordinated curtains. There is a state-of-the-art CD with speakers built into the wall and even a radio mike so that everyone in the room can hear the wedding ceremony.

Chris is no traditionalist when it comes to music during the ceremony. He is quite happy for couples to play Eric Clapton's 'Wonderful Tonight', the theme tune for *Robin Hood, Prince of Thieves*, or anything else they choose.

The second marriage suite is at the other end of the building. It has a completely separate entrance so different wedding parties do not end up bumping into each other. Again it has been tastefully restored with an original slate fireplace, Wedgwood blue wallpaper and large Georgian windows looking out on to the gardens. The walls are decorated with prints depicting wedding scenes.

Finally, the Farley Room is for smaller weddings. It looks as if it was a sitting room in one of the old houses. It is quite small, square and the fireplace has a big wooden surround. The registrar sits in front of a large window giving views over the garden. It would be a lovely room for a couple who were having a quiet second-time-round wedding.

There are weeping willows and a small ornamental pond in the gardens at the front of the building so there are lots of places for photos. Otherwise couples can have their pictures taken with the building as a backdrop. The stucco front has been painted in its original shades of pink. Chris says it looks so beautiful that even couples who have been married at a nearby church come to the register office gardens for their photos. There is good disabled access and plenty of parking. Guests can stay at the nearby Moat House Hotel.

Highfields shows just what can be done if a council is prepared to invest in their local register office. Chris and his staff are keen to give couples a proper wedding in lovely surroundings at a price that they can afford. The policy seems to have paid off. Chris says that quite a lot of couples prefer to come to the register office and spend their money on dressing up or a nice wedding car. He once had a Hells Angels' wedding where the bride sped off on a giant motorbike. 'All my staff do their best to ensure that every couple has a special day,' he says.

Contact: Chris Street
Main road: M5/A41
Station: Sandwell and Dudley
Disabled access: Yes
Parking: Ample

Name: **Dudley Register Office**
Address: **Priory Hall, Priory Park, Dudley DY1 4EU**
Tel: **01384 453374**

Dudley Register Office must have one of the best locations in the country. It is easy to find as it is close to Dudley Castle which dominates the skyline for miles around. You reach it by driving up to the edge of the town and then following the road towards the base of the castle. At this point the castle disappears from view and you start to think you are lost.

However, persevere, because the register office has its own turning off the roundabout leading you into the beautiful Priory Park. The ruins of an ancient priory are off to the right and then Priory Hall, home of the register office, comes into view. It is a grand two-storey, stone-built place complete with castellated walls and turrets.

Priory Hall was originally built as the house for the Earl of Dudley's estate manager. The Earl grew rich from mining so his manager had a pretty stylish house. The building has been substantially preserved and the wedding rooms have been restored to their former glory. The main room seats 75. It has original carved oak panelling and a large stone fireplace. The registrar's table is at one end in front of a large walk-in bay window which gives wonderful views on to the parkland beyond. There are fresh flowers everywhere and the room is furnished with rose-coloured seats and curtains. Although the panelling is dark the picture windows, the furnishings and flowers combine to give the room a particularly warm atmosphere.

The second wedding room is smaller, holding 45 people. It is also panelled and has 3 windows looking out over the park. The main wedding room has an induction loop system and the building has full disabled access. There is plenty of parking in the grounds.

When the time comes to take the photos, couples are completely spoilt for choice. They can stand under the trees or in front of the rose gardens which forms a lovely backdrop. David Chamberlain, the superintendent registrar, says that whilst summer weddings are beautiful the best photos are taken in the autumn when the trees are a hundred shades of orange and brown.

David is a keen supporter of the new wedding law and is glad to see couples coming from miles around to have their big day in such beautiful surroundings. He does his bit to make their day special by wearing morning dress for the ceremony.

Contact: David Chamberlain
Main road: A446
Station: Sandwell and Dudley
Disabled access: Good
Parking: Ample

Name: Braintree Register Office
Address: John Ray House, Bocking End, Braintree, Essex CM7 9RW
Tel: 01376 323463

Braintree Register Office is in a tree-lined street close to the centre of the town. From the outside it looks like a small village school. It is a single-storey brick building with a separate entrance at each end. You almost expect to see the inscriptions 'boys' and 'girls' carved over the doors. A closer inspection reveals that this is more than a school house. There is an imposing colonnaded terrace with a large stone crest mounted over the main entrance.

This strange building is actually a former gymnasium built in 1930 as a showpiece to encourage a healthy lifestyle for the children of the neighbouring school. In 1994 it was converted into one of the country's most unusual register offices.

The old gymnasium is now the wedding room. In the 1930s they believed in the invigorating properties of air and light so the room has huge windows and is flooded with sunlight. At one end there is a balcony but the most impressive feature is the magnificent vaulted ceiling which is nearly 25 feet high. It has ornate white plasterwork picked out of a dark blue background.

The room has pale pink walls, a specially made matching pink and blue carpet and blue chairs. The architecture and the decor combine to create a remarkably tranquil atmosphere, an ideal setting for a romantic wedding.

There is seating for 30 and plenty of standing room for at least another 50. The building has exceptionally good disabled access. The wedding room does not yet have facilities for piped music but the registrar, Mr Bird, is happy for couples to bring their own music along. He is not at all stuffy about what is allowed. He even had a saxophone playing at one wedding.

After the ceremony, photos can be taken outside by the stone columns. To be honest it is not particularly photogenic and you might want to save most of the photos for the reception. There is plenty of parking in the council car park opposite. Receptions can be held in Braintree or outside the town in any number of country pubs.

Contact: Mr Bird
Main road: A120
Station: Braintree
Disabled access: Good
Parking: Plenty

Name: Winchester Register Office
Address: Station Hill, Winchester SO23 8TJ
Tel: 01962 869608

On the wedding morning many a bride or groom may wish that instead of going to the register office they were off to their local for a drink. Well in Winchester their prayers are almost answered. The register office is housed in an old pub!

Just outside the station, only an hour's journey from London, the brand new register office is in what used to be the South Western public house. It first appeared in records back in 1871 under the name of the Railway Refreshment Inn. Until 1992 commuters could stop off on the way home for a quick pint or several. There were even rumours that other more physical pleasures were on offer to weary travellers.

However the building fell into disrepair and in a bold move Hampshire County Council decided to convert it into a brand new register office. The entrance to the building is through what was the door to the saloon bar. Inside it has been tastefully transformed into a reception area with pale cream walls and comfy green armchairs. There is also a gallery above that leads to offices.

As you enter the wedding room you are immediately struck by a sense of tranquillity. The room is decorated in yellow and cream with a blue carpet. It is very tall with a bay window going from floor to ceiling. The window has magnificent stained glass which was specially commissioned for the register office by the county council. A swirling blue motif topped by the image of the rising sun symbolizes the stream of life and the optimism of a new beginning. The stained glass bathes the room in a warm light and the overall effect is increased by the stylish high-backed Rennie Mackintosh chairs.

You might wonder how a pub could be made to look so beautiful. In fact the room has been doubled in height by taking out the first floor. One of the reason why it is so light is because there are small windows high up that would have originally been in the first floor bedrooms.

After the ceremony guests go out through a glass-topped atrium to a small patio. When we saw it the building had only just been opened and the garden looked a bit sad. However over time the shrubs and flowers will mature. Photos can also be taken on the steps outside the stained-glass window.

It has to be said that the outside of the register office is not very picturesque unless you are an architecture freak. Next door is the county's futuristic public records office, all high-tech glass. On the other side is the station. The register office has parking for 4 cars and guests can use the station car park which is empty at the weekends.

Sheila Ractliffe, the registrar, is very excited about the new building which she says is a vast improvement on the old town centre register office. She is keen to help couples have a special day. At present they do not have any piped music in the wedding room and do not have music accompanying ceremonies but in the past they have had pipers and a trumpeter accompanying couples after ceremonies. They have even had a town crier outside announcing the wedding and on another occasion a fireman got married complete with fire engine. Apparently they have also had several dogs at ceremonies, one attired with a bow.

They are very busy at weekends but Sheila says they always make the ceremony special however busy they are. Receptions can be held in Winchester or in several pubs in the nearby countryside. There are numerous hotels and bed and breakfasts in the city and the happy couple can hop on to a fast train to London or Weymouth for their honeymoon.

Contact: Sheila Ractliffe
Main road: M3
Station: Winchester
Disabled access: Yes
Parking: Ample

Name: Coventry Register Office
Address: Cheylesmore Manor House, Manor House Drive, Coventry CV1 2ND
Tel: **01203 833141**

To be honest, Coventry is not the place where you would expect to find a beautiful register office. The city was flattened in the war and unfortunately a lot of the rebuilding was spectacularly unattractive, which all goes to make the city's register office such a delight. When you have finished circulating round one of the country's tightest and most multi-exited ring roads, with a bit of luck you will drop down from exit 5 into New Union Street. Take the first left, then right and 100 yards on the right is a small but perfectly formed medieval building called Cheylesmore Manor House.

Cheylesmore is Coventry's register office and Ray Plant, the superintendent registrar, believes it is the oldest building in the country to be used as such. It is timber framed with an archway running through the middle.

The timber and plasterwork have not been painted black and white but have been left in their original colours. The wedding party comes in through a tastefully designed modern annexe which houses the office staff. A staircase leads up to the first floor and back through to the old building.

The wedding room is quite small and only holds 35 people but it must be one of the best preserved medieval rooms in the country. All the original timbers are uncovered and the plaster has been left unpainted. The registrar's desk is in front of a large chimney breast. On one side the windows look out on to a small courtyard with some very large and aromatic lime trees. It is easy to forget that you are in the middle of a major city.

Ray is very proud of the building and knows all about its history and features. He explains that the notches on the chimney breast originally would have held a large wooden clothes dryer. Fortunately they have not survived as all that washing might remind the loving couple what really lay ahead!

Next door is another room which is used for smaller weddings. It has more exposed timbers and you can see some of the slivers of sandstone which were combined with a mixture of straw and animal dung to make the walls. Don't worry, the animal dung has long since lost its pungent smell.

Unfortunately the 2 rooms upstairs do not have disabled access but if it is required a room downstairs can be brought into use. It also is in the medieval part of the building with plenty of exposed beams but it has rather small windows.

The register office does not have a music system. Ray says that it is partly by choice and partly because of lack of funds. Coventry is an extremely busy office and the normal time allowed for a wedding is 20 minutes. The emphasis is definitely on the more traditional marriage in keeping with the style of the building. They have had a bride in medieval dress but most go for the traditional whites and creams.

There are plenty of hotels in the city which can accommodate guests and put on a reception. Grander events can be held in the medieval Guildhall or at the nearby Coombe Abbey Hotel with its theatrical dining rooms and bridal suites. There is plenty of parking in a public car park just across the road from the register office.

Contact: Ray Plant
Main road: M6/A45
Station: Coventry
Disabled access: Partial
Parking: Ample

Name: **St Austell Register Office**
Address: **12 Carlyon Road, St Austell, Cornwall PL25 4LD**
Tel: **01726 68974**

When it comes to the speeches at the wedding reception there is always some wag who compares you can be sure that the speeches will be littered with criminal references because the register office used to be the magistrates court.

The building is set among a whole complex of council offices in the centre of St Austell. They are not very attractive on the outside, but they do have the benefit of plenty of parking.

Inside it is a different story. Being a magistrates court it was designed to impress all those petty thieves and drunks that the majesty of the law was not a thing to disregard lightly. Nowadays it looks rather different. The guests will be sitting in a large and airy sixties room, tastefully decorated with pink walls and soothing bamboo designs on the tall window screens. These can be lit from behind to create the effect of sunshine streaming into the building.

At one end of the room is a raised platform from which the magistrates used to listen to the excuses and then pass sentence. Today it is decorated with plants and flowers and acts as a backdrop to the ceremony which takes place in front of it in the body of the hall. Because of the layout of the room it is quite possible for the more traditional minded bride to walk down the aisle to be given away.

The room seats 70 people but can take over 100 if the rest are prepared to stand at the back. There is a CD system and the superintendent registrar is happy to play the music that couples want provided it does not have religious connotations. Apparently, Tammy Wynette's 'Stand by your Man' is very popular.

In fact Cornwall seems to be quite progressive when it comes to weddings. In the past they have had a singer contributing to the ceremony. A friend of the couple, she brought her own backing music and sang 'The Power of Love'. They have also had a cowboy wedding. The registrar drew the line at the six-shooter and asked the over-enthusiastic groom to leave it in her office until the time came for the photos.

After the wedding couples can have their photos taken among the trees in the small garden next to the register office. There are numerous nearby hotels for the reception and for guests to stay overnight. The register office has very good disabled access and there is plenty of parking on site.

The new register office is a vast improvement on the old one although very occasionally the registrar gets a local coming to book a wedding who says, 'The last time I was in here I was up in front of the beak.' Nowadays it is much more likely to be a couple who have romantic memories of Cornish holidays.

St Austell Register Office is a fine building and the staff are keen to provide that individual touch which makes a wedding personal and special. It would be an ideal spot for couples who first met on a Cornish beach or want to have a real West Country honeymoon.

Contact: Mrs Alexandra Francis
Main road: A30
Station: St Austell
Disabled access: Yes
Parking: Ample

Name: Chester Register Office
Address: Goldsmith House, Goss Street, Chester CH1 2BG
Tel: **01244 602668**

The day we visited Chester Register Office there was a sleek maroon vintage car with all the trimmings waiting for the bride and groom. It just goes to show that register offices can put on a show with the best of them. The bride emerged looking resplendent in white with her bridesmaids in pink satin and was whisked away to a reception at the nearby Grosvenor Hotel.

Chester Register Office may not be beautiful on the outside, it's a great sixties box of a building, but we all know we should never judge a book by its cover and inside it is a state-of-the-art register office. Lots of dusky pink sofas and soft lighting with delightful flower arrangements all around make it feel really homely. The staff are all cheerful and smiley and about as helpful and friendly as you could hope for.

There are very few restrictions in operation here. Staff have all embraced the new law and are very aware they are a business now. Not only do they go out of their way to be friendly but they will do their very best to make it your day, not theirs. So much so that they recently produced a CD entitled 'Your Wedding' encouraging people to personalize their wedding ceremony with readings, poetry and music. 'We encourage people to make it as much their day as possible. If that involves playing Meat Loaf at the service which happened recently then that's just fine,' says Martin Smith who manages the Registration Service in Cheshire. 'We've had all sorts here,' he says, 'rock and roll weddings, big white weddings and a punk wedding where everything was dark green including the bride's hair!'

The ceremony itself takes place in a huge circular room which is draped with pink curtains. The lighting can be adjusted to be very subdued giving a solemn atmosphere or brighter for a more jolly affair. Every couple has a meeting with the registrar beforehand to discuss the music and readings they want.

Couples all get a copy of Cheshire's glossy pack 'Your Marriage' which tells them exactly what will happen on the day. It lists all sorts of readings, from the film *Carve her Name with Pride* to one from an American Indian ceremony. And of course it includes plenty from Shakespeare and Robert Burns.

There is also a list of enhancements to the wedding ceremony including quotes from Mark Twain about marriage making 2 fractional lives a whole and a quote from John Donne about no man being an island. Heady stuff but you get the picture.

Speaking of pictures it is possible to video the whole ceremony with the agreement of the registrar beforehand. So you can capture your special day on film for the rest of your life!

Contact: Keith Flanagan
Main road: A55
Station: Chester
Disabled access: Excellent
Parking: Locally

AT THE WATER'S EDGE

Here's to matrimony, the high sea for which no compass
has yet been invented!

HEINRICH HEINE

If you love water but don't want to go as far as the coast for it one
of these venues will be ideal. They are all watery places, either
overlooking lakes or in a riverside setting. Some hotels have their
own slipper launches which can be hired and decked out with
balloons and flowers to take you away after the ceremony is all over.
Take heed, however, because although these places may look glorious
in the height of summer, if it happens to rain on your big day you
may be in trouble. So before you get too excited, better check with
the venues that they do have a contingency plan should the English
weather prove true to form!

Name: **Phyllis Court Club**
Address: **Marlow Road, Henley-on-Thames, Oxfordshire RG9 2HT**
Tel: **01491 574366**

On the water's edge at Henley the Victorians built a magnificent Grandstand Pavilion from which to watch the regattas. Fortunately it has been preserved and you can get married here in splendour and style. Rowing buffs, old blues and anyone who just enjoys messing about on the river will consider the Grandstand their idea of heaven.

The Grade II listed pavilion is 2 storeys high and about 100 feet long. The original iron and wood construction has been well preserved. Downstairs it has been glassed in while upstairs is an open deck with a large canopy giving protection from the sun.

Standing on the balcony guests can look to the left down the full length of the regatta course to the Oxfordshire hills. Opposite is the finishing post for the Henley Royal Regatta and to the right is the Leander Rowing Club and Henley Bridge. Below there is a constant flow of eights and fours either training for the next big race or just enjoying a gentle row. Small pleasure launches weave their way up the river trying to avoid the swans.

Here in the elegant white building with the water lapping outside and swans gliding past you can have a truly romantic wedding. The wedding room is downstairs, although the word 'room' doesn't do justice

to the space. There are no brick or timber walls, just delicate Victorian columns and acres of glass. The bride and groom will take their vows against a river backdrop in a room bathed in reflected light. After the ceremony the guests will be able to go upstairs for a celebratory drink before returning downstairs for a slap-up reception.

Any sort of music can be arranged but a string quartet playing Haydn or Beethoven during the ceremony would be perfect. If you have got the money, a trad jazz band would create an excellent atmosphere for the reception. The Grandstand can accommodate about 80 people for the wedding and 150 for the reception.

To give the day an added watery flavour you can arrive or leave by boat – either a rowing skiff pulling away to the strains of the 'Eton Boating Song' or one of those magnificent Thames slipper launches – 15 feet of varnished mahogany and burnished bronze fittings.

Although the Phyllis Court Club sounds like a modern health club stuffed to the gills with exercise machines and leotards it is, in fact, a rather exclusive members' club set in a beautifully preserved Georgian building.

But in spite of being a private club anyone can book a wedding here providing they follow some basic club rules. After 7.30 pm men have to wear a jacket and tie and women cannot wear casual trousers. To be honest, if you want to have a country and western

wedding with blue jeans and rhine-
stones this is not the place. If, on
the other hand, you fancy an Edwardian occasion with striped blaz-
ers, boaters and long floaty dresses
then Phyllis Court is a dream.

While the Grandstand Pavilion is
the jewel in the crown, weddings
can also be held in the club itself.
The Ballroom is a fine Georgian
room that holds about 200 people.
It has pillars at one end with french
windows opening on to the lawns
which in turn lead down to the
river. The smaller Thames Room
holds about 60 people and also gives
on to the lawns.

Phyllis Court has 11 bedrooms
which can be booked by the wedding party. There are no special
bridal suites however. Remember
Phyllis Court is a club and not a
hotel.

Guests can stay in the Red Lion
Hotel or in local bed and breakfasts. The tourist information
bureau keeps a list (01491 578034).
There are plenty of opportunities to
buy last-minute presents in Henley's
numerous antique shops. And if the
groom is still a child at heart his
friends can even buy him some toys
in Henley's very own Meccano
shop.

The club is heavily booked for
events and this is reflected in its
prices – charges leap dramatically if
you use more than one room. Wedding receptions are likely to cost
around £45 per head. Considering
the high standard of the venue, the
bedroom charges are surprisingly
modest at £35–42 per head.

Although Phyllis Court has
several wedding rooms, the Grandstand Pavilion is without doubt the
place to tie the knot. An ideal venue
for an Edwardian themed wedding
with tasteful live music wafting
across the water.

Contact: Sue Gill
Main road: M4/M40
Station: Henley
Disabled access: Yes
Parking: Plenty
Registrar tel no: 01491 573047
Bedrooms: 11
Wedding only: No

Name: Curdon Mill
Address: Vellow, Williton,
Somerset TA4 4LS
Tel: 01984 656522

Curdon Mill is a converted water-
mill situated at the foot of the Quan-
tock Hills amidst rolling farmland
and woodland in the Somerset
countryside.

The red sandstone building is set
amongst the trappings of a working farm and some of the most
delightful countryside in Somerset
provides a delightful backdrop.
The peace is only shattered
occasionally by the white peacocks
which shriek and strut about the
gardens. Inside all is tranquil with
just the sound of the gently flow-
ing stream upon which the mill
sits.

The wedding room is part of the
Dining Room. It is long and narrow
with oak beams and what appears
to be the trunk of a tree supporting

the central part of the ceiling. Farming paraphernalia adorn the walls including a black cast-iron mill shaft which was used in grinding the corn.

The ceremony will be held at the far end of the room in front of an old oak Welsh dresser covered with a collection of plates and jugs. The other end of the room opens out on to a small terrace with spiral steps leading to the gardens. Stone plant pots with a riot of summer flowers create an almost Mediterranean effect on the steps – this is just one spot which would be lovely for photographs.

There is a huge box hedge which almost obscures a small swimming-pool and attractive summer-house on a raised terrace of lawns. Around the side of the mill where the stream runs there is an old tree root which forms a little bridge to the bank on the other side. One couple were so overcome with the romance of the setting that the bride took her shoes off and is captured in her wedding photographs with her bare toes paddling in the stream.

Daphne Criddle who runs the place is a gem. Not only is she a superb cook but she is terribly keen to make your day perfect. She openly admits she adores organizing weddings – it's her favourite part of the job – and before you decide whether Curdon Mill is your choice she will sit you down and go through an extensive collection of wedding albums containing pictures of ones she has already arranged.

Everything is there from where to order fireworks to hiring a horse and carriage.

The largest privately-owned steam railway passes by just a field away. Couples have been known to arrive by steam train with a horse and carriage to pick them up and transport them to the mill. Daphne has organized jazz bands, a barrel organ, fireworks – in fact anything you could want Daphne can sort out.

For larger weddings you can have a marquee on the lawn where the sides roll up and you have a view of the swimming-pool and the Quantocks beyond. Or if you wanted something more intimate you could have a cosy firelit wedding in the restaurant in winter. The maximum number of people for a sit-down meal in the restaurant is 65.

A simple finger buffet with wine will cost around £12.50 a head whereas a full sit-down meal costs around £16.50. Daphne likes to discuss the finer points of the catering individually with each couple. She feels this is really important to get the best out of the day.

For our money the ideal wedding would be a small summer do with drinks out on the steps and patio followed by a reception in the restaurant which serves delicious freshly-made food. It is hard to imagine a more romantic or tranquil setting.

Contact: Daphne Criddle
Main road: A358/M5
Station: Taunton
Disabled access: Partial

Parking: Ample
Registrar tel no: 01984 633116
Bedrooms: 12
Wedding only: No

Name: Oakley Court Hotel
Address: Windsor Road, Water
Oakley, Windsor, Berkshire
SL4 5UR
Tel: 01753 609988

Oakley Court is a huge gothic pile situated on the banks of the Thames just a few minutes away from the M4. More reminiscent of a traditional English boarding school than a luxurious hotel it came as no surprise to discover that at one time it was the location for the film *St Trinians*.

In 1955 Oakley Court was used extensively by Southern Pictures when the Bray Studios moved next door. Around 200 films were made in and around the property including the *Rocky Horror Picture Show*, *Half a Sixpence* and *Murder by Death*.

Downstairs every room is different and it is easy to see how directors had a field day using every part of the hotel in a variety of films. The decor is rather churchy with ornate carved mirrors on the overmantel in the foyer and magnificent coved ceilings and decorative window surrounds. Just the place to curl up on a comfy window seat and watch the boats go by on the river.

Speaking of boats the hotel owns 3 which you can hire throughout the summer, worth bearing in mind if you wanted to arrive at your wedding by slipper launch – or disappear mysteriously after the ceremony for that matter.

The staff are young and trendy but traditional without being snobbish. The day we visited a young man dressed in black uniform greeted us in a cheery transatlantic accent. You also get the impression that the guests are relaxed too. Children rush about everywhere without so much as a raised eyebrow from the staff.

The wedding room itself is in the Windsor Suite which is also used for conferences. It was a bit of a disappointment after looking around the rest of the hotel and gawping at its exquisite decor – no high ceilings or intricate panelling here. Instead the room was long and low and decorated in Wedgwood blue and regency wallpapered. However, since our visit the hotel has told us that it is being completely refurbished to bring it in line with the rest of the hotel's public areas. The room is used to being set up for functions and as such is cleverly designed with partitioned walls so you can have it as large or as small as you like.

Afterwards you can retire to the Conservatory – a beautiful light and airy room where you can have a reception for about 30 guests. Another option is to have an alfresco reception on the lawn in one of the hotel's graceful traditional marquees which could hold anything from 60 to 200 guests. The grounds are quite spectacular with lawns sloping gently down to the river and huge spreading cedar trees to provide shade in the summer.

Oakley Court has an exclusive wedding package which includes the ceremony complete with red carpet, toastmaster, glass of champagne on arrival and half a bottle of red or white wine per person. It also includes the 3-course wedding breakfast, hire of a silver cake stand and knife, place cards, menus and fresh flowers at every table.

You can have anything from a full-blown disco to a low-key harpist to play throughout the meal. Overnight accommodation for the bride and groom is thrown in too. For a party of around 60–80 people that will set you back a mere £62 a head and for more than 100 it costs around £55 a head.

It is worth noting that for an additional supplement you can have a special bedroom suite. These rooms are truly special with a four-poster bed and stone mullioned windows overlooking the river. If you just want to have a wedding at Oakley Court they are happy to do that but will charge you extra for the hire of the room. We would not recommend it as you only really get the full benefit of the venue by using the rest of the hotel.

You could have a wonderful gothic, all-the-frills wedding here for a price admittedly but without all the pomposity of an expensive country house hotel.

Contact: Karen Smith
Main road: M4/A308

Station: Windsor/Maidenhead
Disabled access: Yes
Parking: Ample
Registrar tel no: 01628 21776
Bedrooms: 92
Wedding only: Yes

Name: Ravens Ait
Address: Portsmouth Road, Surbiton, Surrey KT6 4HN
Tel: 0181 390 3554

Ravens Ait is a tiny island on the Thames just upstream from Kingston. Follow a blue sign for the island, wait just by the jetty and pretty soon a little slipper launch will splutter into life and chug over to collect you. From the other side of the river the building itself is nothing much to write home about. But staff at Ravens Ait have been organizing wedding receptions for years and are pretty clued up.

The ait itself has a long and interesting history dating back as far as 1503 when it was rented out to a private individual for £3 per annum. In 1909 Ravens Ait was offered for sale to an outcry from local residents who urged the local council to pledge themselves to preserve the island 'for the benefit of all'.

Kingston Rowing Club shared the use of the island with the Surbiton Swimming Club until 1935 and in 1945 it was bought by the Trustees of the Navy League to provide a boat-house and adventure training centre for the Sea Cadets. The old boat-houses were demolished and the Navy League raised £250,000 to finance a specially designed complex which is what survives today.

In 1976 the Inner London Education Authority bought the centre from the Navy League and it was used primarily as a training and conference centre. Finally in 1989 Kingston Borough Council bought it and operates Ravens Ait as a conference, training and watersports centre for all.

And of course now weddings can be held there and a more watery spot is hard to imagine. The Thames Suite is the first wedding room, actually 2 rooms. Together they can hold 80 people. It is rather like a conference venue with light open brickwork and pine-cladded ceilings, but the view is simply stunning, straight up the river towards London.

The second room is the Lambourn Room which is smaller and more attractive. Again the decor is modern with brickwork and tongue and groove pitched ceilings with inset loft windows. This room opens on to a terrace which overlooks the river. Off to one side is a bar which could serve post-wedding drinks if the weather was bad. The whole room decked out with pedestals of flowers and ribbons and balloons along the walls would be really attractive.

But the best wedding would surely be like the one which had been held the week previous to our visit. A Scottish couple had arrived on the slipper launch which the staff had decorated with white flowers and ribbons. The bride wore a white trouser suit and the groom wore a kilt. Sarah the dog came too, all dressed in tartan. The guests all had coffee in the foyer on a big buffet table. There were 60 guests although only 12 went into the ceremony held in the Lambourn Room. They then came out to the front into the fixed marquee where they had a blessing. Because Ravens Ait does not allow any amplified music outside they had a skiffle band playing jazz and folk music.

After the blessing the band struck up a conga and all the guests trooped out on to the lawn for the wedding photos. 'In the time it took them to have their pictures taken we had set up the patio with candles and flowers and served the reception drinks. After the wedding breakfast the dance floor was cleared in the Thames Suite and they held a huge barn dance in there. All in all an excellent time was had by all,' said Cullum Darwin and Justin Lewis, catering managers.

Prices are from £45 per person including arrival drinks and canapés followed by a 4-course meal. That includes 5-hour room hire, wine and bouquets for the bride and groom's mothers. In the summer you can have a barbecue wedding for around £6.50 a head out on the terrace. In fact there is not much you cannot have at Ravens Ait.

We thought it was very good value particularly if you want somewhere different where you feel very much away from the rest of the world. There is no bridal suite here although there are fairly basic rooms which you could book should someone get too inebriated to get home. Otherwise they recommend taking their fancy white liner down to the nearby Mitre Hotel with whom they have an arrangement. 'We decorate the boat with rose petals and send them off with a bottle of champagne which they can drink on the way,' says Peter Slater. 'If they want to get away from it all the boat can drop them somewhere further down the river and they can make their own way on to wherever they fancy.'

Contact: Peter Slater
Main road: A3
Station: Surbiton
Disabled access: Excellent
Parking: Off street
Registrar tel no: 0181 546 7993
Bedrooms: A few
Wedding only: No

Name: Hambleton Hall
Address: Hambleton, Oakham,
Rutland LE15 8TH
Tel: 01572 756991

The town of Oakham is a bustling little place featuring a picturesque market-place complete with its very own stocks. The local honey-coloured stone gives the town great appeal and you can happily while away a few hours spending your hard-earned cash in many of the local craft shops.

Oakham is in Rutland. Locals all jump on you if you dare call it Leicestershire. The whole region is surprisingly charming and virtually unspoilt – a bit like the Cotswolds without the tourists. Rutland Water is the principal attraction of the area. The largest man-made lake in Europe, it was formed in 1972 as a reservoir to supply the growing demands of the new towns of the East Midlands. All in all it offers 3,100 acres of water where you can sail, fish and generally enjoy yourself.

Hambleton Hall overlooks formally laid out gardens and several acres of fields which slope gently down to the water's edge. You reach the Hall through a winding leafy drive. A huge cedar has pride of place on the front lawn. Above the door as you enter is the inscription 'Fay Ce Que Voudras' which roughly translated means 'Do as you please' – a motto chosen by Walter Marshall when he built the rambling Victorian manor house as a hunting lodge in 1881.

Marshall's fortunes were earned in the brewery business but he moved to Rutland to enjoy the foxhunting. His scrapbooks show that he was suffocated by the prudishness of the mid-Victorian era and liked to cock a snook at the prevailing morality of his age. 'Nunc Hora Bibendi', 'Now is the time for a drink', is another inscription which appears on the sundial on the south side of the house.

As a country house hotel Hambleton Hall is like many others in style but it is one of those rare places where courtesy still counts for something. Discreet but always on hand when you need them, the staff were delightful. When we visited a helicopter was trying to land in the main field. It was drizzling slightly so one of the younger members of staff raced off to find an umbrella and stood in the rain to escort the guests to the hotel. And of course there is the view. Most of the french windows open out on to a terrace overlooking Rutland Water.

The main drawing room is particularly beautiful with cream drapes at the windows and a decor of creams, pinks and blues. The wedding rooms too are all exquisitely furnished. The first is a cosy room with a tall window overlooking the water. The second is much larger and could hold about 40 people. The 2 are interconnecting so for a large wedding they could hold around 60 comfortably.

For a more intimate wedding there is also a very small room called the Study. This is decorated in deep red wallpaper with cream and red drapes at the windows. It overlooks the front of the house and its sweeping drive banked by Cedars of Lebanon.

Jeffrey Crockett who deals with wedding arrangements is pretty switched on. He would like to see couples coming to Hambleton Hall not just to get married but to stay a while to enjoy the Rutland countryside. 'The old days of 350 people in a church followed by a huge do with second-rate food served in a marquee on the lawn are fast dying out,' he says. 'There is much more awareness amongst the British public of what constitutes good food and service and they know they can have quality rather than quantity with a smaller wedding in a beautiful setting.'

We agreed with his recommendation of a spring wedding when the flowers are at their best. The couple can hire Hambleton Hall for exclusive use for 24 hours from £8,000. The wedding might take place in the Study followed by drinks on the terrace overlooking the water. Canapés and aperitifs to follow and then a 3-course meal with coffee and petits fours. A jazz band and dance in the front hall would complete the day and 30 guests can stay at the Hall with the overspill catered for at the nearby Ramjam Inn.

Contact: Jeffrey Crockett
Main road: M1/A1
Station: Oakham
Disabled access: Yes
Parking: Excellent
Registrar tel no: 01572 756547
Bedrooms: 15 double rooms
Wedding only: Negotiable

Name: Close House Mansion
Address: Heddon-on-the-Wall, Newcastle-upon-Tyne NE15 0HT
Tel: 01661 852255

Close House Mansion was built in 1779 and belonged to Robert Bewicke, a former Lord Mayor of Newcastle. The 179-acre estate of mature wooded parkland in which it stands dates back to the 15th century and is today resplendent with both native trees and more exotic species, including monkey puzzles and wellingtonia.

It is the grounds, and the mansion's commanding views across the Tyne valley, that will tempt you to consider choosing Close House for your wedding. Add the possibility of a summer's evening barbecue on the lawns, amid surroundings that have a curiously collegiate air, and you will be sold.

Close House, although only a few minutes out of Newcastle on the A69 dual carriageway, has a truly rural setting, emphasized by the road signs in the grounds that warn drivers not to run over the red squirrels – the Tyne valley and Northumbria remain a haven for these rare animals.

The collegiate atmosphere stems from the mansion's ownership. It was acquired in 1961 by King's College, then part of Durham University and since 1963, the University of Newcastle. As recently as 1994, the mansion underwent a £1m refurbishment programme and is now the venue for both academic and business conferences. The grounds also boast the university cricket pitch, an 18-hole parkland golf course and a helicopter landing pad for a departure in grand style – perhaps to Newcastle Airport and a honeymoon in the sun.

The licence extends to all the principal downstairs rooms, offering space for up to 80 guests at the wedding ceremony, or 124 for the reception (achieved by opening the partition between the Bolbec and Bewicke Rooms). The Calverly Room, normally the restaurant, provides another option.

The Bolbec Room boasts a dance floor, while the Bewicke, with its marble fireplace has a huge bay window that opens to give on to the east lawn, making it ideal for barbecues. From here you have an elevated view across the cricket pitch and golf course to the River Tyne. Taking pictures by the water's edge would involve a real trek and may not be practical for wedding parties.

Perhaps the most pleasant room for the ceremony, however, is the Italianesque Rococo Room, again with a fine marble fireplace. The grounds provide a host of photographic opportunities including a rather fine old orangery.

Where Close House perhaps falls down is that, unlike similar venues, it offers no accommodation on site. There are plans to rectify this by the conversion of nearby stables to provide 45 rooms for conference delegates. These should come into use in 1996 or 1997. And Close House has negotiated a special rate with the Novotel and Newcastle Airport Moat House.

Close House offers a wide selection of menus, ranging from evening buffets, starting at £5.90, wedding breakfast buffets at £14.50 to full wedding breakfasts from £14.95 to £22.50. A total wedding package comes in at £47.85 per person with drinks included. Vegetarian alternatives are available, as are barbecues, a marquee, licence extension (subject to 3 months' notice) and a disco or other entertainment.

For the time being at least, a Close House wedding will suit parties where all the guests can easily travel by car and where someone in each car is prepared to stay sober! Alternatively, collective transport could be arranged. The great attraction will always be the setting – this is a fine building in extensive and beautiful grounds.

Contact: Shirley Filer
Main road: A69/A1
Station: Wylam
Disabled access: Yes
Parking: Ample
Registrar tel no: 01670 513232
Bedrooms: 0
Wedding only: Negotiable

Name: Monkey Island Hotel
Address: Old Mill Lane, Bray-on-Thames, Maidenhead, Berkshire SL6 2EE
Tel: 01628 23400

Monkey Island sits quietly on the Thames just outside Maidenhead. Close to the M4 and only half an hour's drive from the edge of London it seems 100 miles from the hubbub of the big city.

Turning off the M4 you head into the riverside village of Bray and follow the signposts to Monkey Island. Just as you think that you have lost your way there is a turning into a large tree-lined car park. Here you leave your car and walk through the trees until you reach a narrow footbridge suspended over a backwater of the Thames.

Once over the bridge the view opens up to reveal a white hotel and a low pavilion set in extensive lawns which run down to the river on all sides. There are no cars, no motorbikes and no stereos. Instead, peacocks wander across the grass and swans glide on the river.

Monkey Island has a long history. It was purchased by the third Duke of Marlborough in 1723, and later on Edward VII used to visit for afternoon tea. The Duke built two fishing lodges there. No riverside shacks, these are both hexagonal buildings and befitting a duke. The Temple, now part of the hotel, is open at ground level with a billiard room above decorated with an orange plaster ceiling. The original lodge is called the Monkey Room and is part of the pavilion. It is quite small and has a large log fire. The walls and ceilings are decorated with a bizarre set of paintings depicting monkeys playing a variety of sports. It is an ideal spot for members of the family to get together during the reception and reminisce about old times.

Weddings take place in the more modern Pavilion Restaurant which can hold over 100 for the ceremony. It is a large room with french windows that look directly upstream. There is a small garden outside which is ideal for post-wedding drinks at the water's edge. Receptions are held in the River Room which has a domed ceiling and huge windows all around allowing lovely views over the small stretch of water between the island and the far shore. There is a dance floor and the hotel can arrange for a disco or live music.

Larger receptions of up to 250 can be held in the marquee out on the lawn. It is even possible to reserve the whole island for the exclusive use of the wedding party although this option does not come cheap.

The bride and groom can arrive or leave by helicopter, but the watery route is far more romantic. The couple could leave by boat and head off to nearby Oakley Court Hotel, Windsor or pick up a car to take them to Heathrow Airport. According to the manager some couples make a grand exit on the boat and after disappearing into the sunset promptly whizz round the back of the island and start their nuptials in the hotel's own bridal suite.

The hotel has 25 bedrooms, all with private facilities and all overlooking the river. Be warned however, those magnificent peacocks start screeching at each other at about 6 in the morning. Arrangements can also be made to accommodate guests in local hotels and bed and breakfasts. The Waterside Inn nearby at Bray is a very plush restaurant with a few rooms and is owned by the Roux brothers. It would be a real treat for the bride's parents to stay there on the eve of the big day.

Charges for weddings are by arrangement and are likely to vary according to individual preferences. It is possible just to book the wedding room but will cost around £500. The hotel is really suited to combined weddings and receptions and an all-in-package is likely to cost around £65 per head. The bedrooms start at £85 and go up to £145. You will have to pay extra if you have exclusive use of the island so it would be quite easy to run up a bill for £10,000.

The main feature of Monkey Island is its waterside location and the fact that it feels so cut off from the busy world beyond. To get the full benefits you really would need to take over the whole place for the day. It is really suited to a big wedding where a number of guests also need to stay overnight.

Contact: Nicholas Holdsworth
Main road: M4
Station: Maidenhead
Disabled access: Some
Parking: 120 spaces
Registrar tel no: 01628 21776
Bedrooms: 25
Wedding only: Yes

Name: **The Swan Hotel**
Address: **Bibury, Gloucestershire GL7 5NW**
Tel: **01285 740695**

There is something about the rolling green hills, babbling brooks and honey-coloured stone in the heart of the Cotswolds which makes Bibury, a tiny hamlet 14 miles south-east of Cheltenham, quintessentially English. The Swan Hotel stands on the banks of the River Coln, a perfect setting for a typical English country wedding.

The ivy-clad hotel has served many a weary traveller since the 1600s, but its heyday was during the roaring twenties and thirties when fashionable people drove out to the hotel for lunch. Nowadays you're more likely to bump into celebrities like Anne Robinson or Willie Carson who live nearby.

The first thing you notice when you walk into the inn – once used as the local courthouse – is the black lacquered grand piano which has pride of place in the foyer. Unfortunately it plays itself which rather detracts from its grandeur. However there may be some compensation – apparently it can be programmed to play the 'Wedding March' which could mean saving on a pianist!

The hotel is privately run with a staff of 40 and has a relaxed almost casual air about it. Antiques, art deco and contemporary furniture sit happily side by side in the downstairs sitting rooms which overlook the River Coln. Staff and management are so chummy that when the hotel was refurbished 4 years ago the owners commissioned a huge mural which affectionately depicts each member of staff going about their business. It now adorns one entire wall of the bar.

There is a parlour reserved for non-smokers with cosy sofas and comfortable armchairs and a pretty writing room which used to be the village post office. During the winter chestnuts are roasted on the log fires which blaze in every room.

The 18 bedrooms have been individually designed and decorated. Much of the furniture was bought on jaunts around Britain and the owners have mixed and matched fabrics, wallcoverings and lighting much as the fancy took them. Every single item has been individually selected right down to the Egyptian cotton bedlinen. Local spring water and home-baked shortbread together with a selection of books and a very British Roberts radio make each bedroom feel just like home.

The Honeymoon Suite boasts a spectacular period four-poster bed complete with patchwork quilt hand-made by Constance Spry. One unfortunate guest who complained about the 'threadbare bedcover' had to be set straight about its illustrious origins! A happy couple of a more adventurous disposition could probably spend all day in the massive jacuzzi which dominates the black marble bathroom.

Each wedding is tailor-made to suit the couple although staff agree most are pretty informal. Weddings are held in the imposing Georgian Dining Room which can accommodate up to 100 guests. As the bride walks along to take her place beside her husband-to-be she can see the chef preparing the food through an eccentric one-way window into the kitchen.

Across the road at the front of the hotel are delightful gardens on the banks of the river which will form a perfect backdrop for wedding photos. A crystal clear stream packed with trout runs through the gardens before joining the Coln. The hotel enjoys private fishing rights to the river and the chef can often be spotted at dead of night with a torch and a net catching tomorrow's dish of the day!

If the wedding party is still going strong then it's back to the wedding room for the celebrations. It is worth noting that in the restaurant men have to wear jacket and tie but once the carpet is rolled back to reveal a fabulous sprung dance floor everyone can let their hair down.

Horsedrawn arrivals can be catered for and the owners have a garage full of Bentleys which can be lent for the occasion. In fact they have already had one wedding where a jazz quartet met the bride and groom as they arrived in an old Bentley. Apparently the whole village came to a standstill.

The nearest station is Kemble 8 miles away but there is a taxi service or the hotel can arrange a limousine. The Swan also has its own florist and can supply other services such as jazz bands, orchestras and toastmasters.

There is a changing table d'hôte menu with a wide ranging à la carte. Service is crisp and traditional and the cellar houses a large selection of wines and spirits from around the world including many dessert wines and malt whiskies.

For those who want a more informal reception Jankowskis Brasserie offers a cosmopolitan Mediterranean-style menu. In the summer months the brasserie opens out on to the old stable courtyard with its own attractive fountain.

The manager prides himself on arranging individual weddings but a guideline to cost is around £18 a head for a low-key reception in the brasserie to £35 a head for a 5-course sit-down meal. Double rooms range from £115 to £225 for the jacuzzi Honeymoon Suite.

Contact: Mr Sedlacek
Main road: M40/A40
Station: Kemble (8 miles)
Disabled access: Yes
Parking: Limited
Registrar tel no: 01285 650455
Bedrooms: 18
Wedding only: Yes

Name: Armathwaite Hall
Address: Bassenthwaite Lake, Keswick CA12 4RE
Tel: 017687 76551

Novelist Sir Hugh Walpole was enchanted by Armathwaite Hall and its idyllic position on the shores of Bassenthwaite Lake in this peaceful corner of northern Lakeland. To Walpole – famous for his *Herries Chronicle* set in the area – it was pure romance or as he put it so eloquently, 'a house of perfect and irresistible atmosphere'.

A tree-lined drive leads to this four-star country house hotel which has all the features of a 17th-century former stately home. It is set in 400 acres of park and woodland which fall away to the lake. Surrounded by hills with marvellous views of Skiddaw, the Hall is something of a sanctuary, offering just the right amount of seclusion in breathtaking scenery, yet not too far from main road and rail routes. Wordsworth, who was born in nearby Cockermouth, described the area as 'the loveliest spot that man hath ever found', and who are we to argue?

The Hall itself has an intriguing history. There has been a house on the site since the 11th century, although reliable records can only be traced back to 1548. It passed through various hands and was home to many of Lakeland's top families until 1880 when Thomas Hartley, a local mine-owner from Bridekirk near Cockermouth, bought it for £95,000.

Mr Hartley extended and remodelled the Hall into a Victorian country gentleman's residence, the building you see today. He added the rooms that are now the hall, Lake Room, cocktail bar and part of the restaurant. As local MP, Mr Hartley was one of the sponsors of the Fisheries Protection Bill of 1892. When he died in 1926 the estate was sold to a speculator who broke it up and placed it for sale by auction.

Most of the estate was sold except for the Hall and the surrounding 133 acres. It was later saved from demolition by a Keswick hotelier for the princely sum of £5,000. He spent 6 months renovating it before it was opened as a hotel. The Graves family bought it in 1976 and carried out a massive development programme which has brought it up to its present standard. Armathwaite Hall certainly lends itself to weddings for couples who want to indulge themselves in luxurious and elegant surroundings for their special day. Inside you will find wood-panelled restaurants and public rooms, roaring log fires and sweeping staircases all elegantly and sumptuously decorated and furnished.

The Lake Room is the wedding room and, as the name suggests, has stunning views right over the lake. It boasts a wonderful grand piano and seats up to 50 guests for the ceremony. One nice touch is that couples walk down the aisle beneath an arch of flowers provided by the hotel.

Guests can be received either in the gardens, on the terraces or in the grand panelled hall with its large open fire. The hotel's restaurants can seat up to 100 for the reception, be it a wedding breakfast, buffet or formal meal. Armathwaite Hall can also provide an evening buffet with entertainment in the John Peel Suite for those who want to party.

The turreted building has 43 bedrooms, many with four-poster beds and whirlpool baths. All are individually decorated, including studio suites. The Hartley Tower Suite has a sunken bath and its own stone spiral staircase leading to a roof-top patio with views over the lake and woodland – what could be more romantic!

The hotel also has its own indoor swimming-pool and gymnasium and there is a qualified beauty therapist on site for the bride who wants to be pampered before her wedding.

Prices at Armathwaite Hall vary depending on the scale of wedding, when it is and the individual wishes of the bride and groom. As a rough guide, a simple finger buffet comes at around £11.95 per person with a sit-down meal starting at £19.95 per person. Accommodation varies from £100 a night for a basic room with breakfast up to £190 per night bed and breakfast for a Honeymoon Suite.

Armathwaite Hall is an ideal setting for both large and small weddings although a larger affair would probably be better suited to the spacious grounds and buildings.

Contact: Joan Tomkinson
Main road: A66/M6 (24 miles)
Station: Aspatria (9 miles), Penrith (24 miles), Carlisle (26 miles)
Disabled access: Yes
Parking: Space for 100 cars
Registrar tel no: 01900 822274
Bedrooms: 43
Wedding only: No

Name: The Priory at Ware
Address: High Street, Ware, Hertfordshire SG12 9AL
Tel: 01920 460316

This is the wedding venue for canal lovers and particularly for lovers of canal boats. The Priory is in the centre of Ware just a few miles north of London's M25. Its grounds run down to a tributary of the river Lea and it has its own landing stage for canal boats and cruisers thus making it an ideal starting point for a watery honeymoon.

The Priory is a Grade I listed building that started life in 1338 as a Franciscan friary. However, Henry VIII turfed out the monks during the dissolution of the monasteries and it passed into private hands. In the First World War it was used as a hospital and then in 1920 the owner presented the Priory and its grounds to the town.

It has recently been very tastefully refurbished with the help of English Heritage and is now a centre for conferences, local events and activities as well as housing the offices of Ware Town Council. From the outside the two-storey cream building looks rather like a small French château, the only signs of its religious origins being some stone church-like windows on the ground floor.

However once you go inside, the Franciscan heritage is clear to all. The foyer has a flagstone floor and monastic arches complete with some ancient stone figures. The main wedding room is in the Priory Hall on the ground floor. It holds 80–100 people and has some well-preserved Victorian trompe l'oeil wall paintings. There are a number of large church-style stone windows with decorated glass. French windows lead straight out into the gardens. Pale apricot walls complete the light and airy effect.

The old Council Chamber on the first floor is the second wedding room. It is not a great carved-wood Victorian affair. Instead it is a rather small room with a square of committee tables and chairs that seat 25 people. The walls are decorated with pictures of the worthy citizens of Ware who have served their local community as councillors over the years. Three windows look over the gardens and the River Lea.

The third place for weddings is the Hadsley Room along the corridor. A large square room, it has windows on 2 sides and a huge oak beam running across the top with a crown-post supporting the roof. The registrar will conduct the ceremony from a 14th-century Franciscan table which has been in use at the Priory for over 600 years. Although the room is quite large it can only hold up to 40 people for a wedding. Apparently the ancient floor is not very strong and the registrar did not want the bride and groom disappearing in a cloud of dust through the ceiling of the rooms below.

When we visited, the Priory had only just got its licence and staff were beginning to think about arrangements for music at weddings. In the past they have had a harpsichord and a flute player at a reception and said that they would be pleased to help provide couples with any music they needed.

After the ceremony the guests can go out into the gardens for drinks and photographs. A tributary of the Lea runs through the grounds and there are several bridges on to the Priory's very own island which make ideal locations for photos.

The landing-stage is at the end of the gardens. Couples who don't want to go for the full nautical honeymoon can nevertheless make arrangements to arrive or leave by boat. They could then transfer into a car and be off to Stansted Airport which is only 20 minutes away.

Receptions can be held in the Priory Hall. Food is provided by the staff of Byrche's Restaurant which is in another part of the building on the site of a previous Victorian conservatory. This has the advantage that couples who are planning a wedding at the Priory can try out the food when they come to look over the place. Prices for food and wine including the hire of the reception rooms range from about £18 to £50 per head. Smaller weddings could probably make arrangements to have a wedding breakfast in the restaurant.

There is plenty of parking, good disabled access and an induction loop system in the main hall. There is no accommodation at the Priory but there are several local hotels and numerous bed and breakfasts. It is not possible to have a wedding only but it would seem a shame not to make use of the grounds for a reception. Charges start at around £110 for the use of the smallest room for the ceremony.

The Priory at Ware is an ideal spot for a moderately priced summer wedding taking full advantage of the grounds and the water. Canal enthusiasts would be hard put to find a better spot to tie the knot.

Contact: Janet Buttery
Main road: A10
Station: Ware
Disabled access: Good

Parking: Ample
Registrar tel no: 01992 555590
Bedrooms: 0
Wedding only: Yes

A CAPITAL WEDDING

He smiled and took her hand and pressed it. They got up and walked out of the gallery. They stood for a moment at the balustrade and looked at Trafalgar Square. Cabs and omnibuses hurried to and fro, and crowds passed, hastening in every direction, and the sun was shining.

W. SOMERSET MAUGHAM

Someone once said, 'a person who is tired of London is tired of living', and for many people London is the only place to get married. Either they have a connection with the capital, perhaps they worked there once or have friends who still live there, or they have family living in London. Whatever the reason we have tried to give as wide a range of different venues as possible from the very cheapest to the very grandest. If you want to book a wedding in the capital do remember that parking is at a premium so warn guests to take public transport wherever possible. There are obvious advantages having a capital wedding – the world is your oyster as far as restaurants, hotels and nightclubs are concerned And of course there are all the major travel connections if you want to really get away from it all afterwards. The choices are endless.

Name: The Trafalgar Tavern
Address: Park Row, Greenwich,
London SE10 9NW
Tel: 0181 858 2437

You can't miss the Trafalgar Tavern situated as it is right on the banks of the River Thames at Greenwich. You can get to it along the footpath beside the river from Greenwich in front of the Royal Naval College or by road. The tavern holds an important place in the rich history of the area.

It was first established in 1837 but there has been some sort of drinking hole on the site for hundreds of years. It has hosted many a famous personality including Charles Dickens who used it in his novel *Our Mutual Friend* as the venue for a wedding celebration. Perhaps that was where the present owners got the idea from!

It is also where the Whitebait Dinners are held by the Saints and Sinners Club every October. This exclusive club is packed to the gills with famous personalities, MPs and even cabinet ministers and has been meeting here since 1837.

On the ground floor is the pub and restaurant with the private suites upstairs. The Nelson Room which is a regency-style banqueting hall is decorated in creams and red with rich pink drapes. The room is divided into 2 sections one of which has a dance floor and balcony, the other is just a square space. They can be separated by a curtain.

All down one side are windows which overlook the river giving the room a sense of space and light. The ceiling is high with classic mouldings picked out in a square pattern. The room can be used both for the ceremony and the reception. There is a little ante-room where a smaller reception could be held which has a connecting door to the bar.

The bar is totally decked out like a ship with a huge mast and rigging bang in the middle of the room. Two small staircases, one either side, go up to a little balcony which forms a sort of minstrels gallery. The naval theme is continued in the pictures of ships along the walls. You can even hire a resident actor to play Nelson for the night! The room holds up to 50 people.

The Trafalgar Tavern offers a huge range of facilities with a great choice of both catering and entertainment. Their flexible menu can be tailored to your needs and budget. The maximum number of people the place will hold is 300. They have a dance floor and a disco can be hired or they can provide a band. There is a white baby grand piano so you can have live music.

The staff can also arrange flowers and most other extras if you wish. Alison the banqueting coordinator and Mike the banqueting manager are both bright and enthusiastic about their new venture and very keen to help in any way.

Menus at the Trafalgar start at £7 a head for finger buffets, £21 a head for a sit-down meal exclusive of wine, with gourmet buffet at around £25 a head.

The Trafalgar Tavern definitely clings to its naval history and grandeur which sets it apart from your average wedding venue. Each of the rooms has a very individual style and the variety of spaces means most weddings could be accommodated here with ease. Add to this its riverside setting and you have one of the better value venues in the capital.

Contact: Alison Riches
Main road: A102
Station: Greenwich BR
Disabled access: Yes
Parking: Small private car park
Registrar tel no: 0181 854 7205
Bedrooms: 0
Wedding only: No

Name: **Cannizaro House**
Address: **West Side, Wimbledon Common, London SW19 4US**
Tel: **0181 879 1464**

Cannizaro House is a country house hotel with a difference. Its unique combination of town and country makes a very special London venue. Tucked away in the south east corner of Wimbledon Common the approach does nothing to prepare you for such a lovely Georgian building. The back of the house looks out over Cannizaro Park and the rolling lawns help to create the peaceful atmosphere which gives it such a rural feel.

Cannizaro House started life as the home of the Commissioner of Customs for George I and was then owned by the Governor of the Bank of England. Later it became the residence of the Duke of Cannizaro, a penniless Sicilian count who married a wealthy Englishwoman. Thanks to her generous patronage it became a centre of musical life around London.

The late 19th century saw a succession of illustrious residents including Lord Auckland and a dashing Indian maharaja. Later on it became the scene of glamorous garden parties attended by the literati of the day including Oscar Wilde and Henry James. Today the house still plays host to the rich and famous but within the setting of a luxurious hotel.

Grandeur and comfort are the order of the day here. The rooms are all richly furnished. You enter the lounge bar immediately after going through the hotel's reception area and this would be a lovely place to greet wedding guests with a drink, on arrival, particularly in winter. It has a huge fireplace and its thick curtains and carpets and comfy chairs and sofas all serve to create a cosy atmosphere. In the summer you could walk through the double doors at the other end of the room and on to the terrace which looks out over the park.

There are several lovely spots to take photographs within the grounds. The formal sunken garden and gothic aviary would both provide beautiful backdrops for those special photos. There is also an open-air theatre as well as an ornamental pond.

The Queen Elizabeth Room is the

wedding room and holds around 60 people. There are 3 windows down one wall with views out across the park. The alcoves on either side of the windows are filled with flowers. There is a grandfather clock leaning against one wall with a gilt mirror on the other. The lovely mouldings on the high ceiling surround a central chandelier. Although the room is grand and sumptuous, with its thick carpet and curtains, it still has the same cosy feeling as the lounge.

There are 3 main rooms where you can have your reception. The Viscount Melville Suite is made up of 3 interconnecting rooms so it can cater for the smallest party or up to 80 people. The other 2 rooms are smaller. The blue room seats 30 and has a huge bay window overlooking the park. It is rich with oak panelling throughout and has a large stone fireplace at one end. This would be perfect for a winter wedding with a log fire blazing in the grate. For larger parties you could use this room for drinks before the reception.

David Murray is in charge of weddings and is happy to provide almost anything you could wish for. He does not encourage loud music as you might imagine but he can recommend people to play the harp, piano or guitar. He can arrange a competitive wedding package at £70 a head which we would recommend as it includes everything including being treated like royalty!

We thought Cannizaro House could provide a very special wed-

ding for central London. It is appropriate for all sorts of different styles of marriage but a more traditional one would go down best. It would be a lovely place to have a Christmas wedding. The lounge is traditionally decorated at that time of year and would provide a wonderful seasonal backdrop for photographs.

Contact: David Murray
Main road: A3/M25
Station: Wimbledon BR and Underground
Disabled access: Yes
Parking: Up to 90
Registrar tel no: 0181 540 5011
Bedrooms: 46
Wedding only: No

Name: **Sutton House**
Address: **2 & 4 Homerton High Street, Hackney, London E9 1EA**
Tel: **0181 986 2264**

Sutton House is set in the heart of urban Hackney but despite its surroundings it provides a tranquil setting for a wedding party. It comes as a complete surprise as you walk through busy street markets, to find Sutton House tucked away from the roadside. The contrast between the noisy street life outside and the cool, quiet interior gives it a very special atmosphere. It is an urban stately home.

The house dates back to the 16th century when it was the home of Ralph Sadleir, a privy councillor and diplomat. Later it became a merchant's house, a girls' school and then home of some Huguenot silk merchants. It is a fascinating mish-mash of dark oak-panelled rooms ranging from the 16th century to Georgian times.

The wedding room is in the Great Chamber – a large panelled room with a wooden floor which holds 50 people. The heavy almost oppressive character of the dark wood is balanced by the light which streams in through the windows on both sides. Each window has its own window-seat and the whole effect is simple yet stately. Definitely 'seemly and dignified', we could see why it had no problem getting licensed.

You can if you want just choose to have your wedding ceremony at Sutton House. If you do stay for a reception you can use one of 2 Tudor rooms although the panelling makes them rather dark. The large hall is a better size and can hold up to 150. It has a pitched roof with supporting beams. It is rather a functional room of a later period without the romance of the stately home but nevertheless would be great for a reception.

Outside is a small cloistered courtyard which provides a beautiful backdrop for all your wedding photos. Drinks could also be taken out here either before or after the ceremony. Music can be provided but they do not encourage disco music. Acoustic music would fit better with the general ambience of the place.

The key word at Sutton House is flexibility. Carole Mills who organizes the weddings has no hard and fast rules about what you can or can't do although she does point out that, for fire reasons, there is no smoking. She is prepared to do as much or as little towards your wedding as you want. A list of contacts can be provided to help you to arrange cars and flowers or you can leave every last detail up to her.

To hire the wedding room costs £80 with an extra £130 if you decide to hire the large hall. You can get away with catering at around £17.50 a head including wine or a finger buffet starts at around £13.50 a head.

We thought Sutton House was good value and a unique place to have a wedding. If you are on a tight budget it provides a lovely stately home with a relaxed atmosphere at a very reasonable price. It is versatile but we thought it would suit a smaller wedding.

Contact: Carole Mills
Main road: A102/A10
Station: Hackney Central Underground
Disabled access: To reception rooms
Parking: Restricted
Registrar tel no: 0181 986 3123
Bedrooms: 0
Wedding only: Yes

Name: Havering Register Office
Address: Langtons, Billet Lane, Hornchurch, Essex RM11 1XL
Tel: 01708 773481

Langtons in Hornchurch is the register office every registrar in London would give their eye-teeth to get hold of. They all envy the staff there saying that it has everything a register office should have – a lovely building, beautiful grounds and a lake.

They are right, Langtons is a stunning location and for the price of a standard register office wedding couples get the chance to wander round the grounds and end up with photos worthy of a marriage at a stately home. And, if they time it right, they can also have a reception on site for a very reasonable price. The only drawback is that parts of the building are in need of some good decoration to really bring it up to modern standards.

The register office is just opposite the modern Queens Theatre in Hornchurch. When you arrive the first impression is that you must be in the wrong place as the entrance is off the car park at the back of the building. It looks as if you have arrived at the stables. Hardly surprising as that is exactly what the building next door originally was – today it is offices for Havering Council's staff.

The entrance to the register office is through a small Georgian door and along a rather strange glass-sided colonnaded tunnel. It's a sort of early version of a conservatory and is a great spot for photographs. The end of the tunnel opens up into the hall of the house with french windows opposite revealing the fabulous gardens beyond.

Langtons was built as a large Georgian family home for the Massu family. They were Huguenot refugees who had become wealthy silk merchants in the City of London. At the time it was the largest private house in Hornchurch and the locals were suitably impressed by its extensive gardens and ornamental lake.

There are 2 wedding rooms, one either side of the main hall. One has recently been tastefully redecorated in blue with a Wedgwood blue ceiling, blue velvet curtains and a maroon carpet. The registrar's table is at the far end of the room in front of 3 large Georgian windows giving the couple and their guests fabulous views on to the grounds.

The other wedding room has beautiful Georgian proportions, an oak fire surround and equally splendid views over the gardens, this time looking at a Cedar of Lebanon. However, it has to be said that the room does need redecorating. The pale lemon walls and cream regency striped wallpaper combined with some ugly sixties lights do not do justice to the room's potential.

At present the music system is rather limited but the registrars try their best to make sure everyone has a wonderful day. They have had themed weddings including one couple who came dressed as roundhead and cavalier. Another couple wanted to have a candlelit wedding and the registrar arranged for them to have the last wedding of the day. They were married by candlelight at dusk. Whoever said registrars aren't romantics at heart?

After the ceremony the newly-weds and guests leave the wedding room and wander round the grounds to find a good spot for photos. The gardens slope down to a lake with a fountain. On one side is a small orangery filled with exotic plants. If the children are getting bored send them down to the lake to look for terrapins. They were introduced some years ago and to everyone's surprise have flourished.

Langtons also has a function hall in the building that can be hired for wedding receptions. It has a purpose-built bar at one end, holds about 80 people and there are french windows that open on to the grounds. Catering is supplied by council-approved caterers according to your needs.

The weddings are charged at the national standard fees and the hall can be hired for a modest £67.20 for 3 hours or about £120 for an afternoon and evening function.

An ideal arrangement would be to have the last wedding on Saturday followed by drinks in the grounds and a reception in the hall afterwards. But do be warned, Langtons is very popular and can be quite busy on a summer Saturday morning. So if you want to have a really quiet wedding try to arrange it on a weekday.

Contact: Superintendent registrar
Main road: A127
Station: Hornchurch Underground
Disabled access: Yes
Parking: Plenty in Queens Theatre car park

Name: **Templeton House**
Address: **118 Priory Lane, Roehampton, London SW15 5JW**
Tel: **0181 878 1672**

On the edge of Richmond Park is a fantastic listed building set in ornate grounds which for a while was home to the late great Winston Churchill.

The house dates back to 1778 and has been home to a number of distinguished families. In fact it takes its name from one of its owners, Lady Templeton, who lived there in 1786. During the 19th century the house was lived in by Lord Langdale, a well-known law reformer who had originally intended to become a London physician. Early in his medical studies his health broke down and he was forced to give up and take up law. His reputation for fairness and thoroughness grew and he was instrumental in the founding of the Public Records Office.

The 1861 census reveals that after the death of Lord Langdale the house was bought by a general merchant called William Goschen who proved more prolific than his predecessor but 'seems to have had some difficulties in marrying off his daughters', according to the records.

In 1919 when Freddie Guest was the name on the electoral roll at Templeton, Winston Churchill and his wife came to live here for a short while and the 2 families shared the household expenses. In 1930 the Templeton Estate was split up and sold to the Froebel Educational Institute for the princely sum of £14,000. Froebel pioneered a gentle and dignified system of education and chose Roehampton to be the heart of the Froebel movement in this country.

Today the spacious public rooms on the ground floor and the surrounding formal gardens have been opened up as a venue to bring in some much needed cash for the Institute. Weddings are a new departure for them but there is no reason why it should not succeed as the venue is truly glorious.

The Langdale Room was the first room to be licensed. It has cream and beige walls, parquet floors and a rather old woven carpet. Huge casement windows overlook the stone terraces with their iron railings. Beyond you can see the rolling green lawns with their one and only Cedar of Lebanon which looks rather lonely since its partner was demolished in the gales of 1984.

After the ceremony you can come out through the huge double doors into the hall which has white pillars and marble flooring. You could have post-wedding drinks served here. Wedding photos can be taken in the carefully laid out grounds which include 3 lawns, a putting green and a lovely pond.

The second wedding room is the dining room which is almost entirely done out in wooden panelling. The highly polished parquet floors and massive oak table give it the atmosphere of a very grand refectory. The huge Georgian windows bathe the room in light and you could take your vows just in front of them overlooking the garden.

The Churchill Room has beige panelled walls and parquet floors. The ceiling is painted pale and sea green. Great lumbering pieces of antique furniture are all around. The huge bay windows which overlook the garden are bordered by stylish and simple cream and olive green drapes. Circular tables are laid out in here for the reception.

There is a very attractive room upstairs which has been set aside as a changing room for the bride but there are no bedrooms to stay in. The cost of hiring Templeton is £800. Catering is done by Clare Johnston of Clare's Fare who has been doing wedding receptions for donkey's years. Canapés range from £6.50 a head to £8. A full sit-down meal will set you back £20–£25 a head and they will charge £5 a head corkage if you bring your own wine.

We thought Templeton was amazingly good value for the sort of venue it is – a very classy place to marry. We particularly liked the dining room which has a very nice atmosphere and thought a medium-sized wedding here would be ideal.

Contact: Jill Leney
Main road: A3
Station: Barnes or Putney BR or East Putney Underground
Disabled access: Yes
Parking: Good
Registrar tel no: 0181 871 6120
Bedrooms: 0
Wedding only: Yes

Name: The Ritz
Address: 150 Piccadilly, London
WIV 9DG
Tel: 0171 493 8181

There are no words eloquent enough to describe the Ritz Hotel in the heart of London. Opulence, sumptuousness, even extravagance could all be used but somehow the real essence of this extraordinary venue would be missed.

Going through the revolving doors of the Ritz is an almost theatrical experience as you enter a sort of fantasy world from a bygone era inhabited by all sorts of glittering starlets, writers, poets and famous names in politics not to mention royalty. Just sitting in the Palm Court, with its extravagantly sculptured fountain, glass roof and panelled mirrors of bevelled glass, taking tea feels like decadence in the extreme.

César Ritz was born the thirteenth child of a Swiss shepherd. When he was an apprentice wine waiter at the age of 16 he was told by his boss he would never make anything of himself in the hotel business. 'It takes a special knack, a special flair, and it's only right that I should tell you – you haven't got it,' he proceeded to tell young Ritz. Lucky for us the lad went on to prove him spectacularly wrong.

He headed for cosmopolitan Paris where he eventually settled. His special flair became apparent when he took a job at the Hotel Splendide where he quickly recognized the value of the American clientele – he was the only waiter to serve iced water without being asked. It was this attention to detail which was to pay dividends in his later life.

However it was not until 1906 that Ritz was really to make an impression on London society when he opened the hotel which bears his name and where you could get a double room with a private bath for 30 shillings.

The hotel was modelled on the Palace of Versailles, with gold leaf cascading down over doorways, fluted columns and a restaurant which is laden with mirrored chandeliers.

According to Barbara Cartland, after the First World War the Ritz became 'rather a stuffy place but still the place for tea'. She added it was the only place where one could meet young men without a chaperone for lunch and tea, 'so you had lunch with men you were keen on and tea with the rest'.

It was the place to go to keep up appearances even if you could not really afford it. Tea was half-a-crown a head – quite a lot when you consider that 7 shillings would buy you a complete dinner at the Trocadero.

And so it still is, but now if you want to 'keep up appearances' you can get married here. The Trafalgar Suite, where the hallway is decorated in deep blue velvet with ornate gilt wall lights and a white marble floor, is truly spectacular. The wedding room is decorated entirely in cream and gold with huge cream drapes at the windows which overlook Green Park. There is a sense of exquisite opulence about it although the room itself will only hold around 15–20 people. You then wander through to the cream dining room with its beautiful mahogany inlaid table which seats up to 20.

If you fancy something a little more lavish try the restaurant which has been described as the sanctuary of the hotel. Here you can take your vows under the extraordinary ceiling with its trompe l'oeil of a celestial sky. Once married you can move through to the Marie Antoinette Suite done in fabulous tones of dusky pink and great floor-to-ceiling mirrors. Pre-wedding drinks can be taken just outside near the Palm Court.

Needless to say there is nothing the Ritz cannot lay on for you but it does not come cheap. A guideline to costs for 10–24 people is £120 a head, but the food is pretty spectacular and that does include the hire of the room. Optional extras include a wedding cake at around £200, a string quartet from £375 and a dance band from £600.

Kate Walton who arranges the wedding will pull out all the stops to make it a great day. She recommends the Trafalgar Suite for the height of elegance and a more intimate wedding. 'You can have a wedding in complete privacy here making it a stylish, intimate and very personal occasion.'

The Ritz is not the sort of place where you start asking lots of questions about the cost of things and as such would make an ideal venue for someone whose parents were footing the bill and who wanted a delightful setting soaked in atmosphere.

Contact: Kate Walton
Main road: Piccadilly
Station: Green Park Underground
Disabled access: Yes
Parking: Nearby
Registrar tel no: 0171 798 1160
Bedrooms: 130
Wedding only: Negotiable

Name: Westminster Register Office
Address: Westminster Council House, Marylebone Road, London NW1 5PT
Tel: 0171 798 1162

If you are familiar with the streets of London you may well have driven past Westminster Register Office many times without realizing it was there. Set on the Marylebone Road just past Madame Tussaud's the impressive building has 2 huge stone lions guarding its steps.

The main hall is pretty imposing. Two grand marble staircases sweep off to meet on an ornate balcony overlooking the great hall. Photographs of the bride taken on the stairs would be pretty spectacular.

Alison Cathcart is the superintendent registrar here and is terribly enthusiastic about the new wedding law. Young and dynamic she has already ordered Jacques Vert outfits for her female staff, foxglove with a black trim, and smart suits for the men.

Although she believes the registrar's job will become much more interesting now they have the chance to get out and about visiting new venues, she is also extremely proud of the marriage rooms at Westminster – and rightly so.

The first room is quite grand with its cream panelled walls and blue carpet. The vast windows give it plenty of light and the potted plants lend it an informal atmosphere. The registrar sits at a huge mahogany table and formal rows of seats for the guests make it feel a little like a church. This room seats between 25 and 30 guests but for larger weddings the Reception Room can be used.

The Reception Room has a splendid ceiling with all sorts of fancy fretwork and cornicing whilst the walls are wood panelled. This spectacular room seats 50 but can accommodate up to 100 if your guests do not mind standing.

The Waiting Room looks more like a sitting room than a wedding room. Cream walls and a sea green carpet give it an almost Mediterranean air. The cosy armchairs arranged around a small circular table in front of the fireplace make it feel like home. Alison is quite happy to conduct the ceremony in front of the fire with the couple seated in the armchairs. 'The more relaxed they are the better,' she says.

Although the rooms do have some traffic noise it is not intrusive. Photographs can either be taken indoors on the grand staircases or outside on the steps leading down to the road. Fresh flowers are changed twice weekly so they never look sad and Alison is keen for the couple to have music or any readings they may want.

For their reception, couples can whizz round the corner to Baker Street where there is a wide range of restaurants and pubs. Or failing that they could have a big do at one of the posher hotels in nearby Mayfair or Park Lane.

This register office competes with Kensington and Chelsea for their list of famous couples. Two of the Beatles were married here and others include Nicole Farhi, John Hurt and Mel Smith. Never one to miss an opportunity Alison is getting someone to go through the register picking out celebrity names. She thought a hall of fame on the walls might be amusing.

Alison is a great believer that the register office is here to stay. 'Some people want a simple ceremony without a lot of fuss. For example one couple had not even told their family. They just went into the local Alfred Marks office and asked 2 people to be their witnesses. It was still a really lovely ceremony.'

Contact: Alison Cathcart
Main road: Marylebone Road
Station: Baker Street Underground
Disabled access: Limited
Parking: None

**Name: Waltham Forest Register
Office**
**Address: 106 Grove Road,
Walthamstow, London E17 9EY**
Tel: 0181 520 8617

Walthamstow is one of the nicer
suburbs of East London with its
bustling street market and newly-
designed pedestrianized shopping
centre. Walthamstow village dates
back to the Middle Ages and re-
sembles an old-fashioned English
village with olde worlde pubs and
a pretty local church.

The register office is on the
corner of Grove Road and Fraser
Road both of which are fairly
busy. The house itself is a double-
fronted Victorian rectory with a
semi-circular entrance porch. Outside there is a stone lovers' seat
where the happy couple can have
photographs taken with a backdrop
of lovely shrubs and flowers.

The entrance hall could be beautiful and the council has promised
funds for the restoration of its
former Victorian glory. There is a
glorious staircase leading to a balcony which overlooks the hallway.
As soon as you come into the building you are greeted by a cheery
member of staff who immediately
makes you feel at home and is not
the least bit stuffy.

The same goes for Gerald Joseet,
superintendent registrar, who is
keen to encourage people to have
whatever sort of wedding they
want. He helps them make selec-
tions of music which can be played

during the ceremony on the discreetly hidden CD player. They
even had a steel band playing in a
corner one year.

The wedding room itself is
simply but tastefully furnished and
has a lovely set of french windows
opening on to the rose garden at
the back. When we visited the
windows were open and the white
muslin curtains were billowing into
the room in the breeze.

The room is panelled in light oak
and furnished with reproduction
antiques. The whole effect is a little
like a rather comfy sitting room.
After the ceremony the bride and
groom go out of a side door on to
steps under the wrought-iron
canopy where they can have their
photos taken.

If you want something special
staff are on hand to help you. 'We
like to think it is their big day and
we want it to go as smoothly as
possible,' says Gerald. 'We have
had all sorts of marriages here from
simple traditional white weddings
to ethnic weddings and even a wild
west one where they all wore jeans,
check shirts and waistcoats!'

For those who want a small wedding Walthamstow is ideal and if
you want a big bash afterwards
most people go to the Waltham
Forest Assembly Hall which can
cater for up to 1,000. For smaller
receptions there is a wide range of
pubs in the village.

It is also worth noting that
Walthamstow trains some of its
staff in British sign language and
there are others around who under-

stand a variety of languages. (Extensive use is also made of Waltham Forest translation and interpreting service.)

Parking is not brilliant – there is a small car park but we were assured there was no problem parking in the side road. We thought it was a lovely venue for someone on a small budget but who still wants something special.

Contact: Gerald Joseet
Main road: M11
Station: Walthamstow Central BR and Underground
Disabled access: Yes
Parking: Locally

Name: The Kensington Roof Gardens
Address: 99 Kensington High Street, London W8 5ED
Tel: 0171 937 7994

The Kensington Roof Gardens were built in 1938 and were the largest of their kind in Europe standing 100 feet above Kensington High Street on top of what was then one of London's best known department stores – Derry and Toms.

The 1½ acres of fertile gardens were originally designed around 3 themes – the Spanish Garden with its court of fountains and formal design, the Tudor garden constructed in old red brick, and the woodland garden complete with streams, ducks and flamingos.

Since then it has flourished as a private members club on Thursday and Saturday evenings and a fabulous venue which has hosted product launches, corporate parties, wedding receptions, and now of course you can be married here.

The Clubhouse is where you will get married. The room has many moods – bright and airy during the day, or divided into 2 to give a more intimate atmosphere. There is a spacious summery reception area which leads out on to the woodland garden. Potted plants and cool tiling on the floor give it a slightly colonial feel.

The main part of the room has dark blue carpet with a star and moon pattern, the walls are quite simply decorated and the ceiling is low. There is a tremendous feeling of light however as windows fill one side of the room. The second half of the room has a sunken dance floor where the wedding will take place.

It is hard to do credit to the Roof Gardens in so few words – suffice it to say it is an incredibly flexible venue both in terms of space and in imaginative themes. Magicians, stilt walkers, illusionists, clowns and mime artists are just a few of the attractions that have been laid on as part of an event. There is a full disco system and a DJ can be hired for the night. Any sort of music can be catered for from solo musicians to a big brass band.

A sit-down meal at the Roof Gardens will set you back between £25 and £45 a head. During the day there is a minimum spend of £3,000 and night-time rates vary. You cannot hire the venue on Thursday or Saturday nights.

For a stunning location slap bang

in the middle of the city we can't fault the Roof Gardens. It is a unique setting high above the hubbub of life at street level. The gardens are absolutely glorious and if you want truly fabulous wedding photos this is where to go. We would recommend an Arabian Nights themed wedding with the ceremony in the main room followed by a blessing under one of the Moorish arches which are dotted around the place. A dinner and dance in the main room would finish off the day.

Contact: Rachel Ollis
Main Road: Kensington High Street
Station: Paddington BR/Kensington High Street Underground
Disabled access: Yes
Parking: Valet parking in the evening
Registrar tel no: 0171 351 3941
Bedrooms: 0
Wedding only: No

Name: Wandsworth Register Office
Address: Wandsworth Town Hall, Wandsworth High Street, London SW18 2PU
Tel: 0181 871 6120/1

If you want to be sure your wedding is going to go without a hitch you'd better get married in Wandsworth Town Hall. They have the Charter Mark awarded to them by John Major in 1993 and they do their utmost to live up to it. 'We wish you both a happy, carefree and memorable wedding day' is the slogan on their glossy brochure which contains everything you need

to know – from how to avoid the wedding from hell, down to a choice of appropriate readings and music. 'To make the music list easier for people to understand, we wrote a more up-to-date reference next to the original name. So for Ravel's "Bolero", for example, we put the "music from Torvill and Dean"!' says registrar John Charnley.

At Wandsworth weddings are customized for each couple – as long as it can be construed as 'seemly and dignified' – of course. One wedding saw the groom dressed as the lead character in the *King and I* while the bride was resplendent in a tutu. Another had clowns. 'It can be fun but still dignified – the two are not mutually exclusive,' explains John Charnley.

There are 3 wedding rooms, each one elegant but contrasting in design and decoration. The first is the Council Chamber which would be ideal for a traditional wedding where the bride wants to process down the aisle on her father's arm. They even have baby-changing facilities should the couple already have started their family! Over 100 guests fit comfortably in this room with possibly another 30 or 40 on the balcony. The ceiling has an attractive art deco glass dome which gives the room plenty of light.

The other two rooms, each accommodating about 50 guests, are very elegant with wood panelling and leather seats which tone in with each colour scheme. Couples choose their own music and in one room Frank Sinatra was belting out 'New

York, New York' while in the other there were the strains of some rather sombre baroque music. Fresh flowers are replaced twice weekly so that the couple who come in on Monday do not get the wilted bunch from the previous Friday!

The Town Hall has some interesting film connections too. It was used to film Hitler's headquarters and it has also been the White House and Downing Street in its time. The register office has excellent new disabled access and facilities. The Town Hall gardens, central courtyard and art deco marble hallway make excellent settings for photos after the ceremony.

'Couples say they like it here because we understand that it's their wedding. The place is run for them not for the staff,' says Colin Hardy, superintendent registrar. 'Provided you keep within the law and don't trash or trivialize it we will bend over backwards to make sure your day is as special as it can be.'

Contact: Colin Hardy
Main road: Wandsworth High Street
Station: Clapham Junction BR, East Putney Underground
Disabled access: Excellent
Parking: Ample

Name: Brent Register Office
Address: Town Hall, Forty Lane, Wembley HA9 9EZ
Tel: 0181 908 7191

Dedication, proficiency, reliability and adaptability are essential requirements for anyone organizing a wedding and where better to find these qualities than in the staff of the Brent Register Office. Although burdened with as many as 9 ceremonies a day, Mark Rimmer, the superintendent registrar, and his team, do their utmost to make your day as personalized and as stress free as possible.

At first sight Brent Town Hall looks more like a law court than a potential wedding venue. Once inside you are greeted by an equally disheartening mass of signs informing you of local activities and distant offices. Yet once you negotiate your way to the register office the building undergoes a dramatic transformation.

The whole reception area has the appearance of a local surgery waiting room, with bright overhead lighting and blue sofas which surround the central pillars. A large transparent mineral water dispenser with conic paper cups adds the final touch to the professional, if somewhat sterile, ambience.

Things are, however, rarely as they seem and a brief talk to any of the friendly staff shows another picture. Whilst all arrangements are carried out in the reception area, on the day of the wedding guests enter through a small garden gate at the side of the Town Hall. From there they move into an L-shaped waiting room, decked with an array of flowers and comfortable blue sofas.

Here the couple can talk to their guests in the tense moments prior to the ceremony. The guests are then led into the adjoining marriage room. This provides seating for 40 people in the traditional aisle formation with standing room for another 30. The couple can then be married under the council coat of arms which bears a motto with the appropriate words 'forward together'.

The marriage room opens on to some beautiful gardens. After the service guests can roam in a park-like setting which provides a perfect backdrop for wedding photos.

The staff pride themselves on attempting to make your wedding as personal as possible, allowing the couple as much leeway as they can. Ethnic ceremonies, fancy dress and theme or punk weddings have all been catered for in the past. The wedding room itself is equipped with a modern stereo system to allow you to create your own atmosphere.

The wedding room is equipped with a loop system for the hard of hearing and has good disabled access. The high demands on the office mean that time is limited as there can be as many as 3 weddings running simultaneously. Usually guests are only allowed a maximum of half an hour in the marriage room and a further half-hour in the gardens.

Costs here are low. The basic fee is only £25.50. There are a number of nearby hotels where you can have a reasonably priced reception. The Town Hall also has a large function room with a raised stage at one end and seating for around 1,000 people which can be hired for a reception. For those wanting a really lavish do Wembley Stadium is only 5 minutes' walk down the road.

Contact: Mark Rimmer
Main road: A4088
Station: Wembley Park Underground
Disabled access: Yes
Parking: Ample

Name: **Searcy's**
Address: **30 Pavilion Rd, Knightsbridge, London SWIX OHJ**
Tel: **0171 823 9212**

Searcy's is a catering company that has created a Georgian town house in the highly fashionable area of Knightsbridge purely to entertain. It is now a beautifully decorated and elegant London home but it started life as something very different.

Searcy's was founded in 1847 when it was a pastry and confectionery company. 30 Pavilion Road was taken over by Searcy's to be one of their warehouses and it was also the site of their bakery. It first opened its doors to party-goers 30 years ago and has been playing host to private functions ever since.

Its outward appearance is quite misleading, tucked away on a small street behind Sloane Street with a flat façade with plain windows stretching up 5 storeys. It is painted in a rather striking yellow that draws your attention to this corner house. This does nothing however to prepare you for the interior.

Searcy's is now a luxurious venue for the exclusive use of whoever chooses to hire it. By furnishing 30 Pavilion Road with original Georgian and Victorian fittings they have created a sumptuous yet homely atmosphere. It is meant to be seen as a comfortable and convenient alternative to your own home and that is exactly what it feels like.

Whether you want a quiet wedding for 20 or a huge do for 250 the house can be adapted to suit any occasion – and because it was literally designed for entertaining there is plenty of room for dancing with no need to worry about moving the furniture!

You enter through a black door straight into the hallway. This is no ordinary wallpaper-and-stripped-pine-floorboards affair. Instead there is a black and white marble floor and stone walls that have been created by the magic of an artist using the trompe l'oeil technique. This, combined with a roaring log fire in the large marble fireplace and the ornate plasterwork, creates a very special effect. It is a perfect place for drinks or a winter wedding.

To your left there is an entrance that leads off into the Dining Room. Decorated with bottle green fabric wallcoverings it is an ideal place for dancing having its own wooden dance floor. It is quite small and could also be used for an intimate ceremony or reception. It can be made into a bigger space if the hall is used as well.

For a larger party there are 3 rooms upstairs, a Library, a Ballroom and an ante-room that joins the two. The Library has pine panelling and floor-to-ceiling bookshelves lining 2 walls. The shelves contain old, heavily-bound company ledgers. Opposite is a fireplace, again surrounded by books. The red carpet and the subdued lighting from all the lamps around the room together with another log fire create a warm and homely atmosphere.

The Ballroom has a different feel. The walls are a warm yellow, it has a parquet floor, mirrors and chandeliers are Victorian and the light fittings have Georgian sconces. Although they have been imported from other houses they look remarkably comfortable together. The Ballroom is the biggest room in the house and would seat about 70 for the ceremony.

Searcy's is a classy venue that has been furnished with the utmost taste. The whole house is given over to one event at a time so you have the entire place to yourself no matter what the size of your party is. This gives you not only a private venue but also an enormous amount of flexibility. Searcy's has licensed all of its rooms so you can have the ceremony wherever you like.

Searcy's also has 12 bedrooms on the top floors of the house. They are individually decorated with high quality furnishings. The bedrooms are all unusually shaped. One even has a bath in it – ideal for a champagne wedding night! The rooms can be used by the wedding party at a discount. For extra guests Searcy's also owns 2 flats on the Brompton Road for which they charge £100 a night.

A top-class catering company, Searcy's can hardly fail to deliver the goods when it comes to your reception. The maximum number of guests for a seated meal is 150 and for a stand-up do about 250. Remember you have the whole house so you can wander around with your plate of food and choose to sit where you like. There is a large choice on the menus which vary in price – the larger your party the cheaper the prices become. For 50 guests having a sit-down meal, prices would start at about £40 exclusive of wine. For 100 guests this goes down to about £35. A buffet starts at £25 a head for about 50 people and goes down to £17 for 100. To hire the house will set you back £750. This price goes up to £1,000 in December, their busy season.

Searcy's provides you with a warm but grand backdrop for your wedding. It is a venue best suited to a medium-sized wedding and would be wonderful in the winter with the log fires burning and the Christmas decorations making the whole place feel like home.

Contact: James Melville
Main road: Sloane Street
Station: Knightsbridge Underground
Disabled access: Yes
Parking: Nearby
Registrar tel no: 0171 351 3941

Bedrooms: 12
Wedding only: No

Name: **Greenwich Register Office**
Address: **Town Hall, Wellington St, Woolwich SE18 6PW**
Tel: **0181 854 7205**

Greenwich Register Office is housed in Woolwich Town Hall on busy Wellington Street. It has all the bustle of a busy inner city area as shoppers make their way down to Woolwich shopping centre and market.

As you walk up the hill from the shops a perfect example of a Victorian town hall comes into view. It is a redbrick building with a bell tower and dome on top. As with most Victorian buildings the façade is highly decorated, in this case with 3 oval stained-glass windows. The central one is surrounded by a large arch with columns on either side.

You walk up a small flight of steps under a small columned canopy. Once inside there are more stairs and then there is a sight to behold – a perfectly formed jewel of the municipal architect's art. A veritable toytown of a town hall! The sort of place where you expect to be greeted by a proper mayor with a huge gold chain and a three-cornered hat.

Unfortunately in these days of government cutbacks that is not possible but nevertheless Greenwich Council has done a wonderful job preserving the magnificent hall of this building. It has a black and white patterned marble floor leading directly to a small but dramatic marble staircase which dominates the end of the room. Half-way up there is a landing and the staircase divides with the steps leading up to either side of the first floor balcony that encircles the space.

The balcony is supported by columns and topped with semi-circular stained-glass windows. The highly decorated ceiling has 3 domes which combined with the tasteful colour scheme create a real feeling of space and light.

The staircase and hallway make a lovely backdrop for wedding photos. No wonder Greenwich Register Office is now so popular.

It has to be said that whilst the wedding room is very welcoming it is not particularly special. There is plenty of light from the windows and the colour scheme is based around wood panelled walls, pink curtains and a purple carpet. The room is set up theatre-style facing the registrar's desk and can accommodate a fair-sized wedding party.

At the time we visited the registrar, Tony Jarman, was busily organizing himself for an Afro-Caribbean wedding. Tony is proud of the service that his office provides to the whole community. He says that they take a very flexible approach to the wedding ceremony and are always willing to accommodate people's requests for readings and music. As with every registrar he is limited by the time available.

Themed weddings are no problem. In fact over the years he has had couples in all manner of unusual attire. Tony takes the view that it is their day so they can dress how they like. He welcomes the changes to the wedding law but feels that there will always be a place for the local register office that provides a reasonably priced ceremony while still paying attention to the needs of every individual couple.

After the wedding couples on a tight budget could pop over the road to the Director General, one of Woolwich's most famous pubs. Others could go to a number of local restaurants or head off to some of the posher establishments in Greenwich for their reception.

The Greenwich Register Office is a fine venue for a wedding. You can have a friendly ceremony in one of London's smallest and most perfectly formed municipal buildings. And if you want to have some really unusual wedding photos why not head down the road and take a trip across the river on the Woolwich Ferry. Who's to know you're not off to a romantic honeymoon in France?

Contact: Tony Jarman
Main road: A205
Station: Woolwich Arsenal BR
Disabled access: Yes, via lift
Parking: Nearby

Name: Le Gothique
Address: Fitzhugh Grove, Trinity Road, London SW18 3SX
Tel: 0181 870 6567

Le Gothique is situated in a peculiar position – behind a housing estate just off the busy Trinity Road in the heart of Clapham. It is the contrast between this extraordinary gothic building and its surroundings which makes it a truly amazing sight.

It was originally built as an orphanage in 1857 for dependants of servicemen lost in the Crimean War. The gothic cloisters are said to be haunted by Charlotte Jane Bennett who died in a fire in 1862. It was used as a hospital in the First World War and in the Second World War it became a detention and interrogation centre.

After that it fell into disrepair and despite its renovation it still retains a certain air of mystery and uncertainty about it. It must have something to do with the ghost which still haunts its corridors.

Now the building has been transformed and is an unlikely location for a French restaurant which has 3 parts. There is a small bar, a restaurant on a mezzanine level and a garden. The garden is completely enclosed by the building and a covered walkway around it forms the cloisters. Le Gothique were hoping to get it licensed for weddings but this has not proved possible so far.

To get to the garden you go through a rather grand doorway and find yourself in a massive foyer. This has now become the wedding room. The hallway has high white-painted walls and flagstone floors. Straight ahead is a row of archways where the bride and groom could make an impressive entrance into the garden.

The garden itself is charming, a mixture of lawn and gravel with one large tree. There are lots of lovely hanging baskets and the cloisters around it make for a very unusual backdrop for your wedding photos. There is room to seat 80 people but they can cater for more if you have a marquee.

You can hire the whole restaurant for the wedding ceremony and reception although the other two spaces are not nearly as pleasant. Because of the particular type of architecture the ceilings are quite low and there is a slight feeling of claustrophobia about it. The bar area is small but has a door which opens on to the garden and could be a good place for pre-wedding drinks.

The colour scheme throughout the restaurant is red and cream in keeping with the gothic ambience of the place. The menus are spectacular and there is plenty of flexibility. Mark Justin owns and runs the restaurant and is on hand to help you plan the best menu and help with any other wedding arrangements. He has a very business-like manner and is quick to point out the pros and cons of any arrangements. Although Le Gothique is not a large venue there is room for entertainment and certainly music. When we visited there was a barn dance in full swing so the possibilities are endless.

Prices start at around £30 a head which includes aperitif, sit-down meal, wine, the champagne toast and coffee afterwards. They have yet to work out a complete wedding package including the ceremony. The restaurant also hires out a Rolls-Royce for a really grand arrival or departure.

Le Gothique is a flamboyant and outlandish venue and is great if this is what you are looking for. We thought it would be lovely for a summer wedding.

Contact: Mark Justin
Main Road: Trinity Road
Station: Clapham Junction
Disabled access: To the garden and bar
Parking: 100 cars
Registrar tel no: 0181 871 6120
Bedrooms: 0
Wedding only: No

Name: **Burgh House**
Address: **New End Square, Hampstead NW3 1LT**
Tel: **0171 431 0144**

Burgh House is one of those classic English institutions, a beautiful old house lovingly cared for by a group of dedicated admirers and used as a centre for meetings, concerts and exhibitions.

In the heart of Hampstead, it is a magnificent Queen Anne house set back from the road on an imposing corner plot. The four-storey house was originally built in 1703 when Hampstead was a centre for visitors taking the curative waters at the Long Room in nearby Well Walk. The spa's resident doctor was a Dr William Gibbons who lived at Burgh House. Apparently the waters tasted disgusting but judging by the size of his house the good doctor must have made a handsome living out of the water business.

After many changes of ownership the house ended up in the hands of Camden Council who discovered in 1977 that it was riddled with dry rot and promptly closed it. When it looked as if the building was going to end up as commercial premises the residents formed a committee to save it. Being Hampstead it was possible to raise £50,000 in 6 months and soon the building was handed over to the Burgh House Trust.

Today it is an oasis of calm and traditional values just a few yards away from the mayhem of Hampstead High Street. The ground floor has a large hall where 2 ladies sit selling books and pamphlets about the history of the area. Opposite is the Music Room that is used for concerts and meetings. At the back of the house is a gallery space and a small library. The upstairs rooms house the Hampstead Museum, a small exhibition of local history. To finish it all off, the basement has a tea room called the Buttery which offers snacks and cakes to locals weary after battling up the High Street.

Weddings are held in the Music Room at the front of the house. It is a long thin room with 18th-century panelling and a rather splendid marble fireplace topped by a painting of Hampstead Heath. At the far end of the room, sitting in a bay window surrounded by plants, is a small grand piano or to be precise a boudoir grand. There are 5 windows looking out on to the garden which is dominated by a magnificent London plane tree.

The room can take 64 people but would be comfortable with about 50. The grand piano can be hired for weddings if the couple provide a musician. Otherwise a trio or string quartet would fit perfectly with the atmosphere of the room and the house.

After the ceremony the couple can go outside on to the small terrace overlooking the garden for photos. Alternatively the main steps of the house lead up to a magnificent porch and doorway covered in wisteria which would make a lovely backdrop. Other options include an arbour with a bench and a brightly painted hand-cart that used to belong to the local chimney sweep!

Back in the house a buffet can be held in the downstairs hall or library. Sit-down meals can also be arranged in the Music Room. The bookstall is cleared out of the hall when a reception is on, creating a large circulation space and making the place look much more homely. If the reception is held in the afternoon the guests come in the front of the house and visitors to the museum come in via the side entrance. If the reception is held in the evening the wedding party has sole use of the house. Burgh House has good disabled access. For safety reasons there is no smoking and no dancing in the building. The latter because the floor could not take the strain.

Considering its location, hire of the Music Room and hall is very reasonable at £200 for 3 hours and £65 for every extra hour. There is an additional fee of £125 for the wedding if the room is used for a wedding without a reception. If a reception is held at the house the fee drops to £50. Catering is provided by Burgh House's approved caterers and menus can be devised to suit all tastes and pockets.

Parking in Hampstead is never easy and Burgh House is no exception. However, there is a car park within walking distance and the tube is very close. Guests who want to stay overnight can use the nearby Sandringham Hotel.

Pauline Pleasance is Burgh House's administrator. She has been there for 11 years and needless to say is a great fan of the house and its role in the local community. She had organized lots of wedding receptions and is really pleased that they can now offer weddings as well, making life so much easier for couples and their families.

Burgh House is a tranquil spot in the heart of the capital. It would be ideal for an older couple or perhaps a second-time-around marriage with a small number of guests enjoying a quiet meal and drinks accompanied by a pianist or string quartet. It would also be a lovely place for an atmospheric winter wedding.

Contact: Pauline Pleasance
Main road: Hampstead High Street
Station: Hampstead Underground
Disabled access: Yes
Parking: Restricted

Registrar tel no: 0171 860 5600
Bedrooms: 0
Wedding only: Yes

Name: Chelsea Football Club
Address: Stamford Bridge Grounds,
Fulham Road, London SW6 1HS
Tel: 0171 915 1916

If you came out of Fulham Broadway tube station wearing top hat and tails or a wedding outfit most people would think that you were going to a posh wedding at Fulham Register Office just across the road.

But football-mad couples will ignore the register office and turn sharp left down the road to Stamford Bridge, home of Chelsea Football Club. Yes, it is possible to get married in the stand and then go out on to the pitch to have your photos taken. What more could any football fanatic want — provided they are not Millwall supporters.

There are 2 wedding rooms at the club — both are in the brand-new North Stand and both seat 100–120 people. The Tambling and Dixon Suites are pretty much the same. They are large, low function rooms at the back of the stand decked out in Chelsea blue with cream walls and blue banqueting chairs. The registrar has a large mahogany table with a massive flower arrangement and there is even a Chelsea blue cushion for the ring. Unfortunately the rooms do not look over the ground. One looks over the car park and the other a small clump of trees. However the positive side is that there is free parking for all the guests, which is a real bonus in this part of London.

As the rooms look very similar you will probably make your choice depending on whether you are a fan of Chelsea's legendary sixties striker Bobby Tambling or if you think Kerry Dixon was the better player. Music is no problem as the rooms are all wired for sound. Apparently the local registrar is happy for the couple to choose any music they want, as always, within reason. At one wedding they had Whitney Houston's 'I will Always Love You'. Real fans can go for the Chelsea song 'Blue is the Colour' or Glen Hoddle's favourite piece of music 'Jump' by Van Halen, but they would probably have that after the ceremony.

Once the ceremony is over the fun really begins. The wedding party go down the stairs to the North Stand concourse. Photos can be taken in front of the life-size murals depicting action shots of great Chelsea moments. Then it's up the steps and out on to the terrace for photos. Shots can be taken on the hallowed turf but not in front of the goal posts, not because Chelsea are spoilsports, the goal posts are only put up on match days. But there are lots of other possibilities. Photos can be taken coming out of the players' tunnel, in the directors' box and in the dugout in the very spot where Glen Hoddle sits on match days. One enthusiastic bride had her photo taken on the physio's couch and in the players' bath. Fortunately for the groom the bath was empty of water and players at the time!

Receptions can be held in several function rooms. By far the best is Drake's, named after Ted Drake the team manager in the fifties. Built at the back of the stand, it has a sloping roof, a bar on one side, a food counter on the other and a dance floor in the middle. It even has a balcony across the back with another bar area. Being a football club there is also a video wall, so couples can do an instant video replay of their wedding for all the guests and later in the evening watch videos of Chelsea's footballing triumphs!

Debra Ware, who organizes the weddings, says that they have been inundated with requests for information from Chelsea fans, not just Londoners. Some couples are coming all the way from Wales to tie the knot. Unfortunately it is not possible to get married on match days because all the rooms are used for functions or by the supporters' club. However, Debra can give smaller wedding parties a tour of the ground and make sure that couples get all the photos they want.

After the reception most couples head off for their honeymoon, but not, it seems, the dedicated Chelsea fan. The very first couple to get married at Stamford Bridge delayed their honeymoon to make sure they did not miss the next home game.

To cap it all the bride returned to the pitch in her full wedding gear just before the match started and got kissed by team captain Dennis Wise to the roar of the assembled crowd. And every member of the team personally autographed her wedding dress!

Weddings only at Stamford Bridge cost £200. If you have a wedding with a reception the room hire is reduced to £40. Catering charges start at about £15 per head for a buffet with wine and rise to £22 per head for a sit-down meal with wine. There is good disabled access and plenty of hotels just up the road in Kensington and Chelsea.

We think Chelsea Football Club is a great place for keen supporters to have their dream wedding complete with a pitch-shaped cake and photos taken on the turf. Given the location, prices are surprisingly reasonable. And aren't we glad we managed to get to the end of this entry without making any distasteful jokes about the possibility of a certain David Mellor getting married in a Chelsea strip?

Contact: Debra Ware
Main road: Fulham Road
Station: Fulham Broadway Underground
Disabled access: Good
Parking: Ample
Registrar tel no: 0181 576 5217
Bedrooms: 0
Wedding only: Yes

Name: Heathrow Hilton
Address: Terminal 4, Heathrow,
Hounslow TW6 3AF
Tel: 0181 759 7755

Get married at Heathrow – you must be joking! – all those jostling crowds and the roar of the planes – not at all romantic. That was our first reaction. Which just goes to show how wrong you can be. The Heathrow Hilton is a thoroughly modern wedding venue and much better than many we have seen.

Couples who want to check it out should get the tube to Heathrow, Terminal 4. Then head for the departure lounge. At the far right-hand corner a small sign directs you to the Heathrow Hilton. You then follow a long space-age tunnel, all white tubing and metal floors. After a while you begin to think you have wandered by accident on to the set of a sci-fi movie and any moment now an astronaut will float past.

However, you soon emerge blinking into the sunlight at the front of the hotel. This is no standard off-the-shelf corporate rest area but a stunning architect-designed tour de force.

The front has high-tech, dazzling white cladding and a wall of glass supported by a spiderweb of thin metal struts. The revolving doorway is probably the biggest you have ever seen, so big a whole flowerbed goes round with the door!

Inside, the high-tech theme continues. The public areas are all within a huge atrium. A glass lift rises in the centre with 4 balconies reaching out to the white walled bedroom area.

Weddings take place in the Concorde or Heathrow Suites down at the far end of the foyer. Here there is another huge glass wall, this time looking over a small lake with a fountain. The suites have a separate entrance for the bridal car and the hotel provides parking for the guests. Both suites are tastefully designed, modern function rooms. The Concorde Suite is smaller – holding up to 120 people. It has green carpet and mushroom-coloured walls. There are no windows but the ceiling has an art deco design with lots of concealed lighting rather like a modern cinema. The Heathrow Suite is much larger and can take up to 250 people.

After the ceremony, couples can have photos taken outside by the lake with the trees and fountain as a backdrop. There is even a solitary duck to add a bit of natural interest. Once outside you can hear traffic and aircraft noise however, which just makes you realize how well sound-proofed the hotel really is.

There is a light open area outside the Concorde Suite next to the glass wall and the lake which is an ideal place for a buffet – leaving the Concorde Suite for the dancing later on.

We thought couples would want to tie the knot and then have a quick glass of champagne before heading off to a sun-drenched honeymoon. But according to the hotel's banqueting manager, Hayri Alpcan, most couples actually like to get married, have a reception with all the trimmings and stay overnight before leaving the next day refreshed (or not) for their honeymoon.

A wedding only at the Heathrow Hilton will cost you £250–£300 but if you have a reception as well there is no room charge. Catering starts at around £10 a head for a buffet up to £48 for a full sit-down meal. Being an airport hotel, of course there is no shortage of bedrooms including two Presidential Suites which would be ideal for the happy couple on their wedding night.

The Heathrow Hilton is a real surprise – a great building in the most unlikely setting. Its size means it is ideal for a medium to large wedding. Why not get married here in the winter and then fly off for a lovely honeymoon in the Caribbean?

Contact: Hayri Alpcan
Main road: A30
Station: Heathrow Terminal 4 Underground
Disabled access: Good
Parking: Yes for wedding guests
Registrar tel no: 018925 250761
Bedrooms: 400
Wedding only: Yes

A COUNTRY WEDDING

Down the winding Surrey Lanes, past the decorated pubs, and houses set back from the road, with a Bentley instead of a garden in front

DAVID PRYCE-JONES

There is nothing quite as lovely as an English country wedding – particularly in summer. There are literally hundreds of beautiful country house hotels where you can fulfil this dream. Most of them have been doing wedding receptions for years but now are geared up for the ceremony as well. There are also some smaller country houses, manors, barns and genuine working farms. So why not let your imagination run riot with anything from a posh Country Lifestyle wedding to a good old farmer's wedding followed by a barn dance.

Name: Tewin Bury Farm Hotel
Address: near Welwyn,
Hertfordshire AL6 0JB
Tel: 01438 717793

Every registrar we have met has had at least one cowboy wedding. Sometimes it's just the groom arriving in jeans and a stetson. On other occasions the bride, the groom and all the guests are decked out in Levi's, checked shirts and gingham dresses. Sometimes the registrar has to decide whether six-shooters are allowed at the ceremony.

Now country and western fans no longer need to traipse down to the register office wishing they were getting hitched out on the range. Instead they can mosey off to the farm and tie the knot in a stable or barn.

One of the best venues for this type of wedding must be Tewin Bury, a working farm in Hertfordshire complete with some beautifully converted stables and an original timber barn. Of course, you don't have to put on your cowboy gear for a wedding here. It is a lovely spot for a real country wedding.

The farm is just outside Welwyn on the B1000. When you drive there don't follow the signs to Tewin village or, like us, you will get lost. Stick to the B1000 and the farm entrance will soon come into view. Then it's down the drive, across the little River Mimram and into the farmyard where Angela Williams or one of her staff will be waiting to greet you.

A few years ago Angela decided to do a bit of bed and breakfast. It was a great success and over the years has grown so that now Tewin Bury has become a small, and very special, farm hotel. And the Williams family still run the farm.

Weddings are held in the 17th-century brick-built Stables. They have been sympathetically converted to make them suitable for weddings and receptions. Inside, the ancient, weathered brick walls are complemented by a wooden roof and iron chandeliers. At each end there are minstrels galleries. One would provide a perfect place for musicians to serenade the couple and guests.

Compared to the barn this is quite a small space. It seats about 60 people, more if some guests sit in the other gallery. There are small rooms on one side looking out on to the farmyard while on the other side an alcove has a large door opening on to the river bank. In winter the Stables would be cosy, in summer, with the doors open, they would be light and airy allowing all the country noises to float into the wedding room.

After the ceremony the wedding party can have drinks on the river bank or go to the back of the Stables where there is a separate and very cosy bar. Receptions can either be held later on in the Stables or in the Tythe Barn next door.

The barn seems to be virtually unchanged since it was built in the 17th century. It has timber walls and rafters supporting a tiled roof together with a flagstone floor. At one end is a raised area which can be used for a buffet, a bar or a band. It can take 120 people seated or up to 200 for a party. There is some heating in the Tythe Barn but it is really the place for a summer reception. It is also possible to have a barbecue outside to satisfy those guests who work up an appetite in the evening during a barn dance.

Small weddings can have a more intimate do in the downstairs rooms of the farmhouse itself. The lounge, which has an inglenook fireplace and lots of comfy chairs, is the place for a few drinks. Afterwards guests can go into the dining room for a meal.

There are 16 bedrooms at Tewin Bury, including some family rooms. Most are made out of converted farm buildings. That may sound a bit strange but be assured, they all have lots of exposed brickwork, wooden beams, pleasant farmhouse furnishings and ensuite facilities.

It costs £120 to hire the Stables for a wedding. A wide variety of menus can be provided according to taste. To give an idea of prices, hot and cold menus are available starting at around £22.50 a head. Rooms start at £27.50 a night. There is ample parking and considering it is a farm, disabled access is pretty good. There is even a bedroom with disabled facilities.

Tewin Bury Farm is an ideal place for a country and western wedding or a more traditional country wedding with a barn dance to follow. And it is only a short drive up the A1 from London, making it an ideal place for all those urban cowboys to have the wedding of their dreams.

Contact: Angela Williams
Main road: B1000
Station: Welwyn North
Disabled access: Yes
Parking: Ample
Registrar tel no: 01992 555590
Bedrooms: 16
Wedding only: Yes

Name: Preston Priory Barn
Address: Priory Farm, Preston St Mary, Sudbury, Suffolk CO10 9LT
Tel: 01787 247 251

Preston Priory Barn is a traditional timber-framed barn built in the 16th century but rebuilt and extended in the 18th century. The barn is L-shaped and forms two sides of an attractive courtyard. It is at the centre of a 300-acre working farm, although Adrian and Jane Thorpe who own it ensure there is not too much activity while weddings are in progress.

It is deep in the Suffolk countryside not far from the medieval town of Lavenham with its rows of half-timbered houses. Approaching it from Lavenham you drive down a country lane until a sign directs you to turn left into Priory Farm. With some of the venues in this book you drive down a grand, tree-lined avenue or at least a sweeping gravel drive. But here you turn straight into a farmyard – not a sanitized tourist affair but a proper working farm.

Preston Priory Barn is little altered since the days when farm workers flailed corn on the floor. Huge doors open on to the courtyard and at one end 2 sets of doors open out from the side of the building. The other side has a window looking out on to the duck pond so you may hear the occasional 'quack' during the ceremony!

There are old farm implements on the walls and at one end is a raised platform which used to keep the grain dry. Today it makes an ideal area for the bride and groom to take their vows while the guests look on from the main part of the barn. On the platform stands an old farm cart, painted green with red wheels. It has been completely restored and if filled with flowers would make a lovely backdrop to the ceremony.

The barn will seat 150 people and up to 300 standing so you can have a really good party here. Although the building is old some modern facilities have been discreetly added. There are new toilets, a catering-size kitchen, a bar in one corner and a telephone to call taxis. There is even a heating system should you want a winter wedding.

Most couples will want to get married here in the summer. Photos can be taken in the barn or outside in the Thorpes' own garden. In contrast to the ruggedness of the farm buildings the garden is a haven of peace with plenty of places to take romantic shots.

There is a classic English rose garden, some box trees, a stone seat and even an arch in the yew hedge.

Between the barn and the garden is a field where Mrs Thorpe keeps her miniature Shetland ponies. Being naturally curious creatures they like to watch the activity and often end up in the photos!

There is a separate holiday cottage next to the farm which could be booked by close family while guests can stay in local bed and breakfasts or at the Swan or Angel Hotels in Lavenham. On the wedding day the bride can get ready in a spare room in the house which has its own bathroom.

The Thorpes are quite happy to have themed events at the barn. They have already had a rustic wedding. When we visited, one couple were in the process of arranging an 'Alice in Wonderland' day. Medieval weddings can have a hog roast or a spit inside the barn as part of the reception. And of course a square dance or barn dance would be ideal to follow the reception.

At Priory Barn there is no in-house catering and there are no wedding packages. Couples rent out the building and then organize their own food, flowers and entertainment. The Thorpes have lists of recommended suppliers if needed. This makes it a lot cheaper than some of the other venues. To have the barn for an afternoon wedding and evening reception costs a flat fee of £500. If a couple want to have a do-it-yourself event the Thorpes are quite happy to let the organizers come in the day before and clear up on the day after.

Priory Barn is the place for a

couple who want a marriage with a difference. It would be ideal for a country and western wedding followed by a live band in the evening.

Contact: Mrs A. Thorpe
Main road: A1141
Station: Sudbury (7 miles)
Disabled access: Partial
Parking: Ample
Registrar tel no. 01787 372 904
Rooms: None, but a cottage on site
Wedding only: No

Name: **Lythe Hill Hotel**
Address: **Petworth Road, Haslemere, Surrey GU27 3BQ**
Tel: **01428 651251**

Haslemere is a small market town about 40 miles south of London with a history dating back more than 10,000 years to the Stone Age. It was during the 19th century that Haslemere's fortunes changed. With the advent of the railway it was transformed from a tiny village into a thriving market town.

The B2131 out of Haslemere is one of those typically English country roads bordered on both sides by graceful trees. On a sunny day the light filters gently through the leaves and on to the road. It is so quiet it is quite easy to miss the turning for Lythe Hill. Once you find it, however, you are not disappointed.

The historic country house hotel is set in 20 acres of woodland on the border of the Surrey and Sussex hills. The former farmhouse and outbuildings form a picturesque hamlet well off the beaten track. The main hotel building has been converted from the old farm outbuildings – barns, milking sheds, and animal stalls all give the hotel a certain rustic charm. During the 18th century Lythe Hill Farm House was used as a Court House and the convicts were hanged in what is now the kitchen. Little wonder there is a resident ghost!

The listed Tudor farmhouse is separate from the main hotel and dates back as far as 1475. It has been completely refurbished without losing any of its olde worlde charm. Original beams still remain and the old oak door which once served as the main entrance to the house.

There are 3 wedding rooms all in different parts of the hotel. The first is the Hamlet Room in a building on its own, which has recently been refurbished in shades of blue. It provides a delightful setting with its terrace which overlooks a lake and the rolling Sussex/Surrey countryside, and would be perfect for pre-wedding drinks.

The second is the huge Italian Garden Room in the main hotel. This is like a vast conservatory with white walls and hanging plants and a glass roof which lets in plenty of light and gives a rather Mediterranean atmosphere. It has modern wooden beams, polished floors and Georgian-style french windows. If you want a summer wedding but worry about the weather it would be ideal, for, whatever the weather this room appears to be summery.

The room seats up to 95 guests and will cost £100. For larger groups double doors give on to the Petworth Suite and together the 2 rooms seat up to 130 people.

But for a truly romantic winter wedding you would go a long way to find anything better than the Quennell Room. This is in the 14th-century farmhouse and is warm and cosy – all reds and gold and polished wood and brass – with a roaring log fire to complete the effect. Once the wedding ceremony is over guests can move over to the Garden Room with its own cocktail bar and terrace overlooking the Sussex Weald.

To complete your romantic idyll you can stay in an original Tudor bedroom complete with wonky floorboards and fascinating nooks and crannies. The triple brass-bed is the height of luxury and for a small extra charge you can have breakfast in bed with a magnum of champagne. Just the way to start married life!

Kevin Lorimer is the person in charge of weddings and is very keen to make sure you have a perfect day. 'We offer a special honeymoon package which includes a bouquet of red roses, a bottle of champagne, a very special box of chocolates and a gift from us to the bride and groom.'

The hotel is totally geared up for receptions and can cater for anything from a finger buffet at around £15 a head to a formal sit-down meal at around £50 a head. The full-blown meal includes drinks on arrival, a half-bottle of house wine and a glass of sparkling wine for the toast. Children under 10 are charged at half-price and discounted accommodation for the guests can be arranged. There are 40 bedrooms and prices range from £95 to £150 for a luxury garden suite overlooking the lake.

Extras such as the wedding-cake, chauffeur-driven car, music from a harpist or a string quartet and a helicopter for the departing couple can be arranged through local contacts. A changing room is thrown in with the price plus a double room for the night with the compliments of the hotel.

The Lythe Hill Hotel is truly superb for either a grand themed wedding in the Italian Garden Room or a cosy winter wedding in the 14th-century inn. Photographs can be taken alongside the lake with a backdrop of the Sussex countryside or on one of the hotel's many terraces.

Contact: Kevin Lorimer
Main road: A3/B2131
Station: Haslemere
Disabled access: Not good
Parking: Ample
Registrar tel no: 01483 62841
Bedrooms: 40
Wedding only: No

Name: The Manor
Address: Newlands Corner,
Guildford, Surrey GU4 8SE
Tel: 01483 222624

Newlands Corner is a designated area of outstanding natural beauty just outside Guildford, a conservation town with a great history. There are numerous country walks within easy access as well as many local places of interest. The Royal Horticultural Society's famous gardens are at Wisley just a couple of miles up the road and for theatre lovers Guildford, Leatherhead and Farnham all boast excellent facilities.

The first thing you notice about the Manor is a conservatory which looks as if it has been bolted on to the front of the house. Although it seems rather incongruous and not in keeping with the period of the original building it does have its benefits. According to owner Peter Davies, it ensures that even on the rainiest day the bride is guaranteed brilliant photographs.

The manor house itself was built in 1870 and became famous as the country retreat of Lytton Strachey, then editor of the *Spectator*, who regularly entertained Agatha Christie, Virginia Woolf and other members of the Bloomsbury group here. During the Second World War the Manor had a more practical use serving as a hospital.

There are 3 wedding rooms but by far the best is the Bloomsbury Room which is decorated in delicate shades of peach and has huge windows overlooking the 9 acres of parkland. It can hold up to 100 guests. This room is an ideal setting for a traditional white wedding and the chairs can be arranged so that the bride can walk up the aisle on her father's arm.

The second wedding room which has a more informal and cosy atmosphere is in the original wing of the manor house which dates back to 1870. The room can hold up to 30 guests and with its latticed windows and oak beams the whole effect is very romantic.

The third room is the Lytton Strachey Room. It is at the back of the hotel and can take 150 guests. It is on a split level and french windows open on to the gardens.

Whichever wedding room you choose at the Manor you can be sure the service will be tip-top. Peter Davies is a great believer in the old adage 'you are only as good as your last function' and takes his responsibilities in his new role very seriously. His wedding package includes a list for the bride and groom explaining everything the couple need to do for a perfect wedding.

The Manor was the first venue in Surrey to hold a civil wedding and according to everyone concerned it was a roaring success. The couple arrived in a vintage Chevrolet convertible. The bride wore white and came down the aisle to the strains of Handel's 'Water Music' played by the same organist who performed the hymns in the blockbuster *Four Weddings and a Funeral*! After the ceremony, the guests sang 'Love is All Around' and the happy couple exited to the 'Trumpet Voluntary'. 'It provided all the pomp without God, a very special occasion without religion', said the bride.

Needless to say Peter Davies was thrilled. 'We like to think of ourselves as a three-star hotel offering a four-star service.' He is very keen to encourage couples to take advantage of the new law and is happy to provide suggestions to make the day special. From discos and jugglers to live bands and entertainers, he can sort it out for you. If you want to party till dawn that's no problem either. The hotel has a licence until 2 am on Thursday, Friday and Saturday.

Hire of the room will cost £100–£200 and gives you use of the facilities from 9 am through until 2 am the next morning if you want. Catering comes out at around £25 a head plus £6.50 for a finger buffet for late arrivals in the evening. There is ample parking for more than 100 cars and the hotel has 19 rooms for overnight accommodation. Guests can stay locally at the Clavadel Hotel just 3 miles away in the village of Merrow or one of the many reasonable bed and breakfasts in the surrounding area.

Two types of wedding would be superb at the Manor. Firstly a traditional white wedding in the Bloomsbury Room followed by drinks on the lawn, then a sit-down meal in the restaurant and a disco in the evening. Secondly a small wedding with a few close family in the cosy little room followed by lunch for family and friends in the restaurant. The couple could then stay for the whole weekend and enjoy the beautiful walks around the area.

Contact: Peter Davies
Main road: A3/M25
Station: Guildford
Disabled access: Limited
Parking: Ample
Registrar tel no: 01483 62841
Bedrooms: 19
Wedding only: No

Name: Lainston House Hotel
Address: Sparsholt, Winchester, Hampshire SO21 2LT
Tel: 01962 863 588

Lainston House is just outside Winchester close to the A272. It is reached along a winding drive lined with chestnuts and limes and through parkland of mature trees.

The house has roots as far back as 1316 but today's building was built in the 17th century. It has had a chequered history including a period when it was a lunatic asylum, but don't worry about the rooms being haunted. In those days the physician lived in the great house while the patients were housed in huts in the grounds!

Lainston is now a country house hotel and restaurant and a very good one at that. The reason it is included is not because of its fine food and quality rooms – but because it has a Barn in the grounds where you can get married. Mind you this is no tractor and straw Barn. It is an impressive building that has been restored to a high standard in keeping with its surroundings.

The Barn is approached by a covered walkway from the hotel. Originally built in the 17th century, it is now a large function room with half-timbered walls and plenty of wooden beams showing in the roof. A large brick fireplace complete with open fire dominates one side of the room while the brick wall at the end has been cleverly adapted to include a bar and toilets. There is a parquet floor and central heating to keep out the chill in winter.

Many of the original features have been preserved such as the doors which would have originally led up into the old hay loft. At one stage there was obviously some concern that the roof might fall in, so large metal ties were installed to hold the whole place together. The architect has carried it off with style and they now add to the atmosphere of the room.

The Barn is licensed for live music and would be ideal for a country and western wedding or for a traditional barn dance after the reception. It holds 100 people and has good disabled access together with a disabled toilet.

After the wedding photos can be taken in all sorts of places. There are the remains of an 11th-century Norman chapel, some rather fine topiary and an octagonal dovecote. Apparently the dovecote has boxes for 600 doves. When it was built in the 17th century they were a valuable source of winter food.

Post-wedding drinks can be taken back in the hotel. The wood-panelled bar, made from a giant cedar that once stood at the side of the house, opens out directly on to its own lawn. Most weddings would then head back into the barn for a reception and dancing. Smaller parties could have a private dinner in one of the hotel's several dining rooms.

The bride and groom will probably want to stay in the Delft Room, the original master-bedroom of the house. It has 3 large windows looking down over the ornamental drive. Another option would be the Sycamore Room with its huge four-poster, and TV in the bathroom. The guests could stay at Lainston House or in one of the numerous hotels or bed and breakfasts in nearby Winchester.

You can have sole use of the Barn for just £500. Menus start at around £27 and an average reception with wine and all the trimmings is likely to end up costing around £40 per head. Double rooms start at £125 going up to £250 for the bridal suite. Unusually, these prices do not include breakfast.

The Barn at Lainston House is a beautiful place to hold a wedding. The surroundings are lovely but you should not have any illusions about a cheap farmer's wedding. Remember that it is an up-market hotel with prices to match.

Contact: Patsy Enright
Main road: M3/A272
Station: Winchester
Disabled access: Yes
Parking: Plenty
Registrar tel no: 01962 869608
Bedrooms: 38
Wedding only: No

Name: Chiseldon House Hotel
Address: New Road, Chiseldon, near
Swindon, Wiltshire SN4 0NE
Tel: 01793 741010

So many country house hotels are now doing weddings that it is difficult to know what makes one stand out. Chiseldon House is an old building with nice grounds and lovely rooms – but what really makes it special is its secret weapon – Jan Capaldi who manages the weddings!

Jan is a woman with a mission – to make absolutely sure that couples have a day to remember. If they want music they can have it. If they want a steel band no problem. If they want a baroque wedding the hotel will be decked out in the appropriate style. In short anything is possible – and well within the means of most couples.

Chiseldon House Hotel is just off the M4 near Swindon. It was built in 1827 as a private country house with $3\frac{1}{2}$ acres of grounds. It was enlarged at the end of the 19th century and went through various changes ending up as a country doctor's house before being turned into a hotel in the 1980s.

From the driveway the building looks rather small, a little like a French manor house. It is 2 storeys high and built of pale limestone. On the ground floor is an arched terrace covered in wisteria which forms a balcony for the first-floor bedrooms. The hotel's domestic origins are clear to see. There is a small portico leading into the hallway which looks just like part of a private house, albeit a rather fine one. There is a stylish curved staircase and 3 massive French gilded mirrors. To one side the drawing room is tastefully decorated with regency striped wallpaper with a large gracious window looking out into the garden.

Weddings are held in the Borelli Room, which still looks much like the formal dining room of a country house. It is painted Wedgwood blue with 2 alcoves picked out in white and matching blue drapes. The registrar will stand in front of the fireplace next to a mahogany table. The guests will be seated in rows complete with an aisle for the bride to walk down. The room, which seats 65 people, has lovely views out to the front garden. Music can be provided from a CD but Jan is very keen for couples to have live music and can arrange a flautist or a classical guitarist to accompany the ceremony.

There are several options for eating and drinking. Lively groups can have an outdoor reception by the small heated swimming-pool and barbecue. There is even a thatched gazebo for the photos. More formal wedding breakfasts are held in the Orangery Restaurant. Seating 85, it is decorated in turquoise and peach with large murals depicting Wiltshire scenes. Jan fills the whole room with flowers on wedding days making sure that they tone in with the bride's own colour scheme.

Drinks can be taken outside the front of the house on the terrace. If the weather is good it is an ideal spot for a live band.

There is no formal bridal suite but the bride and groom may want to stay in one of the large rooms at the front of the house which have a balcony and a window seat looking over the garden.

Chiseldon House Hotel does not charge for the hire of rooms when a reception is booked with the wedding but there would be some charge for a wedding only. There is a variety of menus which range from £7.50 to £36 a head. Drinks will be on top of this and start at around £7 a head. There is a complimentary room for the bride and groom complete with champagne breakfast while guest rooms cost between £30 and £40 a head for bed and breakfast.

Chiseldon House is an ideal place for a themed wedding and Jan Capaldi will certainly help take the strain out of the preparations. She has already helped organize a baroque event and a 'Tea at the Ritz' wedding is next on the list with everyone in flapper dresses eating cucumber sandwiches, with the piano tinkling in the background.

Contact: Jan Capaldi
Main road: M4
Station: Swindon (8 miles)
Disabled access: Some
Parking: Ample
Registrar tel no: 01793 521734
Bedrooms: 21
Wedding only: Yes

Name: **Marshall Meadows Country House Hotel**
Address: **Berwick-upon-Tweed, Northumberland TD15 1UT**
Tel: **01289 331133**

There was a time when couples used to flee to Scotland to get married. Now they can stop just a couple of hundred yards from the Border to tie the knot at England's northernmost wedding venue.

Marshall Meadows is 3 miles north of the River Tweed at Berwick, the town which has changed hands between the English and Scots 13 times over the centuries. Now firmly in England, in the legislative sense at least, Marshall Meadows is a legacy of the town's stormy past. The grand house was built around 1750 as a home for the marshal of the Berwick army garrison.

Berwick itself is steeped in history having impressive Elizabethan fortifications and fine bridges, and has long been known for some of the country's finest salmon fishing. The rolling heather-clad borderlands end in spectacular cliffs that fall away dramatically to the North Sea just a few hundred yards from Marshall Meadows. So it is fitting, with such a magnificent backdrop, that the hotel can offer couples the next best thing to an outdoor wedding in the airy new Conservatory which is licensed for civil marriages.

There is a definite garden atmosphere here with french widows looking straight on to the hotel's terrace and out over 15 acres of woodland

and matured gardens. Flanked by open farmland and sea views, the terrace is an excellent place for wedding photographs. There is even a swing in a tree where the bride and groom can be snapped.

The Conservatory is one of 4 rooms at Marshall Meadows licensed for marriages. The other wedding rooms are the Music Room – rather austere for a ceremony – the more attractive lounge, with period decor, and the roomy Ayre Suite which, with a capacity of 200, is the ideal venue for large events.

Marshall Meadows was converted to a country house hotel in 1991 having been a fever hospital and a private house in the past. Owners Bryan and Irene Worsell moved up from Kent where they were property developers. Irene was from Berwick and she was keen to get back to her roots. The hotel has been restored to its former elegance by the Worsells who are rightly proud of the buildings and wonderful setting. There are woodland walks alongside Marshall Meadows Burn which meanders down to a small waterfall leading to recently discovered ponds.

The hotel even has its own pet Highland cow and small flock of Jacob sheep. The grounds also boast an all-weather tennis court and a croquet lawn.

Herbs and vegetables grown in the kitchen gardens are used by the hotel's chefs. Menus also feature fresh fish and shellfish from the nearby Scottish fishing port of Eyemouth. This is the place for a couple in search of something just a little bit special for their guests. Otherwise, finger buffets start at about £5 a head, and sit-down breakfasts at £14. With drinks, expect to pay about £20 a head, with the £150 room hire charge waived for larger receptions. You can hire other extras including a single Scots piper or full 20-piece band.

Marshall Meadows would be ideal for the couple wanting all the Scots trimmings without actually going to Scotland (well, not quite, anyway). We felt that a ceremony for up to 40 in the Conservatory followed by photographs on the lawn and a reception in the Music Room would be ideal here.

Contact: Matthew Rudd
Main road: A1(M)
Station: Berwick
Disabled access: Yes
Parking: Ample
Registrar tel no: 01289 306479
Rooms: 18, including 2 honeymoon suites
Wedding only: Negotiable

CHAPTER 8

We want to hear from you

We want to make sure that *Dream Weddings* helps couples have a really special day. That means our information has to be up to date and accurate. We need your help. We would like to hear about your experiences using the venues listed in the book as we will take your views into account when we do the next edition.

So write and tell us whether you received a good service, the staff were really helpful and whether the registrar was willing to make your day special. We would also like to hear if you had any problems, disasters or were let down on the day.

We are keen to encourage more imaginative approaches to the marriage ceremony. So if you had a medieval themed wedding, a gothic event or the registrar allowed you to have a jazz band playing during the ceremony send us the details. If it was really unusual we would love to see a photograph.

Finally, we want to hear of new venues that you think should be in the next edition of the book. If you have heard of a good wedding venue or are the proprietor of somewhere interesting send the details to us.

Dream Weddings
PO BOX 9421
London
N8 7JB

We look forward to hearing from you.

Make Your Wedding Dreams Come True

Win a dream wedding ceremony and reception at The Royal Pavilion, Brighton catered by Letheby & Christopher Ltd.
or
Win a beautiful £1,000 wedding dress and £100 groom dress hire from Pronuptia Youngs.

These prizes are available to the winners until 31 December 1997. See overleaf for more details about the prizes and please note the prize conditions section.

To enter the competition please answer the three questions and tie-breaker below:

Questions

1. *What are the 4 traditional items that should be worn by the bride on her wedding day?*

2. *Which British king had the most wives?*

3. *What is the name of the actress with whom Hugh Grant fell in love in the film FOUR WEDDINGS AND A FUNERAL?*

Tie-Breaker

In no more than 30 words describe why the person you want to marry is your dream partner

Please send your answers on a postcard with your name, address and telephone number to:

DEPARTMENT DW, SIGNET MARKETING DEPARTMENT,
PENGUIN BOOKS LTD, 27 WRIGHTS LANE, LONDON W8 5TZ

The closing date is 31 May 1996. The competition is open to residents of the UK. No person under the age of 18 may enter.

PRIZES

WEDDING DRESS

Vouchers for a £1,000 dream wedding dress of your choice and hire of a groom's outfit to the value of £100 from Pronuptia Youngs.

Outside the competition, for details of your nearest stockist please call 01254 664422.

A DREAM WEDDING AT THE ROYAL PAVILION

The Royal Pavilion in Brighton provides a truly magnificent venue for both wedding ceremonies and receptions and will certainly ensure a day to remember.

Ceremony

The civil ceremony will take place in the elegant Red Drawing Room, normally closed to the general public. Up to 40 people can attend.

Rich in colour, elegance and style, this charming room is a very special royal setting for a wedding ceremony.

Reception

This can be held in the nearby William IV Room, which has hand-painted Chinese wallpaper in shades of soft blues, silver and pink. It offers a picturesque setting for wedding receptions. The room can accommodate 60 guests for a seated event or 70 for a standing buffet.

Alternatively the Queen Adelaide Suite, also within the Pavilion, provides an equally exquisite venue. The suite comprises two rooms with an adjoining balcony which offers sweeping views across the newly restored gardens. This suite can seat up to 55 people on a traditional top-table and 3 sprigs, or up to 90 people for a standing buffet.

For further details and bookings outside the competition please telephone the Public Services Section at the Royal Pavilion (Tel: 01273 603005).

Catering

The catering for the wedding will be provided by top caterers Letheby and Christopher Ltd to the value of £2,500 including VAT.

The make up and style of the catering can be in any format the winner decides, such as formal sit-down meal, buffet, canapé reception, etc. and may include alcoholic beverages. Staff, china, glass and linen are included in the prize menu price.

Outside the competition you can contact Letheby and Christopher caterers at branches covering the following areas:

South - *01273 814 566*

London - *0171 735 6303 (Leiths)*

Thames Valley - *01344 20387*

West - *0121 440 0747*

East - *01638 662750*

North West - *01942 275552*

Scotland - *0141 331 2555*

RULES OF ENTRY

The competition is open to residents of the UK (excluding employees of Penguin Books Ltd, The Royal Pavilion, Pronuptia Youngs and Letheby & Christopher).

No person under the age of 18 may enter.

Only one entry per person.

No proof of purchase is necessary.

All entries must be received by 31 May 1996.

No responsibility can be accepted for entries which are illegible, lost or damaged in the post.

The winners will be the two entrants who submit correct answers to the questions and who in the opinion of the judges submit the best tie-breakers. The judges will decide which prize will be allocated to which winner and their decision is final. No correspondence may be entered into.

There is no cash alternative for either of the prizes.

The winners will be informed by post or telephone by 14 June 1996.

A list of the winners' names and tie-breakers will be available from the Signet Marketing Department (same address as for the competition entries) upon request.

PRIZE CONDITIONS

WEDDING DRESS

This is a separate prize to the wedding ceremony and reception.

The winner will be given a voucher to the value of £1,000 to be redeemed on a wedding dress at participating branches of Pronuptia Youngs.

The winner will also be given a voucher to the value of £100 to be redeemed on any groom's outfit hired from participating branches of Pronuptia Youngs Formal Wear.

The vouchers cannot be used against sale or discounted products.

You can spend your own money together with the vouchers to buy or hire a more expensive garment if you wish.

Vouchers must be redeemed by 31 December 1997.

WEDDING CEREMONY & RECEPTION

The date and time of the ceremony and reception will be subject to availability but must take place before 31 December 1997 on either a Friday or a Saturday.

Ceremony

The civil ceremony will take place in the Red Drawing Room and the Royal Pavilion undertakes to provide correct staffing and cover the cost of a local registrar performing the ceremony (currently £200) free of charge.

The winning couple must give in their legal notice prior to the ceremony and purchase a wedding licence in advance in accordance with UK Marriage Laws.

In addition to the bride and groom no more than 40 people may attend the ceremony to comply with fire and safety regulations.

Reception

The Royal Pavilion will undertake such organisation that is required for the smooth running of the event.

The reception includes free room-hire and staffing for **either** the William IV Room or the Queen Adelaide Suite, seating, tables and a £2,500 contribution towards the cost of the catering by Letheby and Christopher Ltd. The cost of any other equipment, services, photographers, entertainment, flowers, bridal wear etc., must be borne by the winning couple.

The prize is limited to the hire of one reception room only.

The reception room will be available for a 4-hour period.

Dancing is not permitted in the Royal Pavilion and smoking is restricted to the Small Adelaide only. The rooms are licensed to serve liquor by waitress service only.

The Royal Pavilion will require the winning couple to sign a contract and hiring agreement, and to abide by the terms and conditions specified within. The Royal Pavilion is part of Arts & Leisure Services for Brighton Borough Council.

Catering

The catering for the reception must be co-ordinated with the availability of the Royal Pavilion reception rooms.

Letheby & Christopher Ltd. will make every effort to comply with the winner's choice of dates but reserve the right to refuse a date should this not be suitable due to prior commitments.

The prize value of £2,500 is to be taken at Letheby & Christopher's normal selling price as at the date of the wedding reception. This prize value is solely restricted to catering services.

Letheby & Christopher Ltd. shall be the sole caterer for the winner's reception and any expenditure over the prize value of £2500, including VAT, will be the responsibility of the winner.